D1706844

Security in Wireless LANs and MANs

For quite a long time, computer security was a rather narrow field of study that was populated mainly by theoretical computer scientists, electrical engineers, and applied mathematicians. With the proliferation of open systems in general, and of the Internet and the World Wide Web (WWW) in particular, this situation has changed fundamentally. Today, computer and network practitioners are equally interested in computer security, since they require technologies and solutions that can be used to secure applications related to electronic commerce. Against this background, the field of computer security has become very broad and includes many topics of interest. The aim of this series is to publish state-of-the-art, high standard technical books on topics related to computer security. Further information about the series can be found on the WWW at the following URL:

http://www.esecurity.ch/serieseditor.html

Also, if you'd like to contribute to the series by writing a book about a topic related to computer security, feel free to contact either the Commissioning Editor or the Series Editor at Artech House.

For a listing of recent titles in the *Artech House Computer Security Series*, turn to the back of this book.

Security in Wireless LANs and MANs

Thomas Hardjono
Lakshminath R. Dondeti

ARTECH
HOUSE

BOSTON | LONDON
artechhouse.com

Library of Congress Cataloging-in-Publication Data

Hardjono, Thomas.
    Security in wireless LANs and MANs / Thomas Hardjono, Lakshminath Dondeti.
      p. cm. — (Artech House computer security series)
    Includes bibliographical references and index.
    ISBN 1-58053-755-3 (alk. paper)
    1. Wireless communication systems—Security measures. 2. Wireless LANs—Security measures. 3. Metropolitan area networks (Computer networks)—Security measures. I. Dondeti, Lakshminath R. II. Title. III. Series.

TK5103.2.H3684 2005
005.8—dc22   2005048032

British Library Cataloguing in Publication Data

Hardjono, Thomas
    Security in wireless LANs and MANs.—(Artech House computer security series)
    1. Wireless LANs—Security measures
    I. Title II. Dondeti, Lakshminath R.
    005.8

ISBN-10:1-58053-755-3

Cover design by Yekaterina Ratner

International Standard Book Number: 1-58053-755-3

10 9 8 7 6 5 4 3 2 1

To Maria and Elizabeth
— Thomas Hardjono

To Manu and Sridevi
— Lakshminath R. Dondeti

Contents

II   Data Protection in Wireless LANs   91

Preface

Wireless communications are becoming ubiquitous in homes, offices, and enterprises with the popular IEEE 802.11 wireless LAN technology and the up-and-coming IEEE 802.16 wireless MAN technology. The wireless nature of communications defined in these standards makes it possible for an attacker to snoop on confidential communications or modify them to gain access to home or enterprise networks much more easily than with wired networks.

The 802.11 and 802.16 standards considered wired equivalency and secure access as important in the original design itself. Unfortunately, efficiency considerations seem to have sidelined security as a "nice-to-have" component, whereas a "must implement cautiously" specification would have been more appropriate considering the potential threats. To be sure, strong security seems sometimes overly burdensome in terms of both computational as well communication overhead.

Wireless devices generally try to reduce computation overhead to conserve power and communication overhead to conserve spectrum and battery power. Due to these considerations, the original security designs in wireless LANs and MANs used smaller keys, weak message integrity protocols, weak or one-way authentication protocols, and so forth. As wireless networks became popular, the security threats were also highlighted to caution users. A security protocol redesign followed first in wireless LANs and then in wireless MANs.

This book discusses the security threats and requirements in wireless LANs and wireless MANs, with a discussion on what the original designs missed and how they were corrected in the new protocols. It highlights the features of the current wireless LAN and MAN security protocols and explains the caveats and discusses open issues.

This book is divided into four parts. The first part discusses authentication technologies common to security in wireless LANs and MANs. A detailed discussion on EAP and the various methods is included to help readers understand the technologies implemented in the providers' networks to support secure access. The second part discusses the security encapsulation and key management protocols in wireless LANs. Wireless roaming and security issues therein are the topics of the third part. Security issues in wireless MANs and the evolution of the security design in the IEEE 802.16 specifications is the topic of the fourth part. The final chapter provides an outlook in the security area in wireless networks.

Our goal in writing this book is to provide the reader with a single source of information on security threats and requirements, authentication technologies, security encapsulation, and key management protocols relevant to wireless LANs and MANs.

Acknowledgments

This book is the result of our working in the area of WLAN and WMAN security, which necessarily included interaction with numerous persons in various forums and standards bodies such as the IETF, Wi-Fi Alliance, and the IEEE. As such, there are various people whose opinions and views have helped educate us and shape the contents and areas of emphasis of this book.

We therefore wish to thank the following people for their input and positive influence on this book (in alphabetical order): Bernard Aboba, Tim Takao Aihara, Tim Allwine, Phil Hallam-Baker, Blair Bullock, Gene Chang, Leigh Chinitz, David Cohen, Alex Deacon, John Ferguson, Mo-Han Fong, Warwick Ford, Paul Funk, Bill Gage, Jim Geier, Paul Goransson, Amer Hassan, Haixiang He, Russ Housley, Brian Johnson, Marcus Leech, Jeff Mandin, Bob Moskowitz, Al Potter, Kartik Seshan, Joel Short, JunHyuk Song, Dorothy Stanley, Wen Tong, John Vollbrecht, Jesse Walker, Doug Whiting, and Peiying Zhu. We apologize to those whose names we may have inadvertently missed.

We also appreciate Donald Knuth, Leslie Lamport, and countless others who developed the wonderful typesetting system, LaTeX, without which we could not have produced the manuscript in time. Thanks also to Alistair Smith for his assistance with LaTeX in preparing the camera ready copy of this book.

We thank Nicholas Popp and Mahi De Silva (VeriSign) and Don Fedyk and Bilel Jamoussi (Nortel Networks) for their support. Any opinions in the book are ours alone and may or may not represent the opinions of those above or our current or past employers.

We especially thank Rolf Oppliger, Tim Pitts, Julie Lancashire, Tiina Ruonamma, Judi Stone, and Rebecca Allendorf for not giving up on us, and for their assistance in various stages of the publishing process. We are grateful to the anonymous reviewer(s) for their constructive criticism and suggestions, which helped improve the quality of this book.

Lakshminath thanks Thomas for his patience during the manuscript preparation and production process. He also acknowledges the help of Shannon Shean and Valerie Smith of QUALCOMM for their assistance during the manuscript and galley review stages.

It is very difficult to find time to write a book while employed full-time in demanding jobs, and inevitably it is at the expense of the spouses' time. We thank our wives Elizabeth and Sridevi for their love and support during the 18 months that it took to produce this book.

Chapter 1

Introduction

The topic of this book is the security of 802.11 *wireless local area networks* (WLANs) and of 802.16 *wireless metropolitan area networks* (WMANs). These networks are based on the IEEE standards belonging to the 802 family — which include the much-beloved Ethernet (802.3) that is common today in homes and offices. Although the development of the 802.11 technology and standards have been ongoing since the late 1990s, grassroots adoption of "wireless Ethernet" only began in the 2000–2001 timeframe when access point (AP) devices became cheap enough for the home user to obtain.

The convenience of having wireless access to the IP Internet is self-evident. The value proposition in terms of employee productivity has been so compelling that many enterprises began also to introduce the technology into their corporate networks. This enterprise adoption, however, was prematurely halted when security flaws in the WEP algorithm were discovered and published. Various temporary patches were then suggested in order to support existing enterprise investments in WLAN equipment, with the IPsec-VPN (e.g., over the wireless segment) as the most common approach. The IEEE standards community completed the revision of the security-related components of 802.11 in 2004, with conforming products scheduled to be shipped in 2005.

This book aims, in the first instance, to provide a roadmap for readers seeking a deeper understanding of the security aspects of 802.11 WLANs today and the upcoming 802.16 WMANs. In order for this book to be a useful technological roadmap to the reader, the discussion sometimes goes into a considerable level of detail. This is needed because these discussion points explain the solutions adopted by the 802.11 standards community in answer to the poor security design of the first generation of 802.11 specifications and products. As it is widely known today, the security problems of the early 802.11 specifications resulted in insecure implementations, and thus low adoption of the technology by enterprises.

1

Second, the aim of the book is to bring together and explain the other broader areas of networking technology that are being impacted by the advent of 802.11 WLANs and 802.16 WMANs. Clearly the 802.11 WiFi phenomenon has gained a tremendous interest in the IP networking industry, and therefore this phenomenon will clearly have an effect on the other technologies and services in the IP networking industry and even the telecommunications industry. Thus, for example, WiFi roaming at airports was unknown only three years ago. In contrast, today, not only is it becoming commonplace, but WiFi's success has caused a re-thinking among 3G providers about the possible impact of 802.11 WLANs and 802.16 WMANs on the future business model underlying 3G offerings. Along the same lines, WiFi roaming (e.g., at hotels) has displaced a considerable size of the enterprise Internet dial-up market, resulting in many dial-up providers to either embrace WiFi services or to refocus only on the home user dial-up market. Similarly, 802.16 promises an upheaval in the broadband industry, offering ISP newcomers and content providers an opportunity to provide new broadband and content services to the market. The WiMax forum is promoting 802.16-based broadband wireless access (BWA) networks.

This book is not a user guide to specific WLAN or WMAN products, and intentionally avoids specific references to such products. It is also not a thesis on the various engineering solutions that could have been applied to solve the WiFi security problem. Instead, the book attempts to explain what current approaches and solutions have been adopted, and why these were chosen.

The contents of the book are arranged in four parts, where each part groups together topics and issues that are closely related. These parts roughly cover the topics of WLAN authentication and authorization, WLAN security algorithms and protocols, security in WLAN roaming, and security in WMANs. These are described in more detail next.

The first part focuses on the important area of authentication and authorization, with specific attention given to technologies that are relevant to WLANs and WMANs. The chapters covered in this part are as follows:

- *Chapter 2: Authentication in WLANs: An Overview.* Chapter 2 provides an introduction to the area and covers the basic network configuration of a WLAN and describes the entities involved. The chapter discusses some authentication models, identifying 802.1X and the UAM as the predominant models. An important entity in 802.1X is the authentication server (AS), the most common being the RADIUS server. As such, the RADIUS protocol is discussed also in this chapter. Finally, device authentication is also described, analyzing the approach and solution adopted by the cable modem industry. This approach is of importance to both WLANs and WMANs in solving the rogue devices problem.

- *Chapter 3: EAP, TLS, and Certificates.* Chapter 3 brings together three technological ingredients that are are crucial for authentication and for the security of WLANs and WMANs in general. The EAP protocol has now become the basic building block for transporting payloads between entities within the 802.1X context. As such, it is important that the reader obtain a good understanding of this protocol. Various EAP methods for authentication and authorization deploy an underlying TLS session to protect end-to-end communications between the 802.1X supplicant and authentication server. Hence, the chapter provides an introduction to the basics of the TLS (SSL) protocol and its operation. Finally, since the TLS protocol is typically deployed with digital certificates, some basic coverage of PKI and certificates is provided as a continuation of the TLS discussion.

- *Chapter 4: EAP Methods.* Chapter 4 is devoted exclusively to the EAP methods (protocols) that are most commonly cited and used today in the 802.1X context. Those covered are the EAP-TLS, PEAP, EAP-TTLS, EAP-SIM, and EAP-AKA protocols. Since many mobile network operators (MNOs) today are venturing into providing WLAN services — with some repurposing of their authentication infrastructures to support WLANs — some discussion of the EAP-SIM and EAP-AKA protocols is provided, as SIM authentication is the predominant approach used by MNOs.

The second part of this book pertains to data protection in WLANs. The chapters in this part of the book focus on the basic security algorithms used to protect data as it traverses the wireless segment. The chapters covered in this part are as follows:

- *Chapter 5: WEP.* Chapter 5 is entirely devoted to WEP in order to correctly explain its weaknesses and to understand what improvements need to be made. This chapter sets the backdrop to the ensuing three chapters, all of which are devoted to the new algorithms and protocols developed to replace the original WEP algorithm and improve the security of WLANs.

- *Chapter 6: 802.11i Security: RSNA.* One of the stated important aims of the improvements done to the 802.11 specification is to define the notion of the Robust Security Network (RSN). A given RSN allows the creation of security associations — namely, *robust security network associations* or RSNA — only among the intended entities (e.g., clients/STA, APs) in the network. RSNA itself relies on 802.1X to transport authentication services and key management services. Chapter 6 looks into RSNA and provides a discussion on the 4-way exchange used to derive unicast session keys and the protocols used to deliver these keys to their intended recipients.

- *Chapter 7: CCMP*. Chapter 7 covers another important building block of the RSN. Counter mode for encryption in conjunction with CBC-MAC for message integrity — referred to as CCM — is now the preferred approach used to provide cryptographic protection for MPDUs being transmitted via shared WLANs. In this chapter *counter with CBC-MAC* (CCM) is discussed in detail. CCM is a crucial building block because in addition to confidentiality and integrity protection, it provides replay protection, and thus facilitates the controlled and secure access to the network.

- *Chapter 8: TKIP*. TKIP is a stopgap protocol for secure encapsulation of 802.11 frames in legacy 802.11 devices. The aim of TKIP is to patch the many vulnerabilities of WEP using various techniques. However, in designing TKIP one important consideration is the large install base of existing 802.11 hardware. Hence, TKIP was designed so that it could be implemented with only a firmware upgrade. Chapter 8 provides a discussion of TKIP.

The third part of this book focuses on the area of wireless roaming security, covering two chapters on the following topics:

- *Chapter 9: Security in WiFi Roaming*. One of the main attractions of WLANs is the fact that the mobile user can roam from one service provider to another. Chapter 9 introduces the notion of roaming as found in today's dial-up Internet. It then covers the entities involved in roaming, and proceeds to discuss WLAN roaming as defined by the WISPr architecture.

- *Chapter 10: 3G-WLAN Roaming*. Chapter 10 is devoted to the new area of 3G-WLAN roaming, where WLAN services are provided by 3G network operators. The chapter reports the efforts under way in the 3GPP standards community in defining roaming models and interfaces between WLAN and 3G services.

The fourth part of this book is devoted to the security of the emerging area of technology called WMAN or "wireless broadband," based on the IEEE 802.16 standard. The two chapters covering WMAN security are as follows:

- *Chapter 11: An Overview of 802.16 WMANs*. Chapter 11 provides some basic background regarding 802.16, including network arrangement, frequency bands, the MAC security sublayer, and network entry/initialization. The chapter then presents the privacy and key management (PKM) protocol, which is important for authentication between a subscriber station and base station. The PKM protocol, which is derived from a similar protocol used in cable modems, employs device certificates. As such, this chapter looks into the topic of device certificates as found in the cable modem industry.

- *Chapter 12: Wireless MAN Security.* Since security weaknesses were found in 802.11 WLANs, a similar security reevaluation of 802.16 has been under way. Chapter 12 provides a discussion and insight into these recent developments on the security of 802.16.

  Finally, the concluding chapter provides a brief summary of the book and ongoing work in 802.11 and 802.16 networks.

Part I

Authentication and Authorization in WLANs

Chapter 2

Authentication in WLANs: An Overview

2.1 INTRODUCTION

Traditionally, the term *authentication* in the context of computer and network security concerns the ability of a verifier (or prover) entity to ascertain the correct *identity* of another entity claiming to be that identity. Thus, the aim of authentication is for one entity to prove its identity to another based on some *credentials* possessed by that first entity. Examples of credentials include passwords, digital certificates, or even physical keys. The outcome of an authentication process is typically binary, namely success or fail. The process is typically defined and implemented as one or more *protocols*.

The term *authorization* pertains to the rights, privileges, or permissions given to an authenticated entity in relation to some set of resources. In practice, authorization for an entity to take actions (e.g., access network, read files) is preconditioned on a successful authentication. The functions of authentication and authorization are often accompanied by *accounting* (or auditing), with the three loosely referred to as *AAA*.

The level of authorization assigned to an entity when it seeks access to resources is often tied to the type and strength of the authentication protocol used and the type of credential possessed by the authenticated entity. Hence, differing levels of assurance or certainty regarding the outcome of an authentication process can be gained by using different credentials and authentication protocols.

For example, when a password (as a credential) is used with a weak protocol (e.g., plaintext challenge-response), then a low or weak level assurance is obtained as both the credential and the authentication protocol are weak. In contrast, a strong credential such as a digital certificate when combined with a strong authentication protocol, such as SSL or TLS, achieves a higher level of assurance regarding the identity of the authenticated entity.

In today's complex computer and network systems, multiple credentials might be needed for an entity to access multiple resources, each access instance of which

9

may be governed by separate sets of privileges. Thus, often the term *layers* (of authentication and authorization processes) is used to describe complex situations.

In this chapter we look at the broad issue of authentication in wireless LANs, starting with some general security requirements. We look at several models and frameworks for authentication in WLANs. First, the UAM method based on the use of HTTP/SSL is discussed, as it is the most common approach used by many wireless ISPs, due its ease of deployment. Second, the 802.1X authentication framework is discussed, covering the important notion of ports and port-based access control. We provide an overview of the RADIUS protocol as RADIUS is often used as an authentication server in 802.1X implementations as well as in UAM implementations, because of its strong presence in the dial-up world. Finally, we look briefly into device authentication and the issue of rogue 802.11 access points.

2.2   BASIC ENTITIES AND REQUIREMENTS IN WLANS

In the context of IP networks, the first objective of authentication and authorization would be to control *connectivity* to the networks, since networks are considered as resources also. After this primary objective, the second aim would be to control access to resources beyond the network itself, such as other computers and systems interconnected by the network.

The credentials and authentication process used in these two broad classes of access need not be the same. In addition, in the context of authentication and authorization in LANs and WLANs it is useful for us distinguish between the *device* the human user is employing and the *person*, since different credentials and privileges might be assigned to the two entities. In practice, both user and device are authenticated by a *AAA server* through the use of an appropriate authentication protocol. Often, the AAA server also holds the authorization information and other privileges information.

2.2.1   Entities and Functions in a LAN and WLAN

In order to understand further the authentication requirements in WLANs, Figure 2.1 shows a number of entities and their functions in a typical organizational IP network, consisting of LAN and WLANs. For simplicity, no remote offices or campuses are shown, as remote sites today are most commonly connected via secure VPNs to other sites in the same organization.

The entities found within the typical organizational IP network include, but are not limited to, the following:

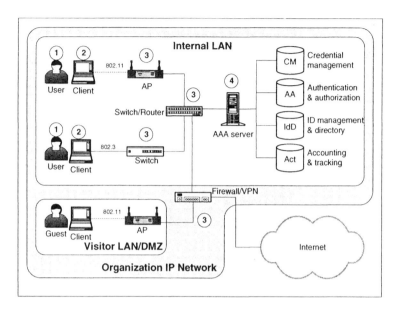

Figure 2.1 Basic entities and functions in a LAN/WLAN.

- *Users and end-user devices*: Human users and end-user devices (e.g., laptop/desktop computers, PDAs, and so on) represent the "consumer" side of the services provided by an organization's IP network (including LANs and WLANs). End-user devices are typically assigned to a person and do not really function to support the operational aspects of the network.

- *Network devices*. Network devices can be loosely defined as those hardware/software systems used to support the operational aspects of an organization's IP network. As such, these devices rightly belong under the authority of the IT and network administrators. The typical nonadministrative (unauthorized) user should not have access to these network-devices. Examples of network devices include 802.11 access points (APs), IP routers, LAN switches, hubs, VPN gateways, firewalls, AAA servers, session controllers, remote access servers (RASs), and others.

- *AAA servers*: The AAA server has a special role in the context of authentication and authorization, as it is the management entity within which access policies are defined and implemented. These policies govern access to the network itself and to resources available on the network (e.g., file servers and printers). In many cases, the AAA server represents the *policy decision point*

(PDP), while other network devices represent the *policy enforcement point* (PEP) [1, 2].

- *Firewalls/VPN gateways*: Firewalls and VPN gateways play a special role as they represent the entry point (exit point) of connections into (out of) an organization's IP network. Many enterprises today perform packet filtering and port monitoring at firewalls and other filter devices. Many firewalls today are tightly integrated to IPsec VPN gateways, as these represent entry points for legitimate users (e.g., employees) who are connecting remotely from remote offices, home offices, public WiFi hotspots, dial-up numbers, and other locations outside the perimeter of the organization's network.

The typical organization network consisting of LANs and WLANs performs a number of important functions pertaining to the operational aspects of the network and security. Some of the security-related functions include the following:

- *Authentication and authorization*: These two functions are interrelated in the sense that authentication establishes the correct identity of an user or device (as known by the network) and authorization determines what resources are available to that identity.

- *Identity management*: Many organizations maintain identities for the users and devices within the network, ranging from the simple user ID to names that carry semantic meaning. Since a human user (and network device) may have multiple identities, both within and outside the organization, some method for identity management must be deployed.

- *Directory services*: Often the function of mapping resources available to a human user is dependent on the identity of the user or device, and on other variables (e.g., which LAN he or she is connecting to or type of access). Directory services embody these functions and in many systems and networks it is tightly related to identity management.

- *Credential management*: Aside from an identity, a user or device needs some form of credential to prove its identity through an authentication process. Credentials today can range from simple passwords, phrases, and digital certificates, to more sophisticated hardware-based credentials, including hardware tokens and smartcards. Since a credential represents the "keys to the castle," its correct and secure management is paramount to the overall security of the organization's resources, including its network.

- *Accounting, auditing, and tracking*: Accounting/auditing, logging, and tracking of connections to an organization's network are functions that are becoming increasingly important to the overall security of the network. All connections, whether from inside the network or from outside must be logged, regardless of whether they were successful or failed attempts. Many corporations today are increasingly deploying *intrusion detection systems* (IDSs), which need this important information for both analysis/forensics and planning defenses against attacks. Some IDS systems today also perform logging of internal connections to resources within the organization, in order to detect unauthorized behavior by employees and intruders.

2.2.2   General Requirements in WLAN Security

The following lists some general requirements with respect to authentication and authorization of devices and human users connected to LANs and WLANs:

*   *Device authentication*
    All devices connecting to LANs and WLANs must be strongly authenticated, based on a strong device credential.

    Device authentication pertains to the correct identification of devices in a LAN or WLAN — both end-user devices (e.g., laptops) and network elements (e.g., switches, routers) — by an authenticating entity (e.g., authentication server). Many corporate networks today demand that as soon as it detects a device being physically connected to the LAN, the device must be immediately authenticated by an authenticating entity, such as an AAA server (e.g., RADIUS [3] or Diameter [4]). Many networks tie this first-step authentication to the granting of an IP address (e.g., via DHCP) to the connecting device.

    One open issue today is the form of identity of the connecting device and the credential that the device needs to possess to authenticate itself to the AAA server. Many LANs and WLANs use the physical layer *medium access control* (MAC) address of the network interface card (NIC) of the device as the identifying information. However, MAC addresses can easily be reprogrammed by the user and thus cannot be relied upon.

*   *User authentication*
    All users connecting to LANs and WLANs must be strongly authenticated, based on a strong user credential.

    An increasing number of LANs require user authentication in addition to device authentication. Ideally, the process of authenticating a user should be preconditioned on a successful authentication of the user's device. This approach has been adopted by a growing number of corporate networks whose user population increasingly use mobile devices (e.g., laptops and PDAs) and whose end-user devices are in fact the property of the corporation. Many corporate networks today disallow personal computing devices belonging to individual employees to be connected to the corporate LAN or WLAN. Strong authentication for users must be the basis for user authorization.

• *Device authorization*
All successfully authenticated devices on LANs and WLANs must have access only to resources for which they have been authorized.

In the context of devices, this may mean that they can only connect to certain LANs or VLANs of a corporate network, and the other resources (e.g., printers and servers) on those allowable portions of the network.

• *User authorization*
All successfully authenticated users on LANs and WLANs must have access only to resources to which they have been authorized.

This requirement is an obvious one, arising from the general need of computer and network security. As this topic is beyond the current work, it will only be treated here minimally and only when necessary.

• *User privacy*
Depending upon the organizational policy, a user's privacy must be preserved when he or she is accessing resources on the network from various parts of the network. Information regarding users and their behaviors must be held confidential and be only accessible to authorized personnel in the organization, such as the IT or network administrator. Thus, although user *presence* may be an important feature of a network, often a user may not wish this information to be known by other unauthorized personnel.

In the next section we look more closely into a number of AAA models proposed for LANs, WLANs, and WiFi hotspots.

2.3 AUTHENTICATION MODELS FOR WLANS

In architecting a secure LAN and WLAN, often a *model* or framework for authentication is needed in order to understand the particular threats being addressed and the remedies being applied to counter the threats. Credentials and authentication protocols are really only effective when they are appropriately selected and deployed within a given model. Over the last few years, a number of models have been proposed for authentication in WLANs. Some of these are as follows:

• *Web-based authentication model*
One of the early ideas for authenticating users was to employ the SSL functionality that was present in Web browsers on the user's client machine. At the other end, a Web server would intercept the user's HTTP traffic and redirect the user to a login page.

At the login page, the user could either enroll for a new account or enter his or her existing account details together with a password. The transmission of the user's identity and password is protected by the underlying SSL (TLS) session, which encrypts the traffic between the browser and the Web server.

Although this method is simple to install and configure, the approach does not result in a negotiated encryption key at the WLAN frame layer (for use by algorithms such as TKIP). Thus, after the Web login phase has been completed, traffic at the MAC layer may remain unencrypted. This approach, which is also the basis of the *universal access method* (UAM), will be discussed in Section 2.4.

- *802.1X authentication framework*
  The IEEE 802 community developed a standard framework for authentication referred to as 802.1X [5]. In this framework, a port-based access control approach is adopted, in which port access is given only to clients (supplicant) that have been successfully authenticated by an authentication server. This framework has also been adopted for WLAN authentication, and more importantly it has been integrated with various key agreement protocols between the client/supplicant and the 802.11 access point for deriving the layer-2 cryptographic keys.

  One important aspect of 802.1X is that it is an authentication framework, within which specific authentication protocols and credentials need to be specified for deployment. Since 802.1X is today rapidly becoming the de facto model for authentication in enterprise WLANs, this approach will be discussed in Section 2.5.

- *The point-to-point VPN model*
  A number of vendors have proposed the use of standard IPsec VPNs to provide for confidentiality (encryption) of data "over the air" (in the wireless segment between the client and access point), obtaining authentication as a beneficial side effect. The argument put forward by proponents of this approach is that strong security can be established at the IP layer (by virtue of IPsec), regardless of the underlying layer-2 security features.

  In this approach, the client is allocated a temporary IP address at which time the client software automatically establishes an IPsec VPN with a *VPN server*. The VPN server can be collocated with the AP or be another entity behind the AP acting as the VPN end point (e.g., an actual VPN box or Web server). Some vendors even combine all functionality into a single product. The physical implementation of the IPsec VPN can vary, though the primary function is to provide an encrypted communication for the wireless segment. All subsequent data traffic from the client is tunnelled through the established VPN.

In this approach, authentication is conducted as part of the IPsec VPN setup. Failure in authentication means that the IPsec VPN fails to be established, and the client's IP address is deallocated. A count may be maintained by the VPN server for the number of allowable failures by the client. As this approach is not new and is based on well-known technologies, it will not be treated further in this chapter.

- *SIM-based approach*
  In the SIM-based approach, authentication is based on a shared key that is contained in the *subscriber identification module* (SIM) used in GSM networks or USIM in UMTS networks. The growing interest among *mobile network operators* (MNO) in providing WLAN services at hotspots to their subscribers — while leveraging their existing infrastructure — has motivated the use of the SIM in the WLAN context.

  This model is interesting because it presents a new effort to repurpose credentials and AAA infrastructures in mobile networks for AAA functions in IP-based WLANs. The client is assumed to be in possession of a U/SIM card when requesting access to a WLAN at a public hotspot. The U/SIM card contains security parameters that are issued and are shared with the authentication database (namely the *home location registry* or HLR) at the operator's home network. Thus, in simple terms the authentication protocol that executes between the client and the HLR actually extends from the WLAN through to mobile home network, through possibly one or more IP networks and PSTNs in between. This topic will be further treated in Chapter 9.

2.4   THE UNIVERSAL ACCESS METHOD

The Web-based approach for authentication was adopted by a number of early providers of WLAN hotspots due to the simplicity of the approach and the fact that no special software or hardware was needed for the user to make use of the hotspot. However, as many providers soon discovered, some standardization was needed across these providers in order to give the subscriber the same look and feel when roaming to different hotspots, and to give the providers some common auditing and billing information for cross-provider roaming.

Within the WiFi Alliance (WFA),[1] which is the WLAN industry governing association, a small group of vendors and ISPs called the *Wireless ISP Roaming* (WISPr) group began developing the *universal access method* (UAM) as the basis for standardizing operational aspect of WLAN roaming. The WISPr group was

1   Before 2003, the WiFi Alliance (WFA) was known as the Wireless Ethernet Compatibility Alliance (WECA). Due to their expanding role beyond certification of 802.11 devices and the better-known term of "WiFi" for 802.11 technology, the name of the alliance was changed in 2003.

chartered by WECA to describe the recommended operational practices, technical architecture, and AAA framework needed to enable subscriber roaming among WiFi-based wireless Internet service providers (WISPs) [6]. The aim of the roaming framework is to allow WiFi-compliant devices to roam into WiFi enabled hotspots for public access and services. Similar to the dial-up case, a roaming user can then be authenticated by either the roamed WISP or by the user's own home ISP/WISP. The user (or his or her employer) would then obtain a single billing statement, clearly showing the WiFi roaming charges. In order to facilitate compatibility with the widest possible range of legacy WiFi products, the WISPr group recommended that WISPs or hotspot operators deploy a browser-based UAM for public access networks. The UAM allows a subscriber to access WISP services with only an 802.11 NIC card and Internet browser on the user's device.

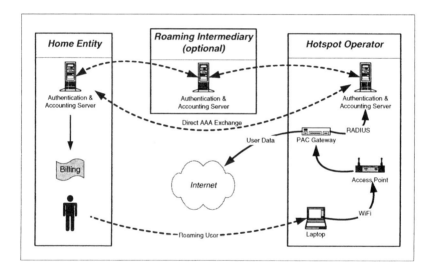

Figure 2.2 The universal access method (UAM).

The basic architecture of the UAM is shown in Figure 2.2. Here, the user is assumed to roam into a hotspot being operated by a WISP. Upon obtaining layer-2 connectivity and an IP address, the user's HTTP traffic is intercepted by a *public access control* (PAC) gateway. The PAC gateway then provides the user with a login (or registration) page, protected using an SSL session.

In recommending the UAM to facilitate WISP roaming, the WISPr group cites a number of benefits to the user and to wireless ISPs. Among others, the UAM allows a subscriber to access WISP services with only an Internet browser and WiFi network interface on the subscriber device, so that all users, regardless of device type or operating system, can participate in WISP roaming. The UAM utilizes home page redirection (automatic redirection of the user's initial HTTP request to an operator-specified Web page), Internet browser-based secure authentication portal, user credential entry, and RADIUS AAA. The UAM represents the lowest common denominator for granting access to a WISP network ensuring that all users can share the same experience [6].

Not surprisingly, the WISPr group did not promote the use of 802.1X even though from a security perspective 802.1X provided a better solution and provides a framework for the negotiation of TKIP keys. The cited reason for this is that 802.1X has not been widely deployed in public access environments. In addition, unlike the UAM, the 802.1X access method requires client software beyond just the Web browser [6].

2.5   THE 802.1X AUTHENTICATION FRAMEWORK

A different approach to authentication and authorization for 802.11 WLANs is that based on the 802.1X standard, which was originally published by the IEEE in 1999, and was revised in 2001.[2]

The original motivation behind 802.1X was the need for "device-level" authentication for network devices connected to an 802.3 (Ethernet) LAN. The basic model adopted was that of the client-server model, in which a client who seeks network access to (or through) a port of another device on the same shared medium must be authenticated by the server. Thus, functionally the authenticating entity (the server) was distinguished from the entity providing the service (or, in this case, the port). This thinking is in line with other existing approaches at higher layers where the server as the decision-maker grants the client access to some service.

With recent developments in newer protocols and architectures, the 802.1X framework has been in fact used with authentication protocols (EAP methods) that employ human credentials, such as passwords and certificates, instead of only for device-level authentication.

One crucial point that distinguishes 802.1X from the UAM approach is the integration of entity authentication with key agreement to establish the master keys subsequently used by the access point and client to encrypt frames when they traverse over the air. In more concrete terms, unlike the UAM approach, after a client has been authenticated by the authentication server (AS) using a given EAP method (e.g., EAP-TLS), the two immediately continue with the derivation of the master keys, which will subsequently be used by the frame encryption algorithm (e.g., TKIP).

2   At the time of this writing, the 802.1X standard was being revised again to reflect some developments in the 802.11i specifications.

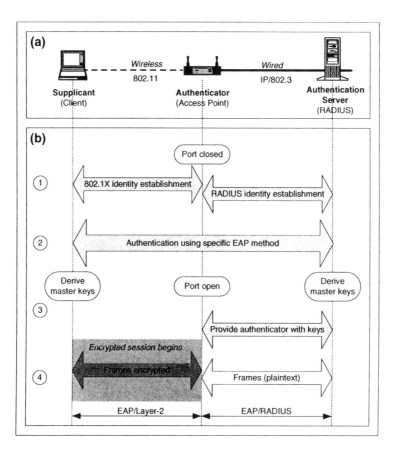

Figure 2.3 (a) Basic entities in 802.1X, and (b) overview of key establishment.

2.5.1 The 802.1X Entities

The 802.1X framework recognizes three primary types of entities or *port access entities* (PAEs). These are the following [5]:

- *Supplicant*: This is the port that wishes to or requests access to the services offered by the authenticator's system. Typically, the supplicant would be the client system, such as a laptop or a PDA.

- *Authenticator*: This is the port that enforces authentication before allowing access to services that are accessible via that port. In the basic WLAN configuration, the AP would typically be the authenticator.

- *Authentication Server (AS)*: This is the entity that performs the authentication function necessary to check the credentials of the supplicant, on behalf of the authenticator. The resulting decision consists of whether or not the supplicant is authorized to access the authenticator's services. The most oft-quoted server is RADIUS [3, 7, 8], though other types of servers could also be used (e.g., Diameter [4]).

These entities are shown in Figure 2.3(a).

From the basic description of the 802.1X entities above, we can get a basic understanding of the behavior of each entity. Thus, for example, a laptop (the supplicant) seeking to gain access to a LAN behind an 802.11 AP (the authenticator) must first execute an authentication protocol against the AS sitting behind the AP. If the authentication process succeeds, the AS signals the AP to open the relevant port on the AP to allow the client access.

2.5.2 The Notion of a Port

An important concept in 802.1X is that of a "port," which is the basis for the *port-based access control* (PBAC) paradigm as specified in the 802.1X standard as a way to provide authentication and authorization to devices attached to a LAN. More specifically, port-based network access control makes use of the physical access characteristics of IEEE 802 LAN infrastructures in order to provide a means of authenticating and authorizing devices attached to a LAN port that has point-to-point connection characteristics (and preventing access to that port in cases in which the authentication and authorization process fails) [9]. Thus, the 802.1X standard applies to both 802.3 (wired Ethernet) and 802.11 (wireless Ethernet) point-to-point connections.

Since a WLAN is considered also to be a LAN, the PBAC approach of 802.1X directly applies to the WLAN situation. The ports of a entity provide the means in which it can access services offered by other entities reachable via the LAN and provide the means in which it can offer services to, or access the services provided by, other entities reachable via the LAN. The PBAC approach allows the operation of a entity's ports to be controlled in order to ensure that access to its services (and/or access to the services of other entities) is only permitted by entities that are authorized to do so [9].

Devices that attach to a LAN have one or more points of attachment to the LAN, referred to in the 802.1X standard as *network access ports*, or simply as *ports*. The notion of a port applies to devices that have a single point of attachment (e.g., network interface card, or NIC, in a laptop) as well as devices that have multiple points of attachment, such as those that provide MAC bridging (e.g., bridges and switches).

The 802.1X standard views ports as being of two types, namely the *protected* and *unprotected*. Authentication applies to requests pertaining to the protected ports, naturally. The unprotected ports could be used by a supplicant (or authenticator) to exchange protocol-related information with other supplicants (or authenticators), though obviously such exchanges must not reveal any sensitive information or parameters that could affect the security of the systems. For cases where the AS is not collocated with the authenticator (e.g., the AP), then these two entities could communicate protocol exchanges using either of the two types of ports. The understanding here is that some higher-level protocol such as EAP/RADIUS would be used between the AP and the AS.

2.5.3 EAP, EAP over LAN, and EAP over Wireless

The 802.1X standard makes use of the *Extensible Authentication Protocol* (EAP) [10] as a way of communicating authentication information between the supplicant (e.g., client, laptop) and the AS, passing through the authenticator (e.g., AP). It is interesting that in this mode of usage, EAP essentially becomes a lowest denomination of "transport" between the supplicant and the AS.

To understand the significance of EAP in this context, it is important to realize that the EAP packets (frames) exchanged between the supplicant and the AS traverse over two different types of communications media:

- Between the supplicant (client) and the authenticator (AP), EAP is layered immediately above the MAC layer (i.e., no IP layer).

- Between the authenticator (AP) and the AS (RADIUS), EAP is over the RADIUS protocol (over IP).

The 802.1X standard defines the encapsulation format, known as *EAP over LAN* or EAPOL, which allows EAP messages to be carried *directly* by a LAN MAC service (i.e., layer-2). The EAPOL encapsulation is used for all communication between the supplicant (i.e., client) and the authenticator (i.e., AP). EAPOL is also referred

to as *EAP over Wireless* or EAPOW, though the intent is clear that the EAP packets
are layered over the MAC layer without the IP layer.

Since an authentication exchange occurs between the supplicant and the AS
(as the decision-maker), during such an exchange the authenticator provides a "pass-
through" or "relay" function. This means that the authenticator needs to repackage
the EAP packets for suitable delivery to the AS. This repackaging must be done
by higher level function in the authenticator. Though not mandated by the 802.1X
standard, the most common way to communicate the EAP frames (coming from the
supplicant) to the AS is through EAP over RADIUS [3, 7, 8]. Note that RADIUS
itself is defined to run over an IP layer, which typically exists between an AP and the
AS in the on-campus scenario (where both the AP and the AS are within the same
subnet), and in the WLAN-roaming scenario (where the AP may be on a different
subnet, network, or even different autonomous system, to the AS).

2.5.4 Supplicant to AS Authentication Protocols

If we view EAP as the encapsulating format (or even as a general "transport"
mechanism) for authentication information exchanged between a supplicant and
AS, the next question would be which authentication protocol is to be executed
between the supplicant and AS (to prove, among others, to the AS that the supplicant
is indeed the entity is claims to be).

The answer is that EAP is extensible enough that the security engineer needs
to "instantiate" EAP with the authentication protocol that she or he wishes to use.
To that extent, the EAP specifications talk about "methods" or "types" that need to
be defined for a particular usage scenario. Note that the EAP methods need not only
be related to security,[3] but can be any other method defined for other functions in a
WLAN. EAP will be further discussed in Chapter 3.

Figure 2.3(b) shows an overview of an authentication process and key generation. This can be better understood by looking at the 802.1X process as consisting
of four phases:

1. *Identity establishment:* In the first phase, the supplicant and the AS begin
   exchanging identity information. This occurs after the 802.11 association.
   This leads to the need of each end point to prove their identities (namely,
   through authentication). Part of this phase is for the AS to indicate to the
   client which authentication method the AS is expecting to use.

2. *End point (mutual) authentication:* In the second phase, the supplicant and
   the AS execute the authentication protocol, expressed as an EAP method.
   Note that not all EAP methods for authentication provide mutually strong

---

3   At the time of this writing, there were over two dozen EAP methods that had been proposed, five or
    six of which were related to security functions.

authentication. For example, a password-based method such as EAP-CHAP does not provide a strong authentication as one side (the supplicant) supplies only a password, which is a weak credential.

3. *Encryption key derivation:* The successful outcome of the authentication process results in both the supplicant and AS deriving some common cryptographic parameter (i.e., keys) that will be used for the basis for deriving (temporal) encryption keys used to encrypt the data in frames for the over-the-air segment of the communications.

    Since the over-the-air segment is the segment between the supplicant and the AP, and since the AP has so far not been involved in key negotiations, the AS must forward a copy of the derived common cryptographic parameter to the AP so that the AP can begin to derive the (temporal) frame encryption keys and itself begin encrypting/decrypting data frames to/from the Supplicant. See Chapter 8 for further information on the key derivation algorithms.

4. *Frame encryption/decryption:* Once both the supplicant and the AP have begun to derive (temporal) keys for the encryption of data in frames, they can begin using the keys to encrypt frames. Note that when frames from the supplicant have been decrypted by the AP, the wired segment of the communications from the AP to the AS is by default in plaintext. Thus, additional security mechanisms must be applied for that wired segment (e.g., encryption in RADIUS or establish IPsec VPNs).

The reader is directed to Chapter 3 for further discussion on how 802.1X functions with the EAP protocol (as transport) and EAP methods (as the authentication protocols).

2.6 THE RADIUS PROTOCOL

The *remote authentication dial-in user service* (RADIUS) [11] is an authentication protocol that has wide deployment in the dial-up Internet services world. Due mostly to its simple password-based authentication method and simple transaction structure, RADIUS has become the de facto "authentication protocol" in the dial-up world for IP connectivity using the *point-to-point protocol* (PPP) [12]. More recently, interest in RADIUS has also been extended to the new area of WLAN authentication. In this section we briefly review RADIUS in order to provide a context for ensuing discussions in the following chapters.

RADIUS follows the client-server model, where a RADIUS client interacts with a RADIUS server, through possibly one or more RADIUS proxies. In the context of dial-up services the client is typically the *network access server* (NAS) that is usually connected to (collocated with) the *remote access server* (RAS), which is essentially the end point of the dial-up connection over the telephone line (PSTN). From the client's perspective a RADIUS-server is responsible for receiving user connection requests, authenticating the user, and then returning all configuration information necessary for the client to deliver service to the user. As such, RADIUS offers functionality beyond just authenticating a user, and provides support for authorization and accounting/auditing (AAA).

RADIUS runs over UDP (instead of TCP) for a number of reasons, though primarily because RADIUS is essentially a stateless transactions-based protocol. More specifically, in its expected usage environment, multiple RADIUS servers may be deployed to provide service reliability. Here, when one server becomes unavailable, a backup server must take on the transactions of the first server. Hence, a copy of the request must be kept above the transport layer to allow for alternate transmission. This points to UDP in the case of RADIUS being a better underlying transport than TCP. However, the use of UDP implies that the end point RADIUS entities must deploy their own reliability mechanisms to handle lost packets. Many RADIUS implementations and deployment cases today just use simple retransmission as a reliability mechanism. Finally, RADIUS was designed with a nonaggressive response in mind. The user is expected not to mind waiting several seconds for an authentication to complete. As such, TCP was deemed to be too aggressive for the needs of RADIUS.

Within the context of the 802.1X authentication framework, RADIUS is the most oft-cited protocol for supporting WLAN authentication. Here, the 802.1X supplicant (e.g., 802.11 AP) is in fact the RADIUS client communicating with the 802.1X AS, which is the RADIUS server. In the context of WiFi roaming, RADIUS is also the most oft-cited authentication protocol since many ISPs and aggregators who are providing new WiFi roaming services typically already have a dial-up infrastructure built using RADIUS, which represents a technology investment these organizations would naturally like to preserve.

From the perspective of protocol extensibility, RADIUS provides an attractive solution as all transactions between the client and server are based on the 3-tuple *attribute-value-length* (AVL) format. As such, a given implementation of RADIUS can introduce its own domain-relevant extensions without affecting other implementations.

In this section, we briefly cover the RADIUS server emphasizing points and issues relevant to the WLAN deployment. For a more comprehensive treatment of RADIUS itself, the reader is directed to the RADIUS-related RFCs (RFC2058 [11], RFC2865 [3], RFC2866 [7], RFC3579 [8], and others) and to the book [13].

2.6.1 RADIUS Packets Overview

RADIUS packets have the format shown in Figure 2.4, where a single RADIUS packet is encapsulated in the UDP data field [3]:

- *Code field*: This field identifies the type of message and is 1 octet in length. Some of most commonly used types of messages are access-request (code 1), access-accept (code 2), access-reject (code 3), accounting-request (code 4), and accounting-response (code 5). Other codes are accounting specific, while others are reserved for future use.

- *Identifier field*: The identifier field is 1 octet in length and is used to match requests and responses.

- *Length field*: This field is 2 octets in length, and indicates the length of the entire packet, including the code, identifier, length, authenticator, and attribute fields.

- *Authenticator field*: The authenticator field is 16 octets in length, with the most significant octet transmitted first. The actual contents of this field are determined by the type of packet within which it is contained.

  When the packet is an access-request packet, this field functions as a *request authenticator* consisting of 16 octets of a random number. In the RADIUS protocol, the NAS and the RADIUS server shares a common secret. That shared secret, followed by the request authenticator is put through a one-way MD5 hash to create a 16-octet digest value. This digest is then XOR-ed against the user's password, the result of which is then placed in the *user-password* attribute in the access-request packet.

  The Authenticator field in access-accept, access-reject, and access-challenge packets is called the *response authenticator*. In this case, the field contains a one-way MD5 hash calculated over the concatenation of the following: the identifier, the length, the request authenticator (from the original access-request packet), the response attributes, and the shared secret (shared between the NAS or RADIUS client and the RADIUS server).

- *Attributes field*: This field contains attribute values that are specific to the packet types.

2.6.2 RADIUS Authentication Approaches

Historically, RADIUS has used two basic authentication approaches, namely, through the use of plain text passwords and the hash of passwords. The second approach uses a keyed hash mechanism based on a shared secret.

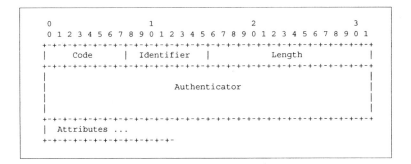

Figure 2.4   RADIUS packet format.

The two approaches are embodied in the two most popular authentication protocols used with RADIUS, namely, PAP [14] and CHAP [15]. In the PAP usage case the NAS (or RADIUS client) sends the client ID (or PAP ID) together with the (plaintext) password within the access-request packet to the server. Since sending plain text passwords from a client to a server is insecure, this practice is discouraged and is no longer used by most dial-up ISPs.

In the CHAP usage case, the NAS first generates a random value and sends it as a *challenge* value to the user, who answers it with a *response*, accompanied by the user name and the CHAP-ID value. The NAS then communicates with the RADIUS server by sending an access-request packet to the Server containing the CHAP user-name and using the CHAP-ID and CHAP response as the CHAP password. The RADIUS server then verifies the password of the user by repeating the hash operation done by the user and compares the result against the stored value. A correct match results in the server returning an access-accept message to the NAS, while an incorrect match results in an access-reject message.

2.6.3   RADIUS Vulnerabilities

The work of [16] provides an excellent summary of the weaknesses and vulnerabilities of RADIUS as defined in RFC2058 [11]. Some of these are as follows:

- *Lack of per-packet authentication for access-request packets.* The access-request message contains a 128-bit pseudorandom number referred to as the *request authenticator* (RA). However, in reality the RA functions more as a nonce, and is used in hiding the user's password in the access-request message. As such, the RA value really does not provide authentication of access-request messages. Note that using RADIUS over IPsec overcomes this problem.

- *Off-line dictionary attacks on the shared secret.* Many implementations of RADIUS only allow shared secrets that are ASCII characters and have lengths less than 16 characters. This limitation results in shared secrets that typically have low entropy. Knowing this an attacker can begin capturing access-request and access-response packets (and also accounting-request or accounting-response packets) in order to then perform off-line dictionary attacks.

- *Off-line dictionary attacks in EAP.* Similar to the previous case, an attacker can also attempt an off-line attack on any packet with an *EAP message* attribute. Note however that since the EAP message attribute uses HMAC-MD5, this type of attack is harder than the previous attack.

The reader is directed to [16] for details on other types of attacks.

2.7 DEVICE AUTHENTICATION FOR NETWORK ELEMENTS

One of the pressing problems in today's deployment of 802.11 wireless LANs in many enterprises is that of the *rogue access point* problem. This refers to the situation in which an employee connects an unauthorized 802.11 AP device to the corporate LAN, effectively creating a security hole in the corporate network. The broadcast nature of 802.11 technology allows a nearby external person to gain access to the corporate LAN and other resources on the LAN. The rogue AP problem is illustrated in Figure 2.5.

The core of the problem is the lack of device-to-device authentication and the need for a network infrastructure in which all network elements are authenticated before they participate within the network.

Before the advent of 802.11 technology in enterprises, all network devices, such as routers and switches, were considered to be "in-the-closet" devices and therefore under the direct control of the network administrator. Although a misbehaving employee could connect a foreign router or switch to the Ethernet port on the wall, the physical limitation of the wired world made it difficult for him or her to provide illegal network access to external persons. The introduction of cheap and small 802.11 APs has introduced potential security holes (literally) in the classic enterprise LAN. Other variations of this attack include an employee converting his or her PC or PDA — which has both a wired NIC and a wireless NIC — into a wireless router or bridge, so that external persons can access the WLAN side of the PC or PDA as a gateway into the corporate LAN.

As a means to secure LANs against unauthorized access, currently many IT administrators perform device identification by maintaining a list of Ethernet MAC addresses that are permitted to connect to the LAN. This approach is no longer viable today from a security perspective, primarily because in many end-user devices the Ethernet MAC address is configurable by the user. Thus, an employee is able to bring an unauthorized device (e.g., AP) into the enterprise premises, reconfigure the device's MAC address to match an existing authorized device, and connect it to the corporate LAN without detection.

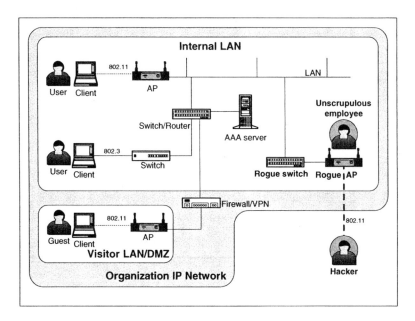

Figure 2.5   The rogue AP problem.

2.7.1   The Rogue Cable Modem Case: A Precedent

In the late 1990s, the cable *multiservice operators* (MSOs) and cable modem manufacturers faced a similar security problem to that of the rogue AP problem. Their problem — which could be dubbed as the *rogue cable modem* problem — consisted of the need to authenticate off-the-shelf cable modem devices when connected by the user to the physical cable.

In the early days of cable modem deployment the home consumer would typically obtain or be assigned a cable modem device from the operator during an installation visit by the operator's technical personnel. In many cases, the consumer was actually renting the cable modem from the operator, though this cost was built into the monthly cable service fee. Any time a cable modem failed through malfunction or wear and tear, the operator would send a technician to install a replacement cable modem device.

This operational model changed somewhat when both operators and manufacturers opted for the off-the-shelf approach. Here, rather than the consumer being leased a cable modem device and having the costly technician to install the device, the consumer would be able to purchase his or her own cable modem from the local electronics store and install the device himself or herself. Furthermore, when the consumer moved to a different town, city, or state, he or she could retain the same cable modem and install it in the new location. Not only would this reduce the operator's costs and encourage manufacturers to reduce the price of the device — effectively making it a commodity — it would also encourage innovation through better features and through combining the device with other devices, such as the *set-top boxes* (STBs).

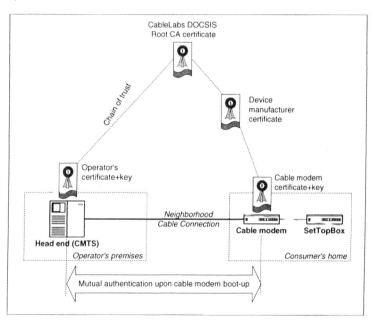

Figure 2.6 Device authentication in cable modems.

In addition to the change in the operational model, the cable operators also required the ability to distinguish legitimate cable modem devices from "cloned" devices, thereby allowing the operator to ascertain legitimate subscribers.

The solution to the problem was to require a cable modem device at the user's home to authenticate itself upon boot-up to the *cable modem terminating system*

(CMTS) device — also called the *head end* — located at the local cable operator premises. The authentication protocol adopted by the DOCSIS1.2 specifications required the cable modem device to engage in an authentication handshake with the CMTS, applying their respective public key pair and their digital certificates. Since the certificate (and public key pair) was embedded within the cable modem device, it was technically difficult or infeasible for a hacker to copy the parameters into a cloned device.

In order to promote interoperability across various cable modem manufacturers and operators, a certificate hierarchy was established under *Cable Laboratories* (CableLabs) as the leading industry consortium.[4] This is illustrated in Figure 2.6. Here each manufacturer is assigned a manufacturer-level key pair and certificate, issued under the CableLabs Root CA. These in turn are used by a manufacturer to issue a device key pair and certificate for each cable modem unit. Currently, there are over 40 manufacturers who are members of CableLabs and who are participating in the CableLabs certificate hierarchy.

2.7.2   802.1X and Device Certificates

The 802.1X authentication framework provides a promising avenue towards solving the problem of rogue devices being attached to an enterprise LAN. A number of authentication protocols in 802.1X (i.e., EAP methods) are certificate-based and can be used for devices as well as users.

In order for a strong authentication protocol to correctly authenticate a device or entity, first a strong identity must be bound to that device or entity. A digital certificate issued to a device and physically embedded into that device provides a strong method for identification. A *device certificate* binds some physical properties or parameters of a device to a private key, expressed in a public-key certificate. The device can be a user device (e.g., laptop, desktop, PDA) or it can be a network device (e.g., access point, router).

The parameters of the device can be a combination of MAC address, product serial number, hash of the driver code, components' serial numbers, and others. One or more of these values can be combined (e.g., through a hash function) to arrive at a unique identity of the device, which is then used as the subject identity in the device certificate.

Thus, a device certificate is aimed in the first place to provide irrefutable proof of the identity of the device when the device engages in a mutual authentication protocol with a "verifying party," which in many cases can be other devices possessing the ability to be an authentication server. Note that it is not sufficient that the device sends a copy of device certificate to the verifier. The device must

---

4   See http://www.CableLabs.org for the DOCSIS specification and other details regarding cable modem device certificates.

engage in the mutual authentication protocol, which involves the device exercising its private key (e.g., sign a nonce) as part of the authentication handshake.

It is therefore crucial that the private keys of devices are not accessible by the human user and hackers alike. This means that for certain types of devices (e.g., network devices), the private key needs to be embedded into an irremovable part of the device, while for other user devices (e.g., laptop), the private key must be stored in special hardware which is not accessible by the user or applications.

2.7.3 Toward a Solution to the Rogue AP Problem

Similar to the rogue cable modem problem, a solution to the rogue AP problem can begin to be solved based on 802.1X, device certificates and a strong certificate-based mutual authentication protocol (e.g., EAP-TLS). The device certificate would bind properties of the AP hardware (e.g., MAC address, serial number) to a private key, expressed in the form of an X.509 certificate. The certificate would then need to be embedded into the hardware of the AP in such a way that the certificate is not removable by the hacker and the private key is not readable or accessible by humans.

In order to make full use of the device certificate inside the AP, there are a number of enhancements that need to be made to the current relationship between the AP and the RADIUS server in the 802.1X framework. These required enhancements are as follows:

- Requirement R1: *AP as supplicant upon boot-up.* An AP must be authenticated by the AS upon boot-up. For this to happen automatically, an AP must have the capability of being an 802.1X supplicant during its boot-up phase.

  This requirement points to the need of APs to contain supplicant code (including EAP peer), with TLS capability. In essence, the same 802.1X port-based access control is applied to APs, where an AP becomes a supplicant and the AS becomes the authenticator to the AP (as well as the AS).

- Requirement R2: *Strong certificate-based mutual authentication between AP and AS.* Using the TLS protocol implementation in the AP, an AP must perform mutual authentication with the AS (RADIUS server) using the device certificate embedded within the AP. The RADIUS server can use the same server certificate that it deploys when engaging in authentication with clients.

- Requirement R3: *Key agreement between the AP and AS.* Currently, in many deployment cases of RADIUS with 802.11 APs, the wired connection between an AP and a RADIUS server must be protected by providing data encryption between the two end points. This is particularly necessary when the AP is located at a remote office or located at a hotspot, which makes the connection somewhat open or susceptible to attacks.

Today, there is no standard automated session key establishment process between an AP and the AS (RADIUS server). Typically, the IT administrator must manually enter keying material (e.g., PIN, password) at both the AP and the RADIUS server. This approach is cumbersome and does not scale for large deployments of APs. It is also difficult to perform for APs that are remotely located.

Device certificates, however, when embedded within an AP lend themselves for additional use beyond mutual authentication between the AP and the RADIUS server. More specifically, as a direct product of a successful mutual authentication handshake between an AP and the RADIUS server (e.g., using EAP-TLS), both ends can now arrive at a common RADIUS session key that is subsequently used by the AP and RADIUS to encrypt traffic between them.

Thus, an automated session key establishment method between an AP and the RADIUS server is a very attractive proposition given the current increase in AP installations.

2.7.4   Toward a Solution for Rogue Network Devices

In addition to the requirements listed above for developing a solution to the rogue AP problem, the general rogue network device needs to be addressed by treating two communicating devices as authentication end points in the classical sense. This means that the notion of state, periodic reauthentication, and session freshness needs to be implemented:

Requirement R4: *Security session maintenance.* After performing mutual authentication (in 802.1X) and key agreement, the supplicant and AS must maintain a fresh security session, with reauthentication at regular intervals.

To understand the relevance of this point, consider the problematic scenario of a basic switch that implements the role of an authenticator, with the AP as the supplicant. In the 802.1X model the switch would be the intermediary between the AP (as supplicant) and the AS. Once the AS successfully authenticates the supplicant (AP), the switch would provide an open port for the supplicant's packets.

The problem, however, is that at this point an attacker (i.e., bad employee) could disconnect the valid supplicant and connect an unauthorized supplicant with a forged MAC address (copied from the valid supplicant). This attack is possible because the authenticator is a switch that acts as a bridge in translating MAC addresses of packets in the two segments of the communications. To the switch (as authenticator), once the supplicant has been authenticated by the AS and a port opened on the switch associated with the supplicant, its role has ended. Here, to the switch the rogue supplicant has the same MAC address as the valid supplicant, and thus the switch continues its bridge function in passing packets to/from the rogue supplicant.

A number of 802.11 hardware vendors are aware of this problem, though a standardized solution has yet to be specified. Recall that this problem is solved in the cable modem case by the CMTS and cable modem device running a (stateful) certificate-based authentication protocol, leading to key agreement. The session is then refreshed after a period of time. A rogue modem cannot be substituted, since it does not have the current session key and session parameters.

2.7.5 Policy-Based Device Authentication in 802.1X

A number of LAN hardware vendors have begun to realize that in the context of authentication, devices need to be treated in the same manner as humans, and that if access policies are used for humans, similar schemes for policy-based access control need to be maintained for all network devices.

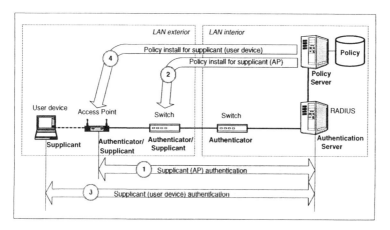

Figure 2.7 Policy-based device authentication in 802.1X.

Figure 2.7 shows a policy-based network device access control model following the 802.1X authentication framework. Here, the fundamental idea is that when an authenticator mediates an authentication session between a supplicant and AS, then besides performing port-based access control for that supplicant, specific policies must be installed at the authenticator (associated to that supplicant). Thus, the authenticator is required to be more intelligent than only performing open/close ports and other basic functions. The authenticator must have a higher level of awareness of the type of device seeking port connection and the type of actions normally allowed for (or capable to be done by) that device.

Note that policy-based access control is not new in the context of higher-level applications and even in the context of network devices. However, previous to the prominence of 802.1X this concept had been applied primarily to users and user devices at the edge of the network.

2.7.6   Further Afield: 802.1X and Trusted Computing

In response to the need of a standardized solution to the rogue AP problem and others, and the need to provide a better security solution for the LAN and WLAN infrastructure, a number of network hardware and software manufacturers have recently joined the *Trusted Computing Group* (TCG) in order to take advantage of hardware-based security solutions.

The TCG — which previous to March 2003 was known as the *Trusted Computing Platform Alliance* (TCPA) — has the general aim of developing *trusted platforms* (TP) based on the use of the *trusted platform module* (TPM) chip and a new hardware architecture for platforms in general. The TPM chip is a piece of silicon hardware that is bound to the motherboard and controls a number of core security functions relating to other hardware components, the BIOS, and the operating system. The TPM (version 1.2) contains a cryptographic engine, random number generator, a number of keys and credentials, and has some limited non-volatile (NV) storage.

Broadly speaking, the design philosophy underlying trusted computing is the combined use of trusted hardware, measurements and attestations in order to establish a system with a hardware-rooted trust. The TPM hardware is an embodiment of the core of this design philosophy. The TPM has a number of functions, including integrity measurement, integrity storage, and integrity reporting of all the events occurring in the platform. Thus, for example, processes that are to run within the system must be integrity-verified by an agent that itself has been measured and is trusted to always behave in the same manner. The various platform state information is recorded within a number of registers during initial platform configuration. During platform boot-up, the process is compared against the known state within registers, ensuring that illegal modifications (e.g., Trojan inserted) are detected. Other uses of the TPM include secure storage of cryptographic keys and certificates.

In the context of LAN and WLAN infrastructure, the TPM provides a promising avenue towards the notion of the *authenticated network* (AN) in which every piece of hardware that participates and composes a LAN/WLAN contains a TPM and is authenticated before it is allowed to gain access to the rest of the network infrastructure. In this way, rogue devices and rogue software (e.g., viruses, Trojans) can be prevented from entering the network and the network truly becomes self-protecting.

The TCG in May 2004 established a *Trusted Network Connect* (TNC) sub-group in order to study further the architectures, designs, and deployment cases for the use of TCG technology to secure the network infrastructure. The reader is encouraged to see [17] for more information on the TCG, the TPM, and more specifically the TNC.

2.8 SUMMARY

This chapter has discussed the issues of authentication and authorization in WLANs, both in the case of on-campus enterprise authentication and in the case of off-campus WiFi roaming. Four models for authentication were described, followed by a further in-depth discussion on two models, namely the UAM authentication and 802.1X authentication.

The Web-based UAM method uses the standard HTTP over SSL connection to deliver the user's password from the client to a PAC Gateway, which then provides or denies further access to the user. Although simple (and it has been deployed by many WISPs), the UAM approach does not integrate the key derivation process needed for the layer-2 frame/packet encryption for the wireless segment of the communication between the client and the AP. As such, for public WiFi hotspots additional security measures — such as running an IPsec VPN — are advised, though VPNs are typically available only for corporate users.

Authentication based on the 802.1X framework standard requires an authentication "method" be used within the framework. The 802.1X framework works on the notion of ports and port-based access control. It promises to be the de facto industry standard for on-campus enterprise authentication of both user and network devices.

Finally, many vendors are beginning to use the 802.1X authentication framework for network element (device) authentication. This interest has been partly driven by the need to solve the rogue AP problem, and the broader rogue device problem. Although 802.1X, some existing EAP authentication methods, and device certificates provide a starting point for solving the rogue AP and rogue device problems, further development and standardization need to be done.

References

[1] R. Yavatkar, D. Pendarakis, and R. Guerin, "A Framework for Policy-Based Admission Control." RFC 2753 (Informational), Jan. 2000.

[2] J. Vollbrecht, "AAA Authorization Framework." RFC 2904 (Informational), Aug. 2000.

[3] C. Rigney, S. Willens, A. Rubens, and W. Simpson, "Remote Authentication Dial In User Service (RADIUS)." RFC 2865 (Standards Track), June 2000.

[4] P. Calhoun, J. Loughney, E. Guttman, G. Zorn, and J. Arkko, "Diameter Base Protocol." RFC 3588 (Proposed Standard), Sept. 2003.

[5] IEEE, "Port-Based Network Access Control," IEEE Standards IEEE Std 802.1X-2001, Institute of Electrical and Electronics Engineers, June 2001.

[6] B. Anton, B. Bullock, and J. Short, "Best Current Practices for Wireless Internet Service Provider (WISP) Roaming," Best Practices Document, Wireless Ethernet Compatibility Alliance (WECA), Wireless ISP Roaming (WISPr) Initiative, Mar. 2002.

[7] C. Rigney, "RADIUS Accounting." RFC 2866 (Informational), June 2000.

[8] B. Aboba and P. Calhoun, "RADIUS Support for Extensible Authentication Protocol (EAP)." RFC 3579 (Informational), Sept. 2003.

[9] IEEE, "Port-Based Network Access Control (revision)," IEEE Standards IEEE P802.1X-REV/D7.1, Institute of Electrical and Electronics Engineers, Oct. 2003.

[10] B. Aboba, "Extensible Authentication Protocol (EAP)." RFC 3748 (Standards Track), June 2004.

[11] C. Rigney, A. Rubens, W. Simpson, and S. Willens, "Remote Authentication Dial In User Service (RADIUS)." RFC 2058 (Standards Track), Jan. 1997.

[12] W. Simpson, "The Point-to-Point Protocol (PPP)." RFC 1661 (Standards Track), July 1994.

[13] J. Hassell, *RADIUS*, Sebastopol, CA: O'Reilly, 2002.

[14] B. Lloyd and W. Simpson, "PPP Authentication Protocols." RFC 1334 (Standards Track), Oct. 1992.

[15] W. Simpson, "PPP Challenge Handshake Authentication Protocol (CHAP)." RFC 1994 (Standards Track), Aug. 1996.

[16] W. Barkley, T. Moore, and B. Aboba, "IEEE 802.1X and RADIUS Security." IEEE 802.11 contribution, Nov. 2001.

[17] "Trusted Computing Group," 2004, http://www.trustedcomputinggroup.org.

Chapter 3

EAP, TLS, and Certificates

3.1 INTRODUCTION

One of the earliest questions with regards to authenticating dial-up users was how to run an authentication protocol with a (dial-up) client when it did not yet have an assigned IP address. This issue was of particular concern since the assignment of an IP address was subject to a successful authentication. However, most of the existing authentication protocols, such as IKE or SSL, were designed to be run over the IP layer with the end points possessing known source/destination IP addresses. This apparent chicken-and-egg problem was solved with the introduction of the EAP protocol, first published as an Internet standard in 1998 in RFC2284 [1] and more recently revised as RFC3748 [2].

In the last couple of years EAP has come to the forefront of discussions, this time on 802.11 WLAN security and 802.1X. This is due to the similarity of the chicken-and-egg problem found in WLANs, namely the question of how a server on an IP network can authenticate an 802.1X supplicant when that supplicant does not yet have an IP address, and whose IP address assigned is in fact subject to a successful authentication by the server.

For the purposes of WLAN security EAP itself can be viewed as a framework within which a security protocol must be instantiated "inside" (on top of) EAP. Thus, with the emergence of EAP came the definition of a number of *EAP methods* which loads EAP with the appropriate security protocol. One important EAP method is EAP-TLS, which is an Instantiation of the TLS (or SSL) protocol inside EAP. More stringent that plain TLS in terms of certificate usage, EAP-TLS mandates the use of digital certificates at both the client and server side.

The purpose of this chapter is threefold. First, it is to provide an overview of EAP and underline its key role in supporting security functions, such as authentication, in WLANs. EAP is an important building block for the 802.1X approach to WLAN security. Secondly, the chapter provides an overview of the TLS (or SSL) protocol in its basic form, as a prelude to the discussion on the EAP-TLS method in the remainder of the book. It is our hope that by understanding EAP and TLS separately the reader can obtain an easier understanding of the EAP-TLS method. The discussion on TLS and EAP-TLS will bring with it some points regarding digital certificates and PKI. As such, the third part of this chapter provides a short introduction to certificates and PKI.

3.2   THE EXTENSIBLE AUTHENTICATION PROTOCOL

EAP is a core component of WLAN technology because it is the lowest common denominator transportation mechanism used by entities in 802.1X that exists in different kinds of networks. In the context of authentication protocols, EAP provides a way to deploy mature and well-understood strong authentication protocols, such as TLS or IKE, in the context of 802.1X and WLANs, by providing a way to "wrap" these protocols' conversations in a common enveloping format independent of the actual underlying communications medium. EAP can be used *directly* above a link layer (layer-2) protocol, such as 802.11 between a supplicant (client) and authenticator (AP). EAP can also be used over the IP layer, or over a higher-layer protocol, such as RADIUS. Hence EAP can be considered as a most useful lowest common denominator transport.

The original aim of EAP was to provide an authentication "framework" for the *Point-to-Point Protocol* (PPP) [3]. The PPP protocol provides a standard method for transporting multiprotocol datagrams over point-to-point links and is the basis for dial-up access to the Internet. EAP can be seen to be a framework because in order to usefully deploy it, EAP needs to be "instantiated" with an actual authentication protocol. On its own, EAP consists only of packet formats and a basic handshake or exchange, which is insufficient to achieve authentication between two entities.

As such, EAP allows the definition of *methods* or *types*, which define a given authentication protocol "wrapped" within EAP. Thus, for example, to implement the TLS authentication protocol, an *EAP-TLS method* needs to defined. Similarly, to run a basic password-based challenge-response protocol such as CHAP, an EAP-CHAP method needs to be defined.

EAP provides its own support for duplicate elimination and retransmission, but it is dependent on the lower layer for ordering guarantees. Fragmentation is not supported within EAP per se, but individual EAP methods may support this. Thus, for authentication protocols that deploy payloads larger than that in EAP, fragmentation support will be needed.

In contrast to many algorithms that are client-initiated, authentication in EAP is initiated by the authenticator. Thus, when an existing authentication protocol is to be defined as an EAP method, additional round-trips may be needed between

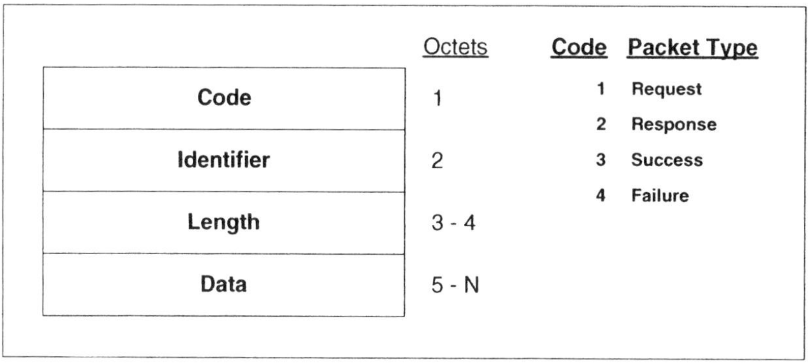

	Octets	Code	Packet Type
Code	1	1	Request
		2	Response
Identifier	2	3	Success
		4	Failure
Length	3 - 4		
Data	5 - N		

Figure 3.1 EAP packet format.

the client and the authenticator. This is particularly true for authentication methods that rely on digital certificates (e.g., EAP-TLS) and chain verification, because such certificate chains may entail more fragmentation and therefore more round-trips. Although extra round-trips may be acceptable in certain environments, for environments with significant packet loss the need for further round-trips may become an issue.

3.2.1 Overview of EAP Packet Format

EAP is flexible precisely because its packets are simple and extensible. Figure 3.1 shows the overall packet format for EAP, together with some codes identifying the different EAP packet types.

The identifier field is one octet in length and is used to match responses with requests. The identifier field and system port together uniquely identify an authentication exchange. During operation, it is the authenticator (e.g., AP) that chooses the value of the identifier field for new EAP requests. To answer a given session, the supplicant must maintain that same value in its EAP response frames to the authenticator.

3.2.2 Basic EAP Exchange

The basic EAP Exchange consists of the exchange of *EAP request* and *EAP response* packets between two *EAP peers*, ending in either an *EAP success* or *EAP failure* packet. In the context of 802.1X the peers can be any two of the 802.1X entities. The basic EAP exchange can be summarized as follows:

- The authenticator sends a *request* to the EAP peer (supplicant) indicating through the type field the kind of request it is making. Typically, the authenticator will send an initial identity request message, though this is not mandated when the identity information is obtained through other means or is simply superfluous.

- The EAP peer (supplicant) sends a reply using a *response* packet, whose type field corresponds to the type field of the request packet.

- The authenticator then sends further requests or information using additional request packets, and the EAP peer replies with a response. The sequence of requests and responses may go on as long as needed, though it must be done in a "lock-step" fashion where a new request cannot be sent prior to receiving a valid response.

- The exchange continues until the authenticator succeeds (or fails) in authenticating the EAP peer (supplicant). At this point the authenticator sends an EAP *success* (or EAP *failure*) packet.

Figure 3.2 shows a basic EAP exchange using *one-time-password* (OTP) as the EAP method for authentication. Here the authenticator initiates the exchange by requesting the identity of the supplicant (Step 1). The supplicant responds with its identity in an EAP response packet, and the authenticator passes the supplicant's identity information to the AS (Step 2). The AS challenges the supplicant (Step 3) using another EAP request packet. The supplicant then provides a password (Step 4) in an EAP response packet. The example shows a successful password authentication, where the AS sends an EAP success packet to the supplicant via the authenticator.

Note that the authenticator started with a port closed state, after which the port is open when the EAP success message was received from the AS. Also, this example shows the typical case where between the supplicant and the authenticator EAP is running over LAN directly (i.e., EAPOL), while between the authenticator and the AS the exchange of EAP frames is carried in a higher-layer protocol such as RADIUS.

In discussions of EAP usage in 802.1X, the supplicant is often referred to as the *EAP peer* when conversing with the authenticator. Thus, the peer of an authenticator is the EAP peer (namely the supplicant).

3.2.3   EAP Peers, Layers, Multiplexing, and Pass-Through

EAP understands the notions of peers and layers. In fact, since EAP is essentially a peer-to-peer protocol, an independent and simultaneous authentication may take place in the reverse direction (depending on the capabilities of the lower layer).

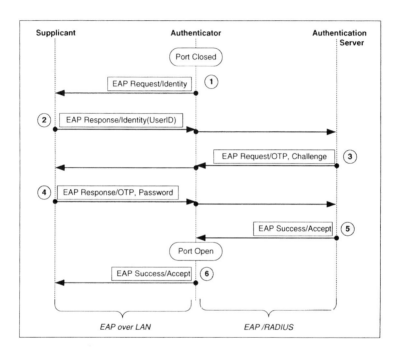

Figure 3.2 Example of basic EAP exchange.

That is, for mutual authentication an entity may ask its peer to authenticate itself, and vice versa, with both conversations occurring at the same time.

For independent and simultaneous authentication to occur, both peers need to be able to act as authenticators (i.e., one to the other) at the same time. This implies that it is necessary for both peers to implement the EAP authenticator layer and the EAP peer layer, and therefore the EAP method implementations on both peers must support both authenticator and peer functionality [2]. Figure 3.3 illustrates different layers where EAP peers can exchange information.

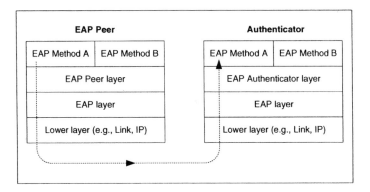

Figure 3.3   Notion of EAP peers.

Since during an authentication exchange in 802.1X the supplicant converses with the AS as the other endpoint of the handshake, an authenticator (e.g., 802.11 AP) must function as a *pass-through* entity. This means that the pass-through authenticator must relay the EAP packets to its corresponding peer. Depending on the direction of the conversation, the peer of the authenticator will be the supplicant on one side and the AS on the other side. The pass-through authenticator must verify the fields of the packets (i.e., code, identifier and length) before forwarding them.

If a given EAP method for authentication is designed in such a way to involve the authenticator entity in the authentication protocol flow (which means it is not a pass-through authenticator), then the authenticator must examine the type field of the EAP packets to see if the authenticator itself needs to take action other than forwarding the packet. If needed, the authenticator may also inspect the EAP method layer header fields. The forwarding model for a pass-through authenticator is shown in Figure 3.4 [2].

In general, since EAP is a peer-to-peer protocol, entities need to implement the EAP authenticator and peer layers as needed. However, in doing so the implementer needs to be aware that not all AAA protocols (and even EAP methods)

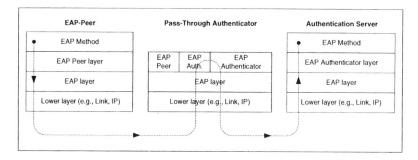

Figure 3.4 EAP pass-through authenticator.

support the same behavior. The reader is directed to [2] for further details regarding EAP and its usage.

3.2.4   Summary of EAP

EAP represents a very useful method to "wrap" authentication protocols — and other protocols — in a common enveloping format independent of the actual underlying communications medium. As mentioned before, EAP can be used directly above layer-2 (MAC layer) and also above the IP layer. As such, EAP can be thought of as a flexible lowest common denominator transport that can connect a supplicant to an AS through an authenticator, where the medium of communication differs in the two endpoints.

Having looked at EAP, in the next section we will focus on the TLS (or SSL) protocol as a preparation for discussing the EAP-TLS method.

3.3   OVERVIEW OF TLS

Since the TLS protocol plays a leading role in a number of prominent EAP methods for authentication, in this section we briefly review the TLS protocol (also known as SSL). The reader is directed to the excellent work in [4] for further details regarding SSL and TLS. Those who are already familiar with SSL and TLS may skip this section.

The *Secure Socket Layer* (SSL) protocol originated from the mid-1990s as part of the Netscape browser (version 1.1 in 1994). The purpose of SSL was to protect HTTP traffic end-to-end, between a browser and a Web server. As such, SSL sits between the higher-layer application (e.g., HTTP and SMTP) and the TCP/IP layer. Application data to be communicated would be fragmented, secured, and then

delivered over TCP (over IP). By late 1995 version 3 of SSL was in use in the
Netscape browsers, which was then the leading browser for the Internet.

Due to the various incompatibilities of the different "versions" or implementations of SSL (e.g., Netscape's, Microsoft's, and others), standardization efforts of
SSLv3 begun in 1996 in the IETF with the formation of the *Transport Layer Security* (TLS) Working Group. The result of the Working Group was the TLS protocol,
and the work was completed in 1999 with the publication of RFC 2246 [5].

Today SSL or TLS is used to provide three main security functions between
a client and server:

- *Authentication*: SSL uses standard public-key cryptosystems (e.g., RSA) to
  support mutual authentication, with the aid of digital certificates. Today, most
  SSL sessions based on RSA only require the Web server to have a digital
  certificate, though the client is not required to have one. Thus, in effect, only
  one-way authentication is provided.

- *Data integrity*: SSL provides message integrity checks to detect tampering of
  data in transit.

- *Data privacy*: SSL provides a means for key negotiation between the client
  and server, with the resulting key used to encrypt the HTTP traffic between
  the two end points.

In this section we use the terms SSL and TLS interchangeably, and unless
specified we will be referring to the standard version of TLS (namely SSL version
3.1) as found in RFC 2246 [5].

3.3.1   The SSL Stack

In order to better understand the various functions embodied within SSL, it is useful
to view SSL as consisting of several component protocols or "layers" of protocols.
Figure 3.5 shows these basic layers.

- *SSL Handshake protocol*: As the name implies, the Handshake protocol is
  used to initiate a session between the client and server, and performs the
  negotiation of the parameters of the session (algorithms, keys, and so forth).

    If the RSA cryptosystem is used, then the RSA-based key agreement
  scheme will be executed between the client and server in the handshake phase.

- *SSL Alert protocol*: The Alert protocol is used to exchange session-related
  messages.

- *SSL ChangeCipherSpec protocol*: The ChangeCipherSpec protocol is used to
  confirm the state that is pending between the client and server.

- *SSL Record protocol*: The Record protocol fragments upper-layer data into suitable units for encryption and integrity protection before delivering the fragments to the underlying TCP protocol. In addition, all the other SSL protocol messages are transported using the Record layer.

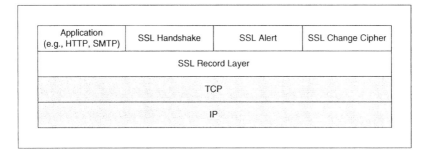

Figure 3.5 The SSL stack.

3.3.2 The Basic SSL Handshake

The basic SSL handshake (based on RSA) is shown in Figure 3.6, which can be better understood as consisting of six steps. These are summarized as follows:

- Step 1: The client indicates to the server which cipher suites (or algorithms) the client supports. The client also includes a random number, which will later be used for key generation.

- Step 2: In response, the server chooses one of the ciphers in the list received from the client. If the RSA key exchange is used for the handshake the server also sends a copy of its certificate (containing its RSA public key) and a random number for the key generation later.

  As an option, the server may request the client to supply it with a copy of the client's certificate.

- Step 3: Upon receiving the certificate, the client verifies the syntax and validity of the certificate. A failure in the server certificate verification leads to an error message from the client and termination of the handshake.

  The client then uses the server's public key to encrypt a random value (the premaster secret), the resulting ciphertext of which is sent back to the server. Since only the server is in possession of its RSA private key, only the server can decipher the message containing the premaster secret.

Note that if in Step 2 the server had requested the client's certificate, the client includes its certificate in its response to the server.

- Step 4: Both the client and server now proceed to compute the encryption key and integrity protection key (i.e., the MAC key) using the random in Step 1, Step 2, and the premaster secret in Step 3.

- Steps 5 and 6: In these last two steps the client and server both begin to apply the algorithm negotiated just previously (in Steps 1 and 2) to the *finished* message, sending it together with a MAC of the previous handshake messages.

Note that for simplicity and clarity of discussion, the basic SSL handshake in Figure 3.6 has omitted the *ChangeCipherSpec* message. The reader is directed to RFC 2246 [5] for a complete description of the *ChangeCipherSpec* message and other functions.

3.3.3   Certificates in SSL

Today, the majority of Web servers running SSL never require client certificates. Thus, only one-way authentication of the server to the client is achieved. In Step 2 of the basic SSL handshake of Figure 3.6, for the RSA-based key negotiation the server always supplies a copy of its X.509 certificate to the client (and possibly a chain of certificates). In Figure 3.6, the server's request for the client's certificate and the client's response is drawn in grey to indicate that these two steps are optional for the client.

In general, when an entity (client or server) obtains a copy of another entity's X.509 certificate (or a chain or certificates), a number of aspects regarding the certificate must be verified. The syntax of the certificate is to be parsed to ensure it conforms to the X.509 format. The validity of the certificate needs to be checked by comparing the expiration date of the certificate with the current date. If a chain of certificates was given, then *path validation* must be performed, which in practice means verifying each certificate up along the chain of issuers. If the certificate was issued by *certificate authority* (CA), then the client/server must see if the CA is included in its list of trusted CAs. Furthermore, the validity and authenticity of the CA certificate itself may need to be verified. Finally, for Web-server SSL certificates, the client should verify the domain name in server's certificate.

One way to verify the validity of a certificate is for the verifier (client or server) to query the CA issuer of the certificate using a certificate status protocol such as the *Online Certificate Status Protocol* (OCSP). Most large CAs provide *OCSP Responders*, which are OCSP servers that, when queried about a certificate, will respond with signed status information (i.e., valid or not valid) regarding that queried certificate.

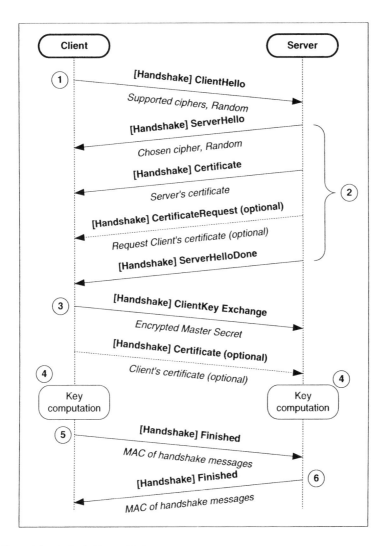

Figure 3.6   The basic SSL handshake.

3.3.4　The SSL Record Layer

An important component of the SSL stack is the *SSL Record layer* or protocol, which has the important function of preparing a message for the lower TCP layer. The SSL Record layer breaks up the data stream into fragments, and for each fragment prepends the appropriate header, computes a digest or MAC and then appends the MAC to the end of the fragment. This process is shown in Figure 3.7.

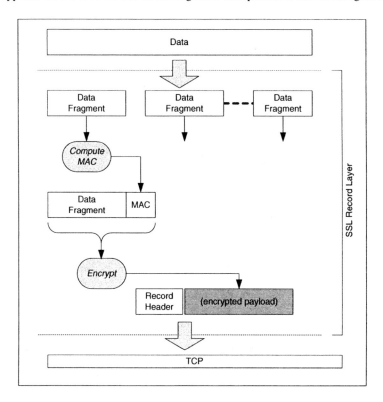

Figure 3.7　The SSL record layer.

In Figure 3.7, the application data is broken into several fragments with padding if necessary. For each fragment, the digest or MAC is computed, and the fragment and MAC are then concatenated and encrypted (becoming the *encrypted payload*). The header is then attached to the encrypted payload, and the unit is thereafter referred to as a *record*. The header identifies the content type (namely, application data), its length, and the SSL version. Note that records can also be used to send control messages, and thus for these types of messages the content type will have the appropriate type code (*alert*, *handshake*, or *change_cipher_spec*).

3.3.5 Summary of SSL and TLS

This section has attempted to provide only an overview of SSL and TLS and show the parts of SSL/TLS that are relevant to EAP authentication methods for WLAN authentication and security.

The important points from this section are the following:

- The fact that SSL/TLS is a well-understood protocol, widely deployed on a daily basis by millions of browsers, and has been standardized makes SSL/TLS an attractive choice for an authentication protocol for WLANs.

- The RSA-based key establishment handshake is an important component of SSL/TLS as it allows for mutual authentication and key agreement between the client and server.

- Certificates play a key role in SSL/TLS. Most Web-server implementations today only deploy server-side certificates, affording therefore server authentication to the client. In deploying SSL/TLS, the implementer needs to consider other PKI-related issues, such as the CA, the certificate hierarchy, and others.

3.4 AN OVERVIEW OF CERTIFICATES AND PKI

The first description of the framework for public-key cryptography was given in 1976 by Diffie and Hellman [6]. It was not until 1978 that the first design for public-key cryptosystems was published. This was the Rivest-Shamir-Adleman (RSA) cryptosystem [7], which is based on discrete logarithm and factorization problems. Merkle and Hellman came up with a scheme [8] using the knapsack problem, while McEliece in [9] designed a system based on error correcting codes. El Gamal used the discrete logarithm problem in the design his public key cryptosystem in 1985 [10]. The idea of using elliptic curves for public-key cryptosystem was proposed by Koblitz [11] and Miller [12].

Although there have been numerous schemes proposed for the basis of a public-key cryptosystem, the most popular public-key cryptosystem today remains the RSA cryptosystem.

3.4.1 Concept of Public-Key Cryptosystems

In private-key cryptosystems, both the encryption and decryption process employs the same key. Since the process is symmetric from both points of view, private-key cryptosystems are also referred to as "symmetric" cryptosystems. In symmetric cryptography, the key must always remain secret.

In public-key cryptography, two related keys are deployed: one to encrypt and the other to decrypt. An important feature of public-key cryptography is the fact that one of the keys is made public (i.e., published) while the other is kept secret. This raises the requirement that it must be computationally intractable to compute the secret key from a public key. Since the keys are different, public-key cryptosystems are also called *asymmetric cryptosystems*. As public-key cryptosystems use two keys, it is possible to make public either the encryption or decryption key.

There are two basic modes for the use of a public-key cryptosystem (e.g., RSA cryptosystem) used between a sender and receiver of a message:

- *Confidentiality*: The sender encrypts the message using the receiver's public key, which is available to all in the form of a certificate. Since only the receiver is in possession of her/his private key, only the receiver can decrypt the message.

- *Authentication*: The sender encrypts the message (or a digest of it) using the sender's private key. The encrypted message together with a copy of the plaintext original message is then sent to the receiver (or broadcasted to the public). Anyone who has a copy of the sender's public key can verify that the message originated from the sender (unmodified), since only the sender could have encrypted it using his/her private key. This is essentially the way to perform digital signatures.

These two modes can be used in sequence (i.e., one process after another) to achieve both authentication and confidentiality. Typically, the confidentiality process is performed first, resulting in a ciphertext, after which the authentication-process is applied to that ciphertext. The receiver would carry out the two processes in reverse.

3.4.2 Digital Certificates and PKI

The notion of digital certificates was first introduced in [13] in which the binding between a public-key pair and its owner is digitally signed by a *trusted third party*. This object is typically referred to as a digital *certificate*. The most common format of a certificate is the X.509 format, defined initially as part of the X.500 directory project in the ISO. The latest version of X.509 is version 3, as found in RFC3280 [14].

The trusted entity that *issues* a certificate and digitally signs it is referred to as a *certificate authority* (CA). When a CA digitally signs a certificate, in effect the CA vouches that a public key belongs to a subject (e.g., person) who is the possessor of the matching private key. Thus, in many circumstances the signer must also deliver a copy of the CA's digital certificate (or pointer to it), together with the signed information and its own certificate.

By definition, the public key of a CA is expressed inside a *Root CA certificate* that is self-signed by the CA. The term "self-signed" means that the certificate — which contains the public key (bound to the CA entity) — is digitally signed by the CA using the private key that matches that very same public key. A *certificate hierarchy* is the term used for the logical tree of certificates, emanating at the root of the tree (which is the CA). Nodes of the tree are public-key pairs (and certificates) whose private key is used to sign/issue other certificates at the next level down.

It is useful to distinguish between a public-key certificate and digital signature. An entity cannot prove its identity by simply showing a certificate (i.e., showing a badge). In electronic communications, an entity must digitally sign a piece of information (e.g., nonce) using its private key in order to prove that it is indeed in possession of that private key. The signed information must then be delivered accompanied with a certificate, or with a pointer to a location where the certificate can be obtained. The signed information can then be verified by anyone, using the (publicly available) public key embodied within a digital certificate. Successful cryptographic verification of the digital signature indicates that the private key used earlier to sign the information indeed matches the public key used to verify the signature.

3.4.3 Role of Certification Authority (CA)

A public-key certificate (or simply "certificate") is the formal embodiment of information regarding a given public key, together with the public key itself and the other parameters supporting the use of the certificate. A certificate is issued by a *certification authority* (CA). A CA is trusted to bind an entity (e.g., person, organization, device) to a public key. To do this, a CA must verify that the information to be placed in a certificate is correct. The CA essentially vouches for the entity identified in the certificate by way of the CA digitally signing that certificate.

Certificates under a CA are typically arranged in a tree-like structure or hierarchic arrangement consisting of a *Root CA* and one or more *subordinate CAs*. The purpose of following a hierarchic arrangement is to provide scalability, ease of management, and security (in the case of stolen or lost private keys). The basic idea is that a higher-level CA would issue certificates for its subordinate (children) CAs, who in turn may use their certificates to issue further certificates for their respective subordinates. Thus, as an example, an enterprise may have an enterprise-level CA, which is used to issue a number of division-level certificates. A division may then issue department-level certificates, each of which may be used to issue employee certificates (where the employees represent the bottom or leaf of the tree/hierarchy). If an employee joins the company or leaves, then only that department's CA needs to take action. If a department-server was hacked and the private key stolen, then only the concerned division would need to revoke the stolen department-level private key (and transition the existing affected valid employee certificates to newly issued certificates).

A Root CA by definition is the end point or root of trust, and thus it self-signs its own digital certificate and makes available the association between its identity and public key through other (possibly nonelectronic) means (e.g., publish in a newspaper or in white pages). Today, there are several different public Root CAs that issue certificates for various areas of application in the open community. In addition, there are thousands of private Root CAs, namely those CAs that are run internally within closed communities or organizations (e.g., banks) and whose certificates may never be used externally or with an external relying party.

3.4.4 Private and Public CAs

A certificate hierarchy under a CA can be deemed to be *private* and *public*, which in practical terms denotes the scope of availability of the (copy of the) Root CA certificate of that CA, and therefore of the trust accorded to it.

In the private case, the Root CA is typically used for intraorganizational needs, and only entities inside that organization will be aware of the existence of the PKI and the Root CA belonging to that organization. Such organizations typically do not have PKI as their business or primary activity.

In the public case, the Root CA certificate is made known as publicly as possible. The organization that is the CA typically has PKI as their core business. In other words, such organizations make a business income from providing PKI-related services. Since digital signatures are legally binding, a public CA must publish its *certificate practices statement* (CPS), which is a legal document. Among other things, the CPS states the functions of the CA, its processes, its services, and its legal obligations as well as liabilities. Copies of the Root CA certificate belonging to a public CA are typically well known and widely distributed, such as within Web browsers. A certificate under a CA typically contains a pointer to the location on the Internet of a copy of the Root CA certificate, as well as a copy of the governing CPS document.

The choice between a public CA or private CA is largely determined by needs. For example, if a company signs electronic documents and e-mails destined for external consumption, then it makes sense to deploy a public CA. In this case, the company would purchase a corporate-level certificate (and key pair) that was issued under (signed by) a respected public CA. The company would then use its corporate-level certificate to issue employee-level certificates, which would be used by an employee for digital signatures and encryption.

When an external recipient sees that employee certificate accompanying a signed e-mail or document, the origins of that certificate can be easily traced, and therefore its genuineness can be established. That is, the recipient can perform *certificate path validation*, which refers to the action of verifying the validity and status of the chain of certificates, from the one in possession to that at the root of trust. In this case, the chain would be verified upwards, starting from the employee certificate, then the corporate certificate (used to issue the employee certificate), and finally to the public CA certificate (used to issue the corporate certificate).

Note that since the corporate certificate was issued by a public CA (whose Root CA certificate is publicly available), the corporate certificate is essentially also public information. It is for this reason that many people use the term *private hierarchy* or *public hierarchy* when they refer to private or public CAs.

3.4.5   The X.509 Format

The current standard for digital certificates is X.509v3, as defined by RFC3280 [14] (and previously by RFC2459). There are a number of fields pertaining to information related to a certificate within version 3 of X.509. These include:

- The version number (i.e., V3);
- The certificate serial number;
- The algorithm ID of the algorithm used to sign the certificate;
- The issuer name of the entity (e.g., CA) that issued the certificate;
- The validity period of the certificate;
- The subject name of the owner of the certificate;
- The public key of the owner, including the public-key algorithm ID;
- The issuer unique ID and subject unique ID;
- Optional extensions, including key usage, which specifies the intended usage of the certificate (e.g., digital signature, encryption).

For a given area of deployment (e.g., banking, device certificates), typically a *certificate profile* is defined for that deployment. A certificate profile defines all the mandatory fields (as demanded by the chosen version of X.509 standard) and the optional fields that are specific to that deployment.

3.4.6　Summary of Certificates and PKI

Public key cryptography represents a very useful technology to provide authentication, confidentiality, and digital signatures. The binding of a public key to an entity (e.g., person, device) is embodied in the form of a digital certificate. Since the private key is a secret parameter, it must be guarded against loss or theft, both of which result in the loss of value of the corresponding certificate, and the need for the certificate to be revoked. The issuer of a certificate is referred to as the CA, which is also the trusted entity that revokes a certificate. Today the predominant format for certificates is the X.509 standard, though XML certificates are also increasingly being deployed. The reader is directed to RFC3280 as well as to [15–17] for an excellent and comprehensive treatment on the subject of certificates and PKI.

3.5　SUMMARY

In this chapter we have discussed three important and related technology building blocks for securing WLANs. These are the EAP protocol, the TLS (or SSL) protocol and digital certificates. These are related in the following way.

EAP has become an important element in WLAN security because it has become the lowest common denominator transportation mechanism used by entities in 802.1X that exist in different kinds of networks. EAP provides a way to deploy mature and well understood strong authentication protocols (such as TLS) in the context of 802.1X and WLANs, by providing a way to "wrap" these protocol's conversations in a common enveloping format independent of the actual underlying communications medium.

The TLS or SSL protocol — which is well-understood and broadly used today in securing Web-browser connectivity — has also been used to provide mutual authentication at the EAP layer, namely in the form of the EAP-TLS protocol. Other EAP methods for authentication have also been proposed recently, many using TLS to establish a secure channel or tunnel between the client and AS. Examples are the EAP-TTLS method and PEAP method. In EAP-TLS both client and server certificates are mandated, while in PEAP and EAP-TTLS only the server certificate is required. It is here that digital certificates and PKI become an important third element for securing WLANs. In itself, the field of digital certificates is broad and well established, and thus it has only received limited treatment here. The reader is encouraged to follow the references provided on digital certificates and PKI in order to gain further understanding of the field.

References

[1] L. Blunk and J. Vollbrecht, "PPP Extensible Authentication Protocol (EAP)." RFC 2284 (Standards Track), Mar. 1998.

[2] B. Aboba, "Extensible Authentication Protocol (EAP)." RFC 3748 (Standards Track), June 2004.

[3] W. Simpson, "The Point-to-Point Protocol (PPP)." RFC 1661 (Standards Track), July 1994.

[4] E. Rescorla, *SSL and TLS: Designing and Building Secure Systems*, Reading, MA: Addison-Wesley, 2001.

[5] T. Dierks and C. Allen, "The TLS Protocol." RFC 2246 (Standards Track), Jan. 1999.

[6] W. Diffie and M. E. Hellman, "New Directions in Cryptography," *IEEE Transactions on Information Theory*, vol. 22, pp. 644–654, Nov. 1976.

[7] R. L. Rivest, A. Shamir, and L. M. Adleman, "A Method for Obtaining Digital Signatures and Public-Key Cryptosystems," *Communications of the ACM*, vol. 21, no. 2, pp. 120–126, 1978.

[8] R. Merkle and M. Hellman, "Hiding Information and Signatures in Trapdoor Knapsacks." *IEEE Transactions on Information Theory*, vol. 24, pp. 525–530, Sept. 1978.

[9] R. J. McEliece, *A Public-Key System Based on Algebraic Coding Theory*, pp. 114–116, Jet Propulsion Lab, 1978. DSN Progress Report 44.

[10] T. El Gamal, "A Public Key Cryptosystem and a Signature Scheme Based on Discrete Logarithms," *IEEE Transactions on Information Theory*, vol. 31, pp. 469–472, 1985.

[11] N. Koblitz, "Elliptic Curve Cryptosytems," *Mathematics of Computation*, vol. 48, no. 177, pp. 203–209, 1987.

[12] V. S. Miller, "Use of Elliptic Curves in Cryptography," *Proceedings of Crypto '85*, pp. 417–426, Springer, 1986. LNCS 218.

[13] L. Kornfelder, "Toward a Practical Public-Key Cryptosystem," B.S. Thesis, Massachusetts Institute of Technology, 1978.

[14] R. Housley, W. Polk, W. Ford, and D. Solo, "Internet X.509 Public Key Infrastructure Certificate and Certificate Revocation List (CRL) Profile." RFC 3280 (Standards Track), Apr. 2002.

[15] C. Adams and S. Lloyd, *Understanding the Public-Key Infrastructure: Concepts, Standards, and Deployment Considerations*, New York: Macmillan, 1999.

[16] W. Ford and M. S. Baum, *Secure Electronic Commerce: Building the Infrastructure for Digital Signatures and Encryption*, Upper Saddle River, NJ: Prentice-Hall, 2000.

[17] R. Housley and T. Polk, *Planning for PKI: Best Practices Guide for Deploying Public Key Infrastructure*, New York: Wiley, 2001.

Chapter 4

EAP Methods

4.1 INTRODUCTION

The *extensible authentication protocol* (EAP) protocol [1,2] provides a very useful means to transport various authentication protocol messages between a client and *authentication server* (AS). A number of EAP methods have been defined to address numerous requirements in WLAN security.

Having provided an introduction to EAP and SSL in Chapter 3, in this chapter we focus on a number of promising EAP methods that pertain to security, in particular to the authentication between the client and AS. The chapter starts with EAP-TLS as the base EAP method that employs the TLS protocol to establish a mutually authenticated secure channel between the two end points. The focus on EAP-TLS provides an understanding for other EAP methods, such as EAP-TTLS and PEAP, which also incorporate the use of a secure channel or tunnel using TLS. The chapter also briefly discusses two EAP methods that implement the authentication protocol used by many *mobile network operators* (MNO), namely EAP-SIM and EAP-AKA. These EAP methods are becoming relevant today as many MNOs are increasingly providing WiFi services as an extension to their GSM and GPRS services.

4.2 THE EAP-TLS METHOD

As mentioned above, EAP provides a way to wrap other protocols, called *EAP methods* (or types), and provide a supporting layer for these protocols to execute. One such EAP method is EAP-TLS.

The EAP method based on TLS (or EAP-TLS) was one of the early EAP methods specified by the PPP-Extentions (PPPEXT) Working Group in the IETF. Published as RFC 2716 [3] in 1999, it represented the first EAP method that made use of the TLS authentication protocol, which was also reaching its final standardization phase in the TLS working group in the IETF.

EAP-TLS was also the first TLS-based EAP method for authentication shipped by Microsoft for the Windows platform, thereby achieving wider availability compared to other more recent proposals. EAP-TLS has found a strong following in many enterprise networks that seek strong security through authentication using strong credentials such as digital certificates. As implemented by Microsoft, EAP-TLS requires both client-side and server-side certificates. For enterprises already running a PKI — either internally or using a public CA — and issuing employee certificates, the step to choosing EAP-TLS is a natural one. The choice of EAP-TLS by enterprises is also made easier by the fact that the Microsoft Windows Server (version 2000 or later) comes shipped with a *CA Server*, which allows enterprises to run their own private CA internally, and have seamless integration with the Microsoft directory-related products (e.g., Active Directory).

4.2.1 SSL Records over EAP

In Chapter 3, we saw that the TLS protocol (namely SSL version 3.1) deployed the SSL Record layer to fragment upper-layer data into suitable units for encryption and integrity protection before delivering the fragments to the underlying TCP protocol. In addition, other SSL protocol messages are transported also using the Record layer. The fact that TLS (SSL) uses a Record layer provides TLS with some independence over the underlying transport protocol used to deliver the SSL Records. Indeed, in EAP-TLS the SSL Records are transported using EAP.

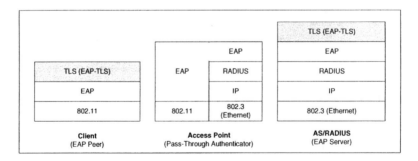

Figure 4.1   Example of layers involved in an EAP-TLS session.

The fact that TLS uses the SSL Record as its unit of transport fits well into EAP's simple packet format. And the fact that EAP can run over layer-2 directly (as in EAPOL) or over the IP layer, provides the ability for TLS (or, more precisely, EAP-TLS) to be run between client and server independent of the underlying transport medium. In the case of the typical 802.11 WLAN setup, this means EAP-TLS over layer-2 between the client and access point (AP), and continuing over layer-3 between the AP and the authentication server (AS).

Figure 4.1 shows an example of the possible layers involved within a typical 802.11 WLAN configuration. Notice that on the client-to-AP side, EAP runs directly over layer-2, without IP. In contrast, on the AP-to-AS side not only is the IP layer involved, but EAP runs over (encapsulated within) a RADIUS protocol layer. Figure 4.1 illustrates the flexibility of EAP as a "transport" for other protocols (EAP methods or types), which in this case is TLS.

4.2.2 The EAP-TLS Exchange

The basic EAP-TLS exchange is shown in Figure 4.2.[1] Here, the EAP-TLS exchange begins after the authentication server (or "server" for short) receives the client's identity in answer to the server's request.

Note that the EAP peers use the *EAP request* and *EAP response* packets to carry their EAP-TLS handshake — or, more precisely, the TLS Records. Note also that the authenticator (e.g., AP) acts as a pass-through device during the EAP-TLS exchange.

The EAP-TLS exchange steps are as follows:

- In step 1 the server signifies the commencement of the EAP-TLS exchange by sending the *EAP-TLS/Start* message within an EAP request packet. Here the EAP type is defined to be "EAP-TLS" with the start-bit being set to indicate commencement. This message from the server does not carry any data.

- In step 2 the client responds to the server by sending the usual TLS *ClientHello* message embodied within an EAP response packet, with the EAP type to be "EAP-TLS." Here, the data field of EAP response packet encapsulates TLS records in TLS record layer format, containing a TLS ClientHello handshake message. As in the basic TLS exchange, the ClientHello message contains the client's TLS version number (version 1.0 or later), a session ID, a random number, and a set of ciphersuites supported by the client.

- In step 3 the server responds with the usual TLS *ServerHello* message, accompanied by several parameters needed by the client, within an EAP request packet (with EAP type being "EAP-TLS"). Similar to step 2, the ServerHello message is expressed in TLS records, and may contain other parameters, such as the server's certificate, the server key exchange parameters, a request for the client's certificate, and the closing *ServerHelloDone* message. As usual,

1   In Figure 4.2. and other figures in this chapter depicting an exchange, the lines and arrows connect the supplicant to the AS directly for clarity. However, the intent is clear that the authenticator is involved in the exchange. if only as a pass-through entity.

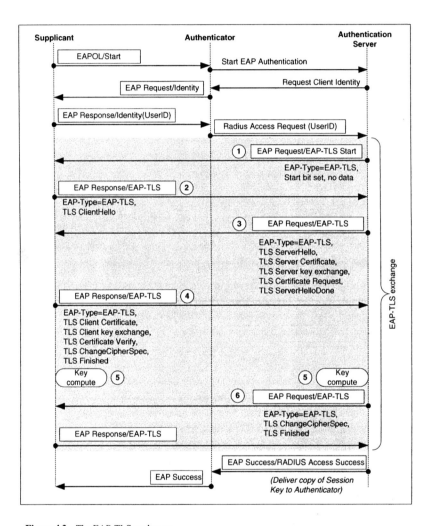

Figure 4.2   The EAP-TLS exchange.

the ServerHello message must have a TLS version number (version 1.0 or later), a session ID and the selected ciphersuite.

- In step 4 the client responds to the server by sending an EAP response packet containing the parameters requested by the server. These include the client's certificate, the key exchange parameters, and the closing "finished" message. The session ID in this message must match that in the previous step (in the ServerHello message), lest the server think this is a new session.

- In step 5 both the client and server now have the parameters needed for each to compute the session key that will later be used for deriving the temporal keys employed to encrypt packets in the wireless segment of the communication (see Chapter 8).

- In step 6, since the server is responding to a current session, the server must include a *ChangeCipherSpec* message with the TLS *Finished* handshake message. The TLS finished message closes the session that was commenced earlier in step 3 with the ServerHello message.

The reader is directed to [4] for more details on the TLS messages and to RFC 2716 [3] for further details on the implementation requirements of EAP-TLS. Further discussion on digital certificates and PKI can be found in Chapter 3.

4.2.3   Summary of EAP-TLS

This section has attempted to provide only an overview EAP-TLS and its exchange. The important points from this section are the following:

- EAP-TLS as specified in RFC 2716 [3] implements the TLS exchange wrapped within EAP packets. The EAP-TLS method provides mutual authentication between the supplicant/client and the AS.

- In EAP-TLS both client-side and server-side certificates are mandatory. One reason for this design decision is the need for strong credentials, something which is true in enterprise networks today. The use of certificates as a strong credential at both end points of the exchange complements TLS (or EAP-TLS) as a strong authentication protocol.

- EAP-TLS is the model for other EAP methods that are also based on TLS. Thus, EAP methods such as PEAP and EAP-TTLS have the same basic exchange behavior and can be seen as building over EAP-TLS.

4.3   PEAP: EAP-OVER-TLS-OVER-EAP

Although the EAP-TLS method provided strong mutual authentication in WLANs through the use of digital certificates, the fact that the client certificates are sent in plaintext over a wireless medium offers the opportunity for attackers to sniff the certificates, and therefore identity of the client. In a wired network such as an Ethernet LAN, sniffing was only cost-effective when the client and the attacker are in the same local subnet. After IP packets leave the subnet, the task is considerably harder to perform.

The *protected EAP* (PEAP) method [5] offers a solution to this need of user identity protection. The current work-in-progress specification for PEAP is version 2 (PEAPv2), which is the version discussed in the current section. The first version of PEAP was initially published in October 2001. Since then, the proposal has undergone considerable improvement. PEAPv2 has now addressed a number of important issues, including the need for protection of the user identity, the need for a standardized mechanism for key exchange, and the need to support fast reconnects.

In this section we discuss PEAP version 2. Unless otherwise mentioned, we will be referring to PEAPv2 as found in [5], which is the latest revision of PEAPv2 at the time of this writing.

4.3.1   Overview of PEAPv2

The idea behind PEAP is to allow additional EAP methods to be run atop (or chained after) an EAP-TLS handshake. That is, other EAP methods or protocols can be "wrapped" within TLS, providing them with the security benefits of TLS. Another way of looking at PEAP is to consider it as consisting of an *inner* EAP being run within TLS, which is in turn run within an *outer* EAP.

One key motivation behind this approach is to allow users to submit their credential (which may contain their identity) after the TLS session has been established, and therefore have their credential passed to the server under the protection (encryption) of the TLS session.

Another motivation for PEAP is to allow the server to request various forms of credentials from the client. In other words, in PEAP multiple authentication methods (e.g., GTC and OTP) can be run under the protection of the previously established TLS session. These can be run sequentially or in parallel. For deployment cases where a client certificate is required, PEAP allows client certificates to be delivered after the TLS session has been established, instead of during the TLS session setup.

Some of the security benefits provided by PEAP are as follows:

- *Identity protection*: The initial *EAP identity request* and *EAP identity response* exchange is sent in plaintext, and thus is open to snooping by an attacker. PEAP supports identity protection by establishing a TLS channel first, before the client's identity is passed to the server.

An additional benefit of this approach is the protection of EAP authentication methods (e.g., password-based) that might be subject to an offline dictionary attack.

- *Negotiation and termination protection*: The negotiation (e.g., ciphersuites) that occurs with EAP (within TLS) is protected from possible downgrade attacks where the attacker replays certain packets to the client/server to force them to use a weaker ciphersuite.

  An additional benefit from using an established TLS channel is the protection of the success/failure indications of the EAP conversation, which may otherwise be open to spoofing (e.g., EAP failure message) by an attacker, which may then in turn lead to to a denial of service.

- *Header protection*: The TLS channel provides protection against the (inner) EAP header being modified in transit (i.e., type-data field within PEAPv2, which includes the EAP header of the EAP method within PEAPv2).

- *Multiple authentication methods*: Since a full (inner) EAP is run within an established TLS session, other EAP methods for authentication can also be thus executed between the client and server. PEAPv2 provides a standard way to chain or *sequence* different EAP methods for authentication, each possibly supporting different forms of credentials. PEAPv2 allows for both *serial authentication* (one EAP method after another), or *parallel authentication* where an EAP method is initiated after another has failed.

  Note that this possibility is attractive to networks where a "machine" credential is used in addition to a "human" credential. For example, for the TLS session establishment (in the outer EAP) a machine certificate could be mandated on the client. If the TLS session establishment succeeds, a human certificate could then be used for the (inner) EAP authentication method (e.g., EAP-TLS).

Other benefits, such as fragmentation/reassembly and fast reconnect, are discussed further in [5].

4.3.2 EAP Methods over TLS: EAP-TLV

A key feature of PEAPv2 is its ability to provide multiple authentication methods over an established TLS channel or session. More specifically, PEAP allows EAP methods for authentication to be run (unmodified) over the TLS channel, either in sequential fashion or in parallel.

In order to provide this ability, PEAP introduces a new EAP method called *type-length-value* (TLV). The purpose of the EAP-TLV method is to carry payloads consisting of other authentication-specific EAP methods. Thus, when we mentioned that EAP runs atop a TLS channel (which runs over EAP, or EAP-over-TLS-over-EAP), what really occurs is that the EAP-TLV method runs inside the top-most (inner most) EAP. In turn, that TLV method carries other EAP methods between the client and server. Figure 4.3 shows a simplified arrangement of layers within PEAP. Note that the bottom-most EAP layer in Figure 4.3 is the outer EAP, whereas the top EAP is the inner EAP.

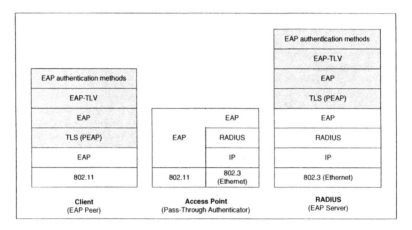

Figure 4.3   Overview of PEAP layers.

The EAP-TLV method is a really only a payload with standard TLV objects, and TLV objects could be used to carry any arbitrary parameters between the client (EAP peer) and the EAP server. The work in [5] defines a number of TLV packets for carrying out a conversation between a client and server. Although a discussion on all of the TLVs are beyond the scope of the current work, some of the TLVs that are relevant for the discussion on the PEAPv2 exchange (Section 4.3.3) are as follows:

- The NAK TLV: The NAK TLV is used by a client to indicate to the server that it does not support a given TLV proposed by the server.

- The crypto-binding TLV: The client and server use the *crypto-binding* TLV to prove to each other that they respectively participated in the same sequence of authentications. This includes starting from the TLS session establishment, all the way to the (inner) EAP authentication methods (which generated keys). The same format is used for *Binding Request* (B1) and *Binding Response*

(B2), with the subtype field indicating them respectively. In phase 2 of PEAP (after the TLS channel is established), the crypto-binding TLV is used to perform cryptographic binding after each successful EAP method (except EAP-TLV) in a sequence of EAP methods.

Other TLVs include the *EAP-TLV request* packet, the *EAP-TLV response* packet, the *Result TLV* packet, the *connection binding TLV* packet, the *EAP payload TLV* packet and the *vendor specific TLV* packet. The reader is directed to [5] for further details on each.

4.3.3   The Two Phases of PEAP

In attempting to understand PEAP, it is helpful to divide a PEAP session into two parts or phases:

- PEAP phase 1: Here a TLS session is negotiated and established. The server authenticates itself to the client using server-side certificate, and optionally the client to the server. The resulting key is used to encipher the exchanges in phase 2.

- PEAP phase 2: Within the TLS session, zero or more EAP methods are carried out between the client and server, with a success/failure indication protected by the TLS session. Identity establishment is part of this phase.

Although it is difficult to discuss PEAP without reference to EAP-TLS (as PEAP also uses TLS), it is helpful to the reader to view PEAP as a different authentication method altogether, rather than seeing it as EAP-TLS augmented with additional steps.

4.3.3.1   PEAP Phase 1

A large part of phase 1 is the establishment of the TLS session. The steps of the session establishment are similar to EAP-TLS, but with some subtle differences. One key difference is possible use of the client's routing realm (part of the *network access identifier* (NAI) [6]) instead of the client's real identity when the client responds with the EAP response/identity message. The actual client identity is established later in phase 2. Thus, this initial identity exchange is used really to route the EAP conversation to the server.

An example of the PEAP phase 1 is shown in Figure 4.4 and is based on RSA and certificates. Note that the client does not send her or his true identity in the EAP response/identity message to the server.

The basic exchange of PEAP phase 1 is as follows:

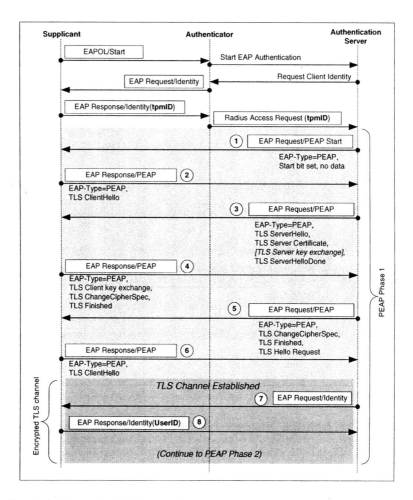

Figure 4.4 Example of PEAP phase 1 exchange.

- In step 1 the server signifies the commencement of the PEAP exchange by sending the *PEAP/start* message within an EAP request packet. Here the EAP type is defined to be "PEAP" with the start-bit being set to indicate commencement. This message from the server does not carry any data.

- In step 2 the client responds to the server by sending the usual TLS *ClientHello* message embodied within an EAP response packet, with the EAP type to be "PEAP."

   Here, the data field of EAP response packet encapsulates TLS records in TLS record layer format, containing a TLS ClientHello handshake message. As in the basic TLS exchange, the ClientHello message contains the client's TLS version number (version 1.0 or later), a session ID, a random number, and a set of ciphersuites supported by the client.

- In step 3 the server responds with the usual TLS ServerHello handshake message, accompanied by several parameters needed by the client, within an EAP request packet (with EAP type being "PEAP").

   Typically, the ServerHello message is followed possibly by a server certificate, a server key exchange message (optional), a client certificate request (optional), a ServerHelloDone (or TLS Finished) message, and/or a TLS ChangeCipherSpec message. As usual, the ServerHello message must have a TLS version number (version 1.0 or later), a session ID, and the seleted ciphersuite.

   Note, however, that for simplicity and clarity in step 3 of Figure 4.4 the server does not send a client certificate message. Unlike EAP-TLS, in PEAP the client certificate request message is not mandated at this point, as the server will later establish the client's identity in phase 2. Even if the server does send a client certificate request, the client need not supply a client certificate in its response in step 4.

- In step 4, the client returns the usual client key exchange message, but does not send any certificates or certificate verification messages.

- In step 5 the server responds with the usual TLS Finished message, but it adds an additional TLS HelloRequest. This TLS HelloRequest message signals to the client that the server wishes to continue to phase 2 under the protection of the (soon-to-be) established TLS channel. As we will see (in phase 2) the HelloRequest message is really a request to renegotiate the authentication protocol.

- In step 6 the client agrees with the request and replies with a TLS ClientHello message.

- In step 7, under the encrypted TLS channel the server requests the real identity of the client.

- In step 8, under the encrypted TLS channel the client responds to the server's request and sends it the client's true identity. In phase 2, the client will also send a certificate to the server.

4.3.3.2   PEAP Phase 2

Phase 2 of PEAP (Figure 4.5) continues from Figure 4.4. Here, the entire conversation between the client and server is protected (encrypted) under the TLS session, and thus achieves the set of security requirements aimed for by PEAP. Note that step 7 and step 8 from Figure 4.4 is repeated in Figure 4.5. Items in italics and square braces are optional.

Phase 2 consists of the following steps:

- In step 9, the server begins to request for the identity of the client, and the client's credentials.

    Previously, in step 7 (in Figure 4.4) the server sent a TLS Hello message, in essence asking for a renegotiation of the authentication method. In step 8, the client agreed with the renegotiation request and responded with a ClientHello message.

    Seeing this ClientHello message, the server now responds by sending a ServerHello message, accompanied by the server's certificate and client certificate request messages.

- In step 10, the client replies with certificate, client key exchange message, and a certificate verify message. Note that this renegotiation occurs within the protected (encrypted) TLS channel, and therefore does not reveal client certificate details.

- In step 11, the server begins to negotiate the additional EAP authentication method (if they are required) using the TLVs, initially sending a crypto-binding TLV (request type B1) with additional parameters (e.g., nonce, MAC).

- In step 12, the client also responds with crypto-binding TLV (response type B2), with response parameters. For simplicity, here the exchange is ended with a success indication for the (inner) EAP authentication.

As Figures 4.4 and 4.5 provide only an overview of a PEAP exchange, the reader is directed to [5] for further details on the PEAPv2 exchange, TLVs, crypto-bindings, and for other noncertificate examples.

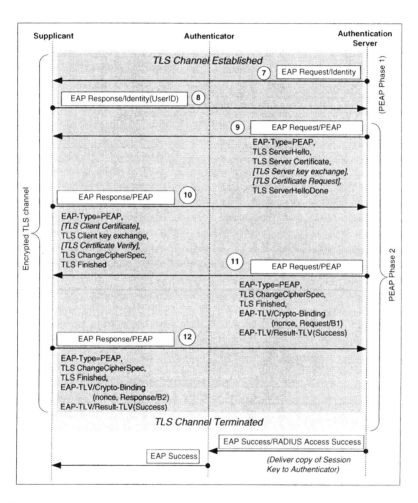

Figure 4.5 Example of PEAP phase 2 exchange.

4.3.4 Summary of PEAP

This section has provided an overview of PEAP version 2, which promises a number of features, improving over EAP-TLS for certain deployment scenarios. These include identity protection, negotiation and termination protection, fragmentation/reassembly, fast reconnect, and others. Key to PEAP's value proposition are that client-side certificates are optional (or if requested, will be provided with identity protection) and that multiple authentication methods can be deployed (phase 2), each established under the protection of the TLS channel in phase 1.

4.4 TUNNELED TLS (EAP-TTLS)

The EAP *Tunneled TLS Authentication* (EAP-TTLS) Protocol [7] is another proposal that uses a TLS channel to protect the exchange of sensitive information between the client (EAP peer) and the server. Both TTLS and PEAP were proposed in the IETF around the same time (mid-2001). In this section we discuss EAP-TTLS as found in [7], which is the latest revision of EAP-TTLS at the time of this writing.

In order to understand the motivations of TTLS and other similar protocols, it is important to understand the WLAN industry status and market situation when the TTLS proposal was first published in the IETF in August 2001. The promise of WLAN hotspot services being provided by traditional carriers and ISPs — as a potential source for new revenue for them — provided an impetus for both WLAN hardware and software vendors alike to offer new protocols and products that would assist such carriers/ISPs in rolling out WLAN services.

TTLS is a proposal from Funk Software (Cambridge, MA), a RADIUS vendor. For many vendors of RADIUS who sell into the carrier and ISP market, it is paramount that the EAP authentication method used in WLAN deployment of RADIUS servers to be interoperable (backward-compatible) with the legacy RADIUS install-base. Thus, although the interaction between the client and RADIUS server through the authenticator in a WLAN is a new feature and required some new protocols (e.g., EAP and EAP-RADIUS), the interaction between the RADIUS server (e.g., RADIUS proxy, RADIUS at a broker, or ISP) and other AAA servers upstream (usually also RADIUS) must remain unchanged. That is, the WLAN-facing aspects of RADIUS could be newly introduced, but the ISP-facing aspects of RADIUS must remain the same in order to support legacy systems.

It is for this reason that TTLS [7] distinguishes between the *TTLS AAA server* and the *home AAA server*. The first refers to the RADIUS server either at a hotspot or at an ISP, while the second refers to the RADIUS server at the "home" or corporate network where user authorization (for WLAN access) would be obtained.

This view is indeed consistent with how RADIUS is deployed today in the majority of the (dial-up) ISPs and other carriers.

In short, the requirements for deployment that EAP-TTLS addresses are as follows [7]:

- *Support for legacy password protocols.* This allows easy deployment against existing authentication databases.

- *Protection of passwords in transit.* Password-based information must not be observable in the communications channel between the client node and a trusted service provider, to protect the user against dictionary attacks.

- *Identity protection.* The user's identity must not be observable in the communications channel between the client node and a trusted service provider.

- *TTLS session resulting in correct key distribution.* The authentication process must result in the distribution of shared keying information to the client and authenticator (i.e., the AP), which will be used by the client and AP to encrypt 802.11 packets for wireless transmission, thereby protecting against eavesdroppers and channel hijacking.

- *Support for WLAN roaming.* The authentication mechanism must support roaming among small access domains with which the user has no previous relationship and which will have limited capabilities for routing authentication requests.

4.4.1 Overview of TTLS

Since compatibility with a legacy install base was an important consideration in the design of TTLS, it features two main aspects:

- *Client-side certificates not mandated.* Its first main feature is the use of TLS without client-side certificates as the basis for establishing a secure channel between the client at the TTLS server. Virtually all of the legacy RADIUS deployments are based on user passwords and not on certificates and PKI. Therefore, mandating user certificates for WLAN access would require many of the existing deployments of RADIUS for AAA to install a PKI just for WLAN purposes, something that would be unreasonable to expect in the immediate future from ISPs and carriers. Note that like PEAP, TTLS is open to client certificates being used. With or without client certificates, the purpose of TTLS is to deliver securely the user password from the client to the TTLS server (under a TLS channel protection), and then onward to the home AAA server for authorization.

- *The use of attribute-value pairs (AVPs)*. Information between the client and TTLS server is exchanged via attribute-value pairs (AVPs), which are compatible with both the RADIUS protocol and the Diameter protocol. Thus, any type of (existing) function that can be implemented via such AVPs may easily be performed over a TLS session, and achieves the highest probability of backward-compatibility to legacy install bases.

Similar to PEAP, the TTLS protocol consists of two phases [7]. In the first phase, the TLS session is established. In the second phase the password and AVPs are delivered. Note that the term "tunnel" here has a different meaning to that used in VPN technology. Here, the tunnel really refers to the encapsulation of AVPs within the TLS records, which are in turn encapsulated within EAP. The two phases are as follows:

- *TTLS phase 1: TLS handshake*.
  In phase 1, TTLS employs the TLS protocol at the EAP layer to establish a secure TLS channel between the client and the server, with server-side certificate used to authenticate the server to the client. Client authentication to the server is optional.

  In performing this handshake, the client must not reveal its identity. Thus, in the EAP response/identity message that the client sends to the server, at most the client should only reveal the realm of the trusted entity (e.g., ISP) that knows the client.

- *TTLS phase 2: TLS tunneling*.
  In phase 2 the established TLS channel is used to "tunnel" information between the client and the TTLS server. Note that the tunnel extends only between the client and TTLS server. A separate protection must be provided for communications between the TTLS server and the home AAA server. The client starts the phase 2 exchange by encoding information in a sequence of AVPs. It then passes this sequence of AVPs to the TLS record layer for encryption, which sends the resulting data to the TTLS server. The TTLS server recovers the AVPs in clear text from the TLS record layer. If the AVP sequence includes authentication information, it forwards this information to the home AAA server.

4.4.2   Example of a TTLS Session

Figure 4.6 shows an example of TTLS phase 1, using the password-based CHAP (or challenge-response) protocol. Here we intentionally chose the CHAP case instead of client certificates for illustration purposes only. The phase 1 shown in Figure 4.6

is fairly similar to that shown in Figure 4.4, and so we will not explore every step of the exchange, but only note certain important differences.

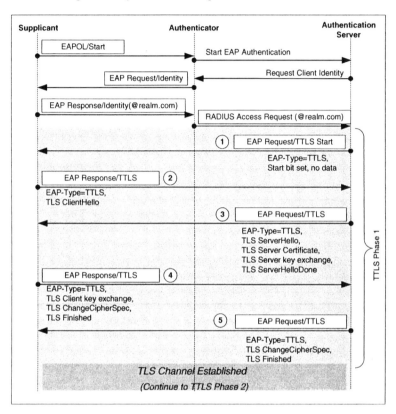

Figure 4.6 Example of TTLS phase 1 exchange.

The use of CHAP becomes apparent only in phase 2, which is shown in Figure 4.7. Note that all traffic in phase 2 is protected under the TLS channel established in phase 1.

Some of the notable aspects of Figures 4.6 and 4.7 are as follows:

- Before step 1, in the EAP response/identity message from the client to the server, the client does not specify its identity, but rather it uses the realm portion only of its *network access identifier* (NAI) [6].

- In step 4 of Figure 4.6 the client does not provide a certificate. Similar to SSL/HTTP and to PEAP without client-side certificates, the client uses the

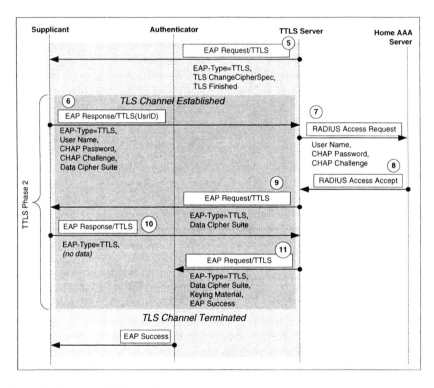

Figure 4.7 Example of TTLS phase 2 exchange.

server's certificate in step 3 to help in the key agreement process, reflected in the client key exchange message.

- In step 6 in phase 2 (Figure 4.7), the client's first tunneled EAP packet will contain the client's actual user name. The user name must be an NAI of the format username@realm, though once phase 1 completes the server already knows the client's realm and needs only the username portion. The realm portion is used by the server to route the authorization request to the home AAA server.

  Another important point about step 6 is the TTLS *data cipher suite* message that indicates the cipher (e.g., WEP, WEP2, AES-OCB) to be used to secure the wireless segment between the client and authenticator (i.e., AP). Here, the client is indicating a list of the ciphers that the client prefers to use. This is the only opportunity that the client has to indicate its preference to the server.

  Note that this TTLS data cipher suite expressed in AVPs should not be confused with the TLS cipher suite selection that was done earlier as part of the TLS session establishment (see Section 3.3). The reader is directed to [7] for further information about the TTLS data cipher suite message and the keying material related to the suite.

- In step 7 and step 8 in phase 2 (Figure 4.7), the TTLS server forwards the user name and the CHAP password to the home AAA server (assuming that the these two entities are not collocated). The home AAA server responds (with an access accept message) in step 8, indicating that authorization is provided for the user.

- In step 9 of Figure 4.7 the server uses another data cipher suite message to indicate the cipher chosen by the server (which will likely be one among the list suggested earlier by the client in step 6).

- Step 10, which contains no data, is essentially used by the client to acknowledge agreement in the cipher selected.

- In step 11, the server indicates to the authenticator (namely the AP) which cipher (e.g., WEP, WEP2, AES-OCB) is to be used by the AP and the client to protect the wireless segment between them. Note that here the AP is given no choice with regards to the cipher selection. The server will reflect the client's choice, and if the client did not indicate its choice in step 6, the server will eventually make the decision for both the client and AP.

4.4.3   Comparison of TTLS and PEAP

The TTLS protocol [7] and PEAP protocol [5] have much in common in terms of the basic philosophy of protecting user identity and providing options for other authentication methods for the client and server. Both are two-part protocols, with the first phase used to establish a TLS channel without client identity (and hence optional client certificate), and the second phase used to deliver the client identity information as well as additional cipher negotiations.

One major difference between the two protocols is the way in which further cipher negotiations are achieved. PEAP introduces a new payload structure in the form of EAP-TLVs, while TTLS uses AVPs. The introduction of EAP-TLVs in PEAP allows a PEAP deployment to choose multiple EAP authentication methods atop the established TLS channel. Admittedly, the layering of EAP-TLV above TLS may add to the complexity of the implementation of PEAP. However, the gain in using EAP-TLV is the ability for a sequence of other EAP methods (even EAP-TLS itself) to be run between the client and server. The choice of AVPs in TTLS is driven by compatibility needs with existing RADIUS and Diameter deployments (both of which are protocols that use AVPs). Further efforts on developing a more general purpose *inner application protocol* for EAP can be found in [8].

Finally, for organizations seeking to choose between TTLS and PEAP, there is the question of availability of the protocols on clients. PEAP is shipped with the Windows 2000 and Windows XP clients. In contrast, TTLS and other EAP methods for authentication would need client side software to be installed. Like many other protocols, market needs will eventually determine which segments of the WLAN market will use PEAP and TTLS, respectively.

4.5   EAP-SIM

As mentioned in Chapter 2, a number of *mobile network operators* (MNO) have begun to provide WLAN services to their GSM customers. These services have primarily been WiFi roaming at hotspots that are either owned and/or operated by these carriers. Naturally, these carriers wish to reuse their existing infrastructure for authentication, authorization, and billing on GSM networks. The credential that GSM networks use is the *subscriber identity module* (SIM) [9], which on the user's GSM handset takes the form of a small removable chip. In general, the SIM chip is relatively tamper proof, in the sense that the cost of breaking the chip far exceeds the value of the parameters stored in it. Newer SIMs based on smartcard technology are beginning to find wider deployment.

In order to use SIM within the WLAN environment, a new EAP authentication method has been proposed in [10], namely, EAP-SIM. In general, the aim is to run

EAP-SIM between the client and the authentication server, which in GSM language is the *authentication center* (AuC) at the operator's *home network* (HN). The AuC is the GSM network element that maintains the authentication parameters for authenticating the subscriber. The SIM protocol is essentially a challenge-response protocol based on a shared secret between the SIM and the HN/AuC.

In this section we discuss EAP-SIM as found in [10], which is the latest revision of EAP-SIM at the time of this writing. We use the terms "client," "user," and "subscriber" interchangeably. When we refer to client or subscriber authentication, what is meant is authentication using the parameters in the SIM unit at the client or subscriber. Unless otherwise specified, the 802.1X authentication server is taken to mean the GSM authentication center (AuC).

4.5.1 Background: The SIM Triplet

In the traditional GSM use of the SIM protocol, the subscriber is associated with three parameters that are used in the following manner. The SIM unit and the home network (HN) share a common key K_i that is unique per user, which is stored in the SIM unit. Both use a keyed-hash algorithm called A3 (authentication) and A8 (encryption-key derivation) [9] to compute other parameters.

When the subscriber requests authentication, the home network sends a random *RAND* to the subscriber for challenge-response. The subscriber's SIM unit uses algorithm A3 to compute the value $SRES = A3(RAND, K_i)$. The home network independently does the same computation to get *SRES*. The subscriber then sends its *SRES* value to the home network. A match in *SRES* values by the AuC means authentication is successful.

To encrypt data in GSM networks, both the SIM unit and home network uses algorithm A8 and key K_i to derive key K_c. Signaling data can then be encrypted using K_c end-to-end. When the subscriber roams to a *visited network* (VN), the triplet $(RAND, SRES, K_c)$ is sent by the home network to the visited network so that the visited network can perform the authentication on behalf of the home network. Note that for roaming, a triplet can only be used once since the visited network does not know the secret value K_i. This means that for each authentication done by a visited network, a new triplet must be obtained by the visited network from the home network.

Note that in the WLAN case, the key K_c is used for deriving keying material (not for encryption directly), and as such it is crucial that K_c remain a secret.

4.5.2 EAP-SIM Overview

Figure 4.8 illustrates a generalized high-level exchange among the entities involved in the EAP-SIM protocol in WLANs. In the first step, the client (assumed to contain a SIM and have a secure interface to it) receives the usual identity-request message from the authentication server (AS), which in this case is assumed to be a RADIUS AAA server.

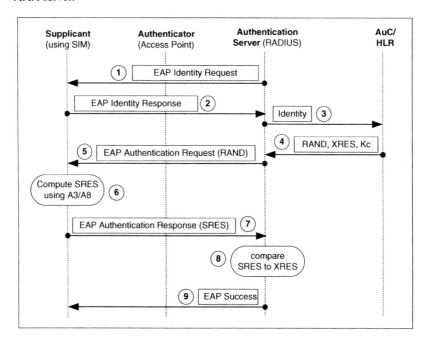

Figure 4.8   Overview of EAP-SIM.

The client obliges and returns the requested identity, which in step 2 of Figure 4.8 can consist of either the *international mobile subscriber identifier* (IMSI) or a pseudonym if client privacy is required. The AS passes the identity information to the authentication center (AuC), which may or may not be collocated with the *home location registry* (HLR) of the client's home GSM network (step 3). In step 4 the AuC/HLR returns a triplet (corresponding to that client) to the AS. The AS passes only the *RAND* value to the client, and keeps the *XRES* and K_c parameters. The *RAND* is indeed the challenge given to the client.

Note that in EAP-SIM, the terminology is slightly modified. The AuC/HLR issues the *XRES* parameter (instead of the *SRES* as in traditional GSM). However, the basic behavior of the protocol remains the same.

The client inputs the received *RAND* value into the SIM, which contains the A3 and A8 algorithms and contains the key K_i that is unique to that SIM. The SIM outputs the value *SRES*, which is then sent by the client to the AS (in step 7). In step 8, the AS compares the response *SRES* from the client with the precomputed value *XRES* received earlier (in step 4) from the AuC/HLR. A match means that the client correctly responded to the challenge, and the AS issues the usual EAP success message and delivers keying material to the authenticator (i.e., AP). Note that in effect the AuC/HLR is treating the AS in the WLAN almost as a visited network (in GSM language).

4.5.3   Example of an EAP-SIM Session

Figure 4.9 shows a more complete example of an EAP-SIM session.

- In step 1 the client responds to the usual EAP identity request message with an EAP identity response message containing either a temporary identity (pseudonym) or an IMSI.

- In step 2 the server signals the start of the EAP-SIM exchange with a SIM-start message containing a list of versions of SIM supported by the server. This is encoded in the attribute-value pair (AVP) payloads of the message (AT_VERSION_LIST). The same message also carries attributes for requesting the client's identity.

- In step 3 the client responds also with a SIM-start message, containing among others the version (of SIM) chosen by the client and a nonce selected by the client (AT_NONCE_MT). Later, the selected version number will be used as input to the computation of the keying material (as a way to protect against cipher downgrade attacks).

- In step 4 if the server is not in possession of the SIM triplet associated with the client, it requests the triplet to the authentication center (AuC) of the client's HLR. The form of this request is transport-specific and is not defined as part of the EAP-SIM specifications.

- In step 5 the AuC/HLR returns the SIM triplet $(RAND, XRES, K_c)$ to the server. Again, the form of this request is not defined as part of the EAP-SIM specifications. Note that between 1 to 5 triplets may be obtained at a time.

- In step 6 the server issues an EAP request/SIM challenge message to the client containing the *RAND* value, and a message authentication code (MAC) attribute (AT_MAC) to protect the challenge from modifications in transit. Note that the nonce from the client (in step 3) is also used as input to the MAC computation.

- In step 7 the client runs the GSM A3/A8 algorithms for the *RAND* value received from the server in step 6, resulting in the *SRES* value. (If there are multiple *RAND* values received, then the client needs to run the algorithms for each of these, producing multiple respective *SRES* values.)

The client then computes its copy of the MAC, which is then compared against the received MAC from the server in the previous step. A mismatch results in an error message being sent by the client to the server, and the exchange terminates immediately. Note that since the *RAND* value given by the server to the client in step 6 is accompanied by the MAC that protects it, and since the nonce (in step 3) from the client contributed to the computation of the MAC (in step 6), the client is able to verify that this EAP message is fresh (not a replay) and that the server possesses valid GSM triplets for the client. In other words, the client sees the (indirect) effect of its nonce from step 3 coming back to itself in step 6.

The client also decrypts the temporary identifier and saves it for the next authentication.

Finally, the client computes one MAC for all the *SRES* values it received, and sends the *SRES* values and the MAC to the server in an EAP response/SIM challenge message.

- In step 8 the server compares the received MAC for the *SRES* (namely MAC_SRES) with its *XRES* received from the AuC/HLR. If they match, then the server issues an EAP success message with keying material to the authenticator (AP), which in turn sends an EAP success message to the client.

  Using the keying material, the AP can now derive the master keys to be used to generate packet encryption keys for wireless traffic between the client and the AP.

4.5.4   Security Issues with SIM over 802.11 WLANs

The SIM authentication protocol was designed for the GSM network, which has a number of different characteristics compared to WLANs and the IP network. The security of the common key K_i, which is shared between the subscriber's SIM unit and the home network, relies on the fact that the SIM hardware is relatively difficult to break. Also, in a GSM network the SIM triplet traverses over a network that is not public or open. In addition, eavesdropping a GSM call-setup process via frequency sniffing is somewhat more difficult compared to sniffing a WLAN.

In contrast to GSM networks, within a WLAN environment such as a WiFi hotspot, the SIM handshake traverses over possibly three different segments. In the first segment, the SIM handshake runs over an 802.11 network from the client to the AP. This segment is easy to eavesdrop by any attacker in the range of the AP. The second segment is over an IP network, from the AP to the AS. In the third segment, it traverses from the AS to the AuC. Although the last hop from the AS

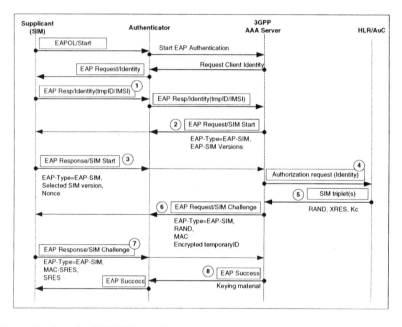

Figure 4.9 Example of EAP-SIM procedure.

to the AuC may be over a private and closed network, attacks can occur in the first two segments.

Note that in EAP-SIM the SIM handshake does not run over a previously established TLS channel (as in PEAP or TTLS). As such, the parameters of the SIM protocol is open to eavesdropping at the vicinity close to the AP.

From the perspective of security another deficiency — which is really due to the history of GSM — is the lack of mutual authentication between the subscriber and the GSM network. In the SIM protocol there is only a one-way authentication from the subscriber to the GSM network. The network (or the AuC) does not authenticate itself to the subscriber, as the challenge ($RAND$) only goes one way, from the AuC to the subscriber. Finally, another deficiency in SIM when used over a WLAN is that the effective strength of the key K_c is only 64 bits [11].

The work of [10] has begun to address some the security issues of the SIM protocol in GSM when carried over into the WLAN world (in the form of the EAP-SIM method). It is important to remember that the designers of EAP-SIM are somewhat constrained by the need to have interoperability of EAP-SIM with the existing GSM authentication infrastructure. As such, only the WLAN side of the architecture is open to modifications, together with EAP-SIM itself. To address the weak key issue in SIM, in EAP-SIM several $RAND$ challenges are used for generating several 64-bit K_c keys, which are then combined to constitute stronger keying material (see step 5 of Section 4.5.3). To address the lack of mutual authentication, in EAP-SIM the client issues a nonce to the network, namely, NONCE_MT in step 3 of Section 4.5.3. This is done in order to contribute to key derivation, and to prevent replays of EAP-SIM requests from previous exchanges. The NONCE_MT can be conceived as the client's challenge to the network. EAP-SIM also extends the combined RAND challenges and other messages with a message authentication code in order to provide message integrity protection along with mutual authentication.

The interested reader is directed to [10] for a further detailed description of EAP-SIM and its differences from the base SIM protocol as found in GSM networks. In the next section, we look at the EAP-AKA method for authentication, which addresses the weaknesses of the EAP-SIM method.

4.6 EAP-AKA

In addition to EAP-SIM, another EAP method for authentication that originated from mobile network operators (MNO) is the EAP *Authentication and Key Agreement* (AKA) protocol [12]. AKA is the mechanism for authentication and session key distribution in *universal mobile telecommunications systems* (UMTS). UMTS is a global third generation mobile network standard. The UMTS AKA is based on symmetric keys and runs typically in a *UMTS subscriber identity module* (USIM) [13], which is based on smartcard technology.

In this section we briefly review EAP-AKA as found in [12], which is the latest revision of EAP-AKA at the time of this writing. We will also note its differences from EAP-SIM.

The behavior of EAP-AKA is similar to that of EAP-SIM, as shown in Figure 4.8. The EAP-AKA method is intended for *third generation* (3G) networks, instead of GSM (which can be considered to be *second generation*, or 2G). From the perspective of security, two of the more interesting differences between EAP-AKA and EAP-SIM are the number of parameters returned by the HSS/HLR — a quintuplet (vector) instead of a triplet — and the fact that the client now authenticates the network. That is, EAP-AKA provides mutual authentication between the client (i.e., USIM) and the 3G network (i.e., the HSS/HLR network element in the home network). This is achieved by the UMTS network sending an authentication token value (AT_AUTN) to the USIM at the client, allowing the client to verify that it is conversing with the correct UMTS network.

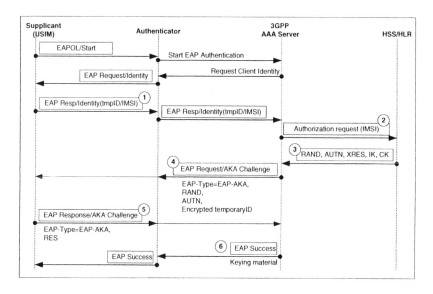

Figure 4.10 Example of EAP-AKA procedure.

An example of an EAP-AKA exchange is shown in Figure 4.10. The basic steps of the exchange are as follows:

- In step 1 in response to the EAP request/identity message, the client sends an EAP response/identity message with a temporary identity in the NAI format [6]. Alternatively, the IMSI may be used as an identity. Which 3G AAA server handles the authentication is determined by the client's NAI.

- In step 2 the 3G AAA server checks to see if it has the authentication vector $(RAND, AUTN, XRES, IK, CK)$ associated with the client. If it does not possess the vector, it requests it from the HSS/HLR using the client's IMSI that is known to the server.

- In step 3, illustrating the case where the 3G AAA server does not possess the client's vector, the HSS/HLR returns the correct vector to the server. The HSS/HLR also selects a new temporary identifier for the client. New keying material is derived from the parameters IK and CK, which is then used to encrypt the temporary identifier

- In step 4 The server forwards only the $RAND$, $AUTN$, and the (encrypted) temporary identifier to the client via an EAP request/AKA challenge message.

- In step 5 the client, upon receiving the parameters, feeds them into the UMTS algorithm in the USIM unit. The USIM performs a verification of $AUTN$ to authenticate the UMTS network (i.e., its HSS/HLR). If the $AUTN$ is correct, the client then proceeds to compute RES, IK, and CK [13].

  The client then derives keying material from the parameters IK and CK, which is used to decrypt the temporary identifier. It keeps the temporary identifier for future authentication events. Finally, the client answers the earlier challenge by sending the computed RES value to the 3G AAA server

- In step 6 the server compares its $XRES$ value (for the client) that was received in step 3 from the HSS/HLR against the RES value received from the client in step 5. If the comparison matches, the client is authentic and the server returns an EAP success message with keying material to the AP, which in turn sends an EAP success message to the client.

4.7 EAP-FAST

Another recent proposal for an EAP method is the *EAP flexible authentication via secure tunneling* (EAP-FAST) [14] from Cisco Systems. The introduction of EAP-FAST was driven by a number of factors. One factor was the security weaknesses that were discovered in Cisco's proprietary LEAP protocol, and thus the need to replace LEAP for the 802.1X case. Another factor was the wish to do away with server-side certificates (which is mandatory in PEAP), in addition to doing away with client-side certificates. This is achieved in EAP-FAST by using a preshared secret as a premaster secret.

Similar to PEAP, one motivation for EAP-FAST is to retain the use of user names and passwords. This removes the burden from the AS of performing PKI related functions (e.g., client certificate checks and path validation), and requires only the AS to have access to a database of user names and passwords. As described in [14], this move away from certificates is also motivated by the need to minimize usage of computational and power resources, particularly on the client side (e.g., PDAs and computationally lightweight devices).

Like PEAP, EAP-FAST also aims to provide broader functionality within the established tunnel [14]. Thus, for example, once the tunnel is established it should be possible for multiple (differing) authentication protocols to be executed between the client (EAP peer) and the AS, or between the client and some remote authentication entity behind the local AS. Note that in the EAP-FAST model, this entity behind the AS is refered to generally as the *inner method server* (IAS), focusing on the fact that an inner EAP method may run within the established tunnel. In practice, depending on the network topology, the inner method server and the AS may be collocated. Similar to the PEAP layers, EAP-FAST also features the use of an EAP-FAST layer over EAP (over the physical medium or "carrier protocols," including EAPOL, RADIUS, and others). In contrast to PEAP, however, above the EAP-FAST layer another TLS layer is introduced, above which a TLV layer is used to transport the other inner EAP methods.

In EAP-FAST a credential is refered to as the *protected access credential* (PAC), which consists of three components. These are the *PAC key*, the *PAC opaque* and the *PAC info*. The PAC key is a preshared secret between the client/peer and the AS, while the PAC opaque contains the client identity. The PAC info contains information identifying the *PAC issuer* as the authoritative credential issuer (and other supporting parameters, such as the key lifetime). The PAC itself is a 32-octet key which is randomly generated by the AS as the trusted entity in the network. The PAC corresponds to the TLS premaster secret within the TLS protocol. Note that the PAC can be provisioned in-band or out-of-band, but must always consist of the above three components.

Similar to TTLS and PEAP, EAP-FAST first establishes a tunnel between the client (peer) and the AS in order to protect subsequent conversations between the client and the AS, possibly performing further authentications and authorizations. The tunnel establishment uses the PAC to initiate an authenticated key agreement exchange, resulting in the tunnel. An important event that occurs in this phase is the generation of the *master session keys* (MSKs) which will be used to derive further session keys between the client and AS.

The reader is directed to [14] for further details on EAP-FAST. Since conceptually EAP-FAST is very similar to EAP-TTLS and PEAP, the reader is directed first to those earlier works for a broader understanding of tunneling in EAP and its benefits.

4.8 RADIUS SUPPORT FOR EAP

With the growing popularity of EAP as a way to allow various authentication methods to be used between the client (EAP peer or supplicant) and the AS, extensions have been defined in RFC3579 [15] for RADIUS itself to support EAP. The aim of the extensions is to use RADIUS to shuttle RADIUS-encapsulated EAP packets between the authenticator (or the NAS) and the AS. Two new attributes were introduced into RADIUS in RFC3579 in order to achieve this effect, namely the *EAP message* attribute and the *message authenticator* attribute.

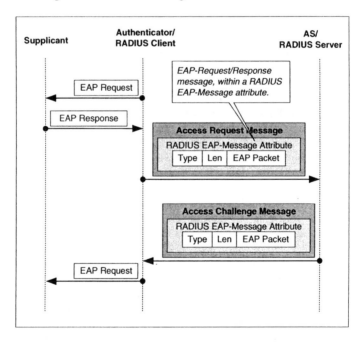

Figure 4.11   RADIUS support for EAP.

In order to appreciate the convenience and usefulness of EAP over RADIUS, it is important to understand the context of usage of the two attributes. In the context 802.1X, when communicating with the RADIUS server, the authenticator (e.g., AP) would in fact be a RADIUS client. Thus, the authenticator has two roles. On one side the authenticator acts as a RADIUS client when communicating with the RADIUS-server. On the other side it acts as the usual 802.1X authenticator when interacting with the 802.1X client or supplicant.

In this dual role, the authenticator essentially acts as an intermediary between the EAP peer and the RADIUS server. It is in this intermediary function that the EAP message attribute is used to encapsulate EAP packets that are being exchanged between the two end points (namely the EAP peer and RADIUS server). In this way the authenticator would be "blind" to the method-specific exchanges occurring between the EAP peer and the RADIUS server, and thus be able to "support" any EAP method for authentication. This is illustrated in Figure 4.11.

The other new attribute, namely the *message authenticator* attribute, is used to authenticate and integrity protect access requests in order to prevent spoofing. The attribute is used in any *access message* (i.e., access request, access accept, access reject, or access challenge) that includes an EAP message attribute. Both the RADIUS client (namely the authenticator) and the RADIUS server must verify the value of the message authenticator if that attribute is present in any received access request message. A RADIUS client must additionally verify the value in the case of the message authenticator attribute being present in access accept, access reject or access challenge messages. The main purpose of this message authenticator attribute is to detect and thwart "rogue" authenticators (NAS) that are setup to launch an online dictionary attack against the RADIUS server. As such, the attribute really does not protect against offline attacks (e.g., intercepting CHAP challenge and response packets).

The reader is directed to RFC3579 [15] for further details on the two RADIUS attributes and their specific usages.

4.9 SUMMARY

This chapter has devoted considerable focus on a number of key EAP methods for authentication. Those that have been discussed are EAP-TLS, protected EAP (PEAP), tunneled TLS (EAP-TTLS), EAP-SIM, and EAP-AKA.

The PEAP and EAP-TTLS methods provide an illustration of the use of tunnels within an EAP conversation. The tunnel approach allows further EAP methods to be conducted under the protection of the tunnel, either using AVPs (in EAP-TTLS) or TLVs (in PEAP). The EAP-SIM and EAP-AKA methods have the potential of becoming the authentication protocols favored by MNOs who provide WLAN access services. Their importance cannot be underestimated, since GSM networks today have a worldwide subscriber population of over 1 billion users.

It is difficult at this current point in time to predict which EAP authentication method will become the de facto method used by the WiFi industry, as a number of factors influence the adoption of any given EAP method.

One factor is the physical location of the user, namely on-campus enterprise or off-campus roaming. For example, many enterprises use EAP-TLS for on-campus WiFi access as it provides strong client authentication using client certificates. EAP-TLS is also supported in most recent versions of the Microsoft Windows operating system, and hence removing the need for the enterprise to obtain third party supplicant software. However, in an off-campus WiFi roaming case, most WiFi hotspot providers today do not support EAP-TLS due, among others, to the need to also support server certificates and PKI management. Other factors influencing the choice of EAP methods include the EAP methods being promoted by WLAN and network equipment vendors, the success of 3G networks, the emergence of 802.16 networks, privacy issues, and other factors.

The growth of the Internet, its services, and supporting technologies may require various protocols (EAP methods) to be available to cater for the specific local network topologies and needs. As such, the development and maturity of several EAP methods may be desirable, provided that they possess strong security features and can be deployed readily.

References

[1] B. Aboba, "Extensible Authentication Protocol (EAP)." RFC 3748 (Standards Track), June 2004.

[2] L. Blunk and J. Vollbrecht, "PPP Extensible Authentication Protocol (EAP)." RFC 2284 (Standards Track), Mar. 1998.

[3] B. Aboba and D. Simon, "PPP EAP TLS Authentication Protocol." RFC 2716 (Experimental), Oct. 1999.

[4] E. Rescorla, *SSL and TLS: Designing and Building Secure Systems*, Reading, MA: Addison-Wesley, 2001.

[5] A. Palekar, D. Simon, G. Zorn, J. Salowey, H. Zhou, and S. Josefsson, "Protected EAP Protocol (PEAP) Version 2," draft-josefsson-pppext-eap-tls-eap-07 (work in progress), Internet Engineering Task Force, Oct. 2003.

[6] B. Aboba and M. Beadles, "The Network Access Identifier (NAI)." RFC 2486 (Standards Track), Jan. 1999.

[7] P. Funk and S. Blake-Wilson, "EAP Tunneled TLS Authentication Protocol (EAP-TTLS)," draft-ietf-pppext-eap-ttls-05 (work in progress), Internet Engineering Task Force, July 2004.

[8] P. Funk, "TLS Inner Application Extension (TLS/IA)," draft-funk-tls-inner-application-extension-01 (work in progress), Internet Engineering Task Force, Feb. 2005.

[9] ETSI, "GSM 03.20 (ETS 300 534): Digital Cellular Telecommunication System (Phase 2); Security Related Network Functions," GSM technical specification, European Telecommunications Standards Institute (ETSI), Aug. 1997.

[10] H. Haverinen and J. Salowey, "EAP SIM Authentication," draft-haverinen-pppext-eap-sim-12 (work in progress), Internet Engineering Task Force, Oct. 2003.

[11] U. Blumenthal and S. Patel, "EAP-SIM Security Analysis: Keyspace and Mutual Authentication Weaknesses," *Proceedings of the 57th IETF*, (Vienna, Austria), July 2003.

[12] J. Arkko and H. Haverinen, "EAP AKA Authentication," draft-arkko-pppext-eap-aka-11.txt (work in progress), Internet Engineering Task Force, Oct. 2003.

[13] 3GPP, "3GPP TS 33.102 V5.1.0: Technical Specification Group Services and System Aspects; 3G Security; Security Architecture (Release 5)," 3GPP Technical Specification, 3rd Generation Partnership Project (3GPP), Dec. 2002.

[14] N.Cam-Winget, D. McGrew, J. Salowey, and H. Zhou, "EAP Flexible Authentication via Secure Tunneling (EAP-FAST)," draft-cam-winget-eap-fast-00 (work in progress), Internet Engineering Task Force, Feb. 2004.

[15] B. Aboba and P. Calhoun, "RADIUS Support for Extensible Authentication Protocol (EAP)," RFC 3579 (Informational), Sept. 2003.

Part II

Data Protection in Wireless LANs

Chapter 5

WEP

5.1 INTRODUCTION

Wireless networks make it easy for an attacker to read, modify, or drop packets, as the attacker often needs only to be in the vicinity of the communicating entities. In contrast, an adversary may need to gain entry to a physical access controlled building, wiring closet, or a network device to attack a wired network. The IEEE 802.11 standard attempts to emulate the physical attributes of wired medium in designing the wired equivalency privacy (WEP) suite of security protocols and data transforms.

WEP consists mainly of an entity authentication protocol and a data security transform. The authentication protocol has two modes: open-system and shared-key authentication subtypes. The open-system authentication protocol is a 2-way handshake initiated by the entity requesting service. It consists of the requester asserting its identity and the responder returning with "successful" or "unsuccessful," only on the basis of whether open-system authentication is supported or not. In other words, open-system authentication protocol does not provide any security whatsoever. The shared-key protocol is a 4-way exchange, also initiated by the entity requesting service. It consists of request, challenge, challenge-response, and result messages in that order. The responder challenges the requester to provide proof of possession of the shared secret. The requester encapsulates the challenge-response message using the WEP transform to prove that it knows the WEP secret key. The responder decapsulates the message using its local copy of the shared secret key and compares the decrypted text with the original challenge text. If there is a match, the requester is granted a connection.

The data security transform, comprising the WEP encapsulation and decapsulation processes, is the other component of an 802.11 security solution. The standard recommends that the authentication protocol be used in conjunction with the data security transform.

WEP uses RC4 (Ron's code: a proprietary stream cipher designed by Ron Rivest of RSA Labs and later released into public domain) as the cipher to protect 802.11 frames. The WEP encapsulation process is designed to be "reasonably strong," self-synchronizing (considering that MPDUs may be dropped or arrive out of order, the receiving entity must be able to decapsulate an MPDU independent of prior or future MPDUs), efficient, and easy to implement in hardware or software. Thus, an initialization vector (IV) for the RC4 cipher accompanies each MPDU, along with a key ID (shared-key ID used to encapsulate the current MPDU), and an integrity checksum to protect against MPDU modification en route. Briefly, the key and the IV are input to the RC4 encryption algorithm to generate a pseudorandom keystream for MPDU encapsulation. A checksum is computed over the MPDU using CRC-32 for integrity protection. The checksum is then appended to the MPDU and is XORed with the keystream to generate the ciphertext. WEP decapsulation follows the reverse process, where, upon decryption of an MPDU, the received checksum is compared with the locally computed checksum, to verify the MPDU's integrity.

WEP design contains several well-publicized flaws. The nature of the flaws will be clear as we delve into the design details. The design goals themselves are suspect: the stated goal is wired equivalency privacy, which in itself is hard to capture. The choice of cipher, and especially the use of a stream cipher for encapsulating packets, also makes it easy for an attacker to cryptanalyze WEP encapsulated MPDUs. The choice of integrity algorithm, CRC-32, which is linear, makes it easy for an attacker to modify encrypted MPDUs without the receiver being able to verify whether the packets are legitimate or not.

5.2   THREAT MODEL

First, we consider an ideal threat model for 802.11 wireless communications, followed by the threat model addressed by the WEP design. Wireless communications may be between two STAs, or between an AP and one or more STAs. In most cases (assuming for instance that there is no Faraday cage enclosing one or more of the communicating devices), wireless signals in the frequency range supported by 802.11, 2.4–5 GHz, can be captured from locations that are in the order of 100 meters away from the transmitting entity. Thus, an adversary can potentially listen in on 802.11 MPDUs without having to gain physical access to a secured facility. So even if the goal is wired equivalency, 802.11 MPDUs need protection from external snooping. Therefore confidentiality is a requirement.

An adversary may also be able to assume the transmitter's identity by jamming the transmitter and sending 802.11 frames to another device claiming to be the transmitter. Thus host authentication as well as message integrity is a requirement.

If the MPDUs are encrypted and integrity protected, an adversary may be able to replay old MPDUs and hope that they will be accepted as new. Thus, replay protection might be a requirement.

Finally, an adversary may be able to launch an assorted variety of denial of service (DoS) attacks. DoS protection in wireless networks should be addressed on a case-by-case basis. For instance, an adversary may replay legitimate MPDUs to cause a receiver to decrypt, verify integrity, and check for replays (which will fail) to drain the battery of the receiver. Denying service to a particular device might be easier for the adversary than attacking the protocols; the adversary may simply jam the device and disallow it from communicating at all.

In summary, secure 802.11 communications require confidentiality of MPDUs, mutual authentication of the communicating entities, integrity and replay protection for the MPDUs, and finally protection against DoS attacks.

5.2.1 Threat Model Addressed by the WEP Design

The WEP designers' main goal was to create "wired equivalency" for 802.11 networks [1]. WEP supports initiator authentication only. In other words, only the entity requesting the service needs to prove possession of the shared key. The network (or the AP) does not authenticate to the entity requesting service.

WEP designers also considered confidentiality and integrity protection as requirements. However, the choice of algorithms and the security encapsulation itself are not even strong enough to protect against an adversary equipped with a desktop PC.

WEP supports confidentiality using the RC4 stream cipher. WEP also supports message integrity. However, CRC-32, the integrity protection algorithm used as part of WEP encapsulation, is not a method that can product a cryptographic checksum. The checksum is encrypted, which provides some protection; however, a fairly simple attack circumvents this limited protection. WEP does not provide replay or DoS protection.

5.3 ENTITY AUTHENTICATION

IEEE 802.11 specification requires that all wireless devices requesting service run an authentication protocol. There are two options for a STA to authenticate to another STA or an AP: first, the requesting STA may use open-system authentication or shared-key authentication. In open-system authentication, the requesting entity asserts its identity and if the receiver supports open-system authentication, it returns a message indicating successful authentication. In shared-key authentication, the requesting STA is required to provide proof of possession of a shared secret key.

Open-system authentication is a 2-way exchange, whereas shared-key authentication is a 4-way exchange. In either case, the authentication messages are defined as a subtype within management messages. They contain the following fields:

- Message type: *Management*

- Message subtype: *Authentication*

- Information items:

    - Authentication algorithm. This field contains the value 0 for open-system authentication and 1 for shared-key authentication.

    - Station ID assertion (optional). This information is required in Message 1 and is the same as the SA field of the MAC header, and optional in all other messages.

    - Authentication transaction sequence number. The sequence number is initialized to 1, and increased by 1 for each subsequent authentication message. This field has the values 1, 2, 3, or 4.

    - Authentication algorithm-dependent information. This field is not required in case of open-system authentication, and generally is included in the first and last messages of either mode of authentication. In the shared-key authentication mode, this field contains the challenge text.

5.3.1 Open-System Authentication

Figure 5.1 illustrates open-system authentication. This is a 2-way exchange starting with the requester sending its MAC address (SA in the MAC header field). If the responder supports open-system authentication, it takes the requester's asserted identity to be the actual identity, and returns "successful." If the AP does not support open-system authentication, it returns "unsuccessful."

5.3.2 Shared-Key Authentication

Shared-key authentication requires WEP support. The goal of this exchange is for the STA requesting 802.11 service to provide a proof of possession of a secret key it shares with the authenticating entity, an AP or a STA. Shared-key authentication is a 4-way exchange and contains the following steps:

1. Identity assertion. The first message is from the STA requesting service to the STA or AP providing the service or wireless connection. The algorithm identification is 1 to indicate the shared key mode, and also contains the requesting STA's asserted identity.

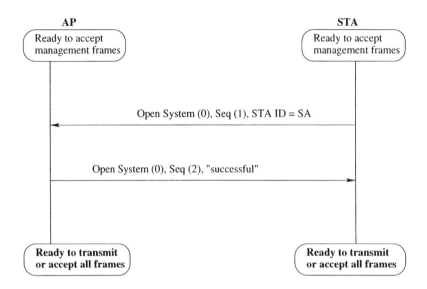

Figure 5.1 Open-system authentication in 802.11.

2. Challenge. The responding STA or AP challenges the requester to prove that it actually holds a copy of the mutually shared key. For this purpose. the responder sends a random challenge text as part of the algorithm-dependent information in the authentication frame.

3. Challenge-response. The requester responds to the challenge by constructing an authentication frame, with a sequence number of 3, and the received challenge text in the algorithm dependent information field. It then encrypts the authentication frame using WEP. The WEP encryption key is the shared secret key and thus only an entity holding the key can respond to the challenge of message 2.

4. Result. The final authentication message contains the result of the exchange. The responder decapsulates message 3 using WEP with its local copy of the shared secret key. If the integrity checksum matches and if the received challenge text is identical to the original challenge, the STA requesting service would be considered legitimate and the responder grants the requested service.

Figure 5.2 illustrates the 4-way exchange for shared-key-based authentication in the 802.11 specification.

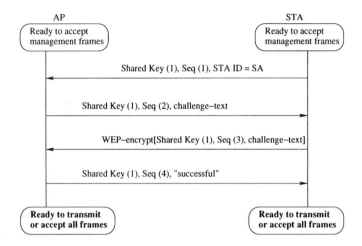

Figure 5.2   Shared-key authentication in 802.11.

5.4   WEP ENCAPSULATION AND DECAPSULATION

WEP encapsulation protects initial device authentication frames as well as MPDUs. It is a prudent practice to use separate keys for different purposes such as authentication and data encapsulation, but we will discuss this and similar design and protocol flaws in detail in Section 5.5.

5.4.1   WEP Design Requirements

The 802.11 MPDUs may arrive out of order or may be lost in transmission due to interference. Therefore, the receiver should be able to decrypt each MPDU independent of other MPDUs preceding or succeeding the current MPDU. This is called the *self-synchronizing* property.

The 802.11 security protocol suite should provide confidentiality, integrity protection to the MPDUs, and allow only authenticated entities to gain access to the DS. Thus, the WEP encapsulation process should be strong enough to force an adversary to resort to brute-forcing techniques to break the protocols or the encryption algorithms.

The design must allow an efficient software or hardware design of the encapsulation and the decapsulation processes.

Finally, note that WEP encapsulation is optional in the 802.11 specification. Wireless devices may use open-system authentication and transmit and accept plaintext MPDUs. In some cases, higher-layer security encapsulation may be employed to control access and to protect data. Note that higher-layer security protocols do not protect MAC layer headers and messages, which may provide an attacker with several vulnerabilities to exploit. For instance, it is possible to modify the address fields, or send bogus disassociate messages and cause denial of service. These type of attacks might be simpler to launch compared to signal jamming, for example, which may require slightly expensive devices.

5.4.2 WEP Shared Secret Keys

The WEP header contains a 2-bit field to carry key ID. This allows 802.11 devices to configure four different shared secret keys. The AP may divide the devices it serves into as many as four groups, and assign and share separate shared secret keys with devices in each group. The shared key can be either 40 bits or 104 bits in size. The original standard specifies the 40-bit key and a revision specifies the longer key.

Sharing host authentication keys with a group of devices or users is not a recommended practice in general. Notice that such sharing allows any device in the group to claim to be one of the other devices.

For strong security, the shared key must be randomly generated and must contain sufficient entropy. Passwords or shared secrets generated from short passwords are not recommended. Instead, a longer passphrase should be used as a seed for a key generator. The key generator could be publicly specified, but should be computationally complex. Since the shared-key generation is an offline process, it does not impact legitimate users, but requires significant computing resources for an adversary to develop a database of keys of, say, all passphrase combinations from a dictionary.

5.4.3 WEP Cipher: RC4

RC4 is the cipher used in WEP encapsulation, as it is freely available, easy to implement in hardware or software, simple, and efficient. Considering that typical 802.11 devices are expected to be priced very modestly, this might be considered an appropriate choice.

However, RC4 is a stream cipher and comes with some caveats. In RC4, a session key is used as a seed to generate the keystream of necessary length; the keystream is XORed with the plaintext to derive the ciphertext. If the same session key is used to encrypt two different streams, XORing the resultant ciphertext streams is equivalent to XORing the two plaintext streams. If a portion of one of the plaintext streams is known, it is easy to derive the other plaintext stream.

RC4 works well in TLS for example, and is the protocol of choice in many SSL/TLS deployments. SSL/TLS runs over TCP and, thus, in order and reliable reception of TLS encapsulated packets make RC4 an excellent choice in that context.

Recall however that 802.11 communication channels are lossy and in some cases with high drop rates; out-of-order MPDU reception is also plausible. To account for this, WEP uses a per-MPDU RC4 key and generates a separate keystream per MPDU. For this purpose, WEP concatenates a per-MPDU initialization vector (IV) to the WEP key. The IV is 24 bits in size, and the shared secret key occupies the rest of the 40 bits to form a 64-bit per-MPDU key, or 104 bits to form a 128-bit per MPDU key. The self-synchronization property requires the IV to be included with the encapsulated MPDUs, and thus increase in IV would result in increase in overhead.

The length and selection of the IV have serious security implications. The 24-bit IV implies that 2^{24} MPDUs can be encrypted with a given key, and after that the key must be changed. Unfortunately, the 802.11 standard does not specify a rekeying mechanism. The shared secrets are established via an external secure channel and any rekeying would have to occur externally as well. In most deployments, key establishment is manually done, and thus is very time-consuming or even implausible in large deployments.

WEP does not specify an IV selection method. Two communicating entities can take advantage of encapsulating 2^{24} MPDUs with the same key only if the IV is used as a counter. A random IV selection might result in IV reuse after encapsulating fewer than 2^{12} MPDUs.

In summary, WEP uses a per-MPDU IV to generate a per MPDU key and keystream. The per-MPDU RC4 keystream is XORed with the plaintext MPDU to generate the corresponding ciphertext. The IV length and selection process are issues of concern.

5.4.4   WEP Integrity Algorithm: CRC-32

WEP specifies CRC-32 as the integrity algorithm. The checksum is computed over the MPDU, concatenated to the MPDU, and the MPDU plus the checksum are encrypted using RC4.

Unfortunately, CRC-32 is not a keyed integrity algorithm and thus an adversary can easily generate a correct checksum. Since RC4 is a stream cipher, the encryption does not afford any significant protection.

5.4.5   WEP Encapsulation

WEP encapsulation is a fairly simple process, and consists of the following steps.

- Integrity protection. First, CRC-32 is used to protect the MPDU. The integrity check vector (ICV) computed using CRC-32 is concatenated to the end of the MPDU, thereby resulting in adding four octets to the outgoing MPDU.

- Keystream generation. WEP keystream generation can proceed independent of the CRC-32 generation process. First, a fresh 24-bit IV is concatenated to the shared secret key to form a 64-bit or 128-bit WEP key or *seed*. The IV forms the lower-order octets of the WEP key whereas the secret key forms the higher-order octets. Specifically, bits 0 through 23 of the IV form the bits 0 through 23 of the seed, and bits 0, 1, 2, ... of the secret key form the bits 24, 25, 26, ... of the seed.

  The seed is input to the RC4 pseudorandom number generator (PRNG) or simply keystream generator. To encrypt an 802.11 MPDU, we need a keystream of length $d + 4$ octets, where d is the length in octets of the MPDU. The additional four octets of keystream are to encrypt the CRC-32 checksum. See Figure 5.3 for an illustration.

- Ciphertext generation. The penultimate step is to derive the ciphertext by combining the keystream with the MPDU concatenated to the ICV using the logical XOR operation.

- Header generation. The final step is to put together the WEP header, which consists of the 24-bit IV and another octet with bits 0 and 1 representing the key ID. Thus the header adds another 4 octets to the length of the outgoing MPDU, bringing the overall packet expansion due to WEP encapsulation to 8 octets.

  The IV and the key ID are in the clear, and in fact not protected at all. The IV in the header allows the WEP encapsulation and decapsulation process to be stateless and accounts for the potential packet loss and out-of-order delivery. The key ID also serves the same purpose. Thus, upon reception of an MPDU, a receiver uses the WEP header to determine the IV and the secret key to use decapsulate the encrypted MPDU.

  Figure 5.4 illustrates the packet formats before and after WEP encapsulation and the encrypted and CRC-32 protected portions of a WEP encapsulated MPDU.

5.4.5.1   Guidelines on IV Usage

WEP uses a 24-bit IV to generate a per MPDU seed. A given IV and key combination generates the same seed and the same keystream. This is simply because the IV is concatenated to the key to form the seed and the seed is supplied to the RC4

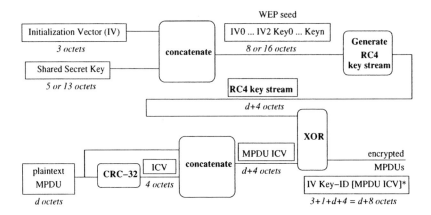

Figure 5.3 WEP encapsulation process.

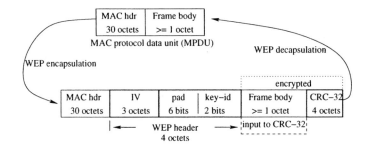

Figure 5.4 WEP encapsulated MPDUs.

PRNG to generate the keystream; in other words there is no other input to affect the process.

From the previous section, we know that the keystream is XORed with the plaintext MPDU to obtain the ciphertext MPDU. Thus, if an IV and key combination were to be reused, say to encrypt two different MPDUs, an adversary can XOR the two encrypted MPDUs to obtain the XOR value of the two plaintext MPDUs. If the adversary further knows or has an idea of the contents of one of the MPDUs, it can simply derive the other MPDU.

Therefore, the IV length allows only 2^{24} MPDUs to be encrypted with a given secret key. To take advantage of the entire IV space, it is best for the sender to use monotonically increasing values for the IV.

However, the 802.11 standard allows several devices — at least a sender and a receiver — to use the same set of four keys (four is the limit on the number of keys supported by a device, considering the length of the key ID field). The 802.11 specification does not describe an IV space management scheme to avoid reuse. The IV space itself is limited however, so any efforts in that direction would be ineffective.

Note that the 802.11 standard is quite liberal in specifying guidelines for IV use. For instance, the standard suggests that the IV should be changed periodically. From the discussion above, it is clear that that is not sufficient. An IV value cannot be reused with the same key.

5.4.6 WEP Decapsulation

The WEP decapsulation process is quite similar to the encapsulation process and in fact reuses the keystream generation step. WEP decapsulation consists of the following steps:

- First, an encrypted MPDU contains the IV, and the key ID of the shared secret key used to generate the RC4 keystream. Using the key ID, the receiving STA or AP looks up the shared secret key, and concatenates the IV in the WEP header to the local copy of the secret key. The receiver then uses the seed formed by concatenation to generate the keystream.

- Next, the receiver XORs the keystream with the received MPDU minus the WEP header (first four octets after the 802.11 MAC header). The result is the plaintext MPDU and the ICV. We will call this ICV_r as it is the received ICV.

- The receiver then proceeds to compute the ICV of the decrypted MPDU using the CRC-32 algorithm. The computed ICV_c must be identical to the received ICV_r.

- Finally, the receiving STA/AP compares ICV_c and ICV_r. If the two ICVs match, the MPDU is accepted; otherwise, it is dropped. Figure 5.5 illustrates the WEP decapsulation process.

5.5   DESIGN FLAWS IN WEP

WEP is a flawed security protocol. The authentication algorithm, the data encapsulation method, the choice and use of the RC4 cipher, incomplete IV usage guidelines, and finally the use of an inappropriate algorithm for integrity protection are all flawed at some level and help potential attackers to subvert the intended security properties.

The various flaws of WEP are highly publicized, and several attacks have been well documented [2–6]. The attacks range from simple operations to cause

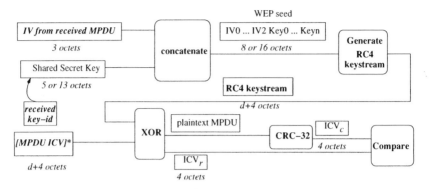

Figure 5.5   WEP decapsulation process.

packet modification without the receiver being able to detect it, to attacks based on the fundamental weaknesses in the RC4 key scheduling algorithm (KSA).

5.5.1   Lack of Proper Integrity Protection

WEP uses CRC-32 for integrity protection. CRC-32 is not a keyed integrity algorithm and is highly susceptible to collisions, and thus is ineffective as an integrity algorithm. The combination of a stream cipher and CRC-32 makes it possible to launch fairly simple packet modification attacks on WEP protected MPDUs.

Given an encrypted MPDU, one needs to simply generate a random bit string of the same length as the MPDU (minus the 4-octet MAC header, and the trailing 4 octets, where the ICV is present) and compute the CRC-32 checksum on the random string. The adversary can then simply XOR the random bit string along with the corresponding CRC-32 value to the encrypted MPDU and the ICV. Since CRC-32 is linear, this packet modification attack would go undetected during the WEP decapsulation process: the received and the compute ICV would match, but the decrypted MPDU is not what was sent originally by the sender.

5.5.2   Improper Use of RC4

WEP's use of RC4 has several serious flaws. First, RC4 is a stream cipher and the key should be used only once to generate the keystream. To achieve the self-synchronization property, 802.11 proposes the use of a per-MPDU IV to generate a per-MPDU seed and a corresponding keystream. Thus, MPDUs may be encrypted with a potentially different IV (a 24-bit component) and a key that remains constant (40-or 104-bit component). It is clear that keys generated following this process may be "related." RC4 is susceptible to related key attacks.

Furthermore, Fluhrer, Mantin, and Shamir [4] prove that RC4 KSA has two major weaknesses that may make it plausible for an attacker to derive the key from the encrypted traffic. First, there are several weak keys; next, the first few bytes of the keystream may be used in statistical analysis to derive the secret key. Whereas an adversary might not have ready access to the keystream, educated guesses on the first few bytes of the MPDU are not hard to make. Consider that the first few bytes in several cases may contain well-known packet headers. Furthermore, the shared-key authentication protocol encrypts the third message whose contents are all known or are part of the second message (for instance, the challenge text), which is in the clear.

In summary, RC4 itself has some vulnerabilities that an attacker might exploit, and WEP's design of reusing the key with an IV increases the potential for related keys. The 802.11 protocols also provide opportunities for the attacker to gain access to cleartext and the corresponding ciphertext.

5.5.2.1 Vulnerabilities Associated with the IV

There are several problems associated with the IV. First, the 802.11 standard is quite casual about the IV usage. In particular it suggests that the IV is selected at random and should be changed periodically. These guidelines are insufficient.

First, the IV must not be reused with the stream cipher. A simple technique would then be to use a monotonically increasing value as the IV. However, considering that secret keys may be shared among several entities — at least between two, a sender and a receiver — IV space management can be quite complex.

Random IV generation increases the possibility of an IV collision or reuse with the same key. Due to the birthday paradox [7] result, there is a 50% chance of IV collision after about $1.2 \times \sqrt{2^{24}}$ or approximately 5,000 MPDUs have been encapsulated using randomly generated IVs.

5.5.3 Lack of Replay Protection

WEP does not support replay protection. Thus even if confidentiality and message integrity were effective, an adversary can replay previously sent packets. The receiver would have no way of telling that the packet is legitimate or a replay. An integrity protected sequence counter is used to provide replay protection (alternatively, time stamps may be used where the sender and the receiver are time synchronized).

5.5.4   Lack of Mutual Authentication and Key Management

The shared-key authentication mechanism only allows the responder to authenticate the initiator, but not vice versa. This allows any STA to claim to be an AP or a STA that the initiating STA wants to communicate with.

Notice that IV is only 24 bits in size. In other words, the IV space can be exhausted fairly quickly, considering that IV space is shared and the high bandwidth rates supported by 802.11g and 802.11a. When the IV space is exhausted, the secret key must be changed. However, the 802.11 standard does not specify a protocol for rekeying. In most implementations, there is no external secure protocol to facilitate rekeying, and thus the keys are typically changed manually and thus quite infrequently. This increases the chance of key and IV pair reuse and thus makes WEP encapsulation vulnerable.

5.6   SUMMARY

The 802.11 specification correctly recognizes that wireless communications are more vulnerable to eavesdropping, packet modification, and other attacks compared to wired LANs. However, the conclusion was to provide only "wired equivalency," which is an ill-defined goal. In addition, the choices for encryption and integrity algorithms are not well thought out and are inappropriate for packet-based transmission as in 802.11 networks.

In this chapter, we described the algorithms and protocols that are part of the WEP design, explaining the security properties in each case. We concluded the chapter with a summary of the flaws in the WEP design.

The various vulnerabilities of WEP are well publicized in the literature and the IEEE designed a new standard called robust secure network association (RSNA) with two new data encapsulation protocols, namely, TKIP for legacy devices with RC4 in the hardware, and CCMP for new devices with AES as the encryption and integrity algorithm. This chapter mainly serves as a reference to WEP, the various flaws in the design, and their implications.

References

[1] IEEE, "IEEE Wireless LAN Edition, A Compilation Based on IEEE Std 802.11-1999 (Reaffirmed 2003) and Its Amendments," tech. rep., IEEE Press, New York, 2003.

[2] C. He and J. C. Mitchell, "Security Analysis and Improvements for IEEE 802.11i," *Proceedings of Network and Distributed System Security Symposium (NDSS)*, (San Diego, CA), Feb. 2005.

[3] A. Stubblefield, J. Ioannidis, and A. D. Rubin, "Using the Fluhrer, Mantin, and Shamir Attack to Break WEP," *Proceedings of Network and Distributed System Security Symposium (NDSS)*, (San Diego, CA), Feb. 2002.

[4] S. Fluhrer, I. Mantin, and A. Shamir, "Weaknesses in the Key Scheduling Algorithm of RC4," *Proceedings of the Eighth Annual Workshop on Selected Areas in Cryptography*, (Toronto, Canada), Aug. 2001.

[5] N. Borisov, I. Goldberg, and D. Wagner, "Intercepting Mobile Communications: The Insecurity of 802.11," *Proceedings of the Seventh Annual International Conference on Mobile Computing and Networking*, (Rome, Italy), July 2001.

[6] J. Walker, "Unsafe at Any Key Size: An Analysis of the WEP Encapsulation." IEEE TGi doc 802.11-00/345r0, Oct. 2000, http://www.ieee802.org.

[7] "Birthday Paradox." Wikipedia entry, http://en.wikipedia.org/wiki/Birthday_paradox.

Chapter 6

802.11i Security: RSNA

6.1   INTRODUCTION

Wireless LAN devices or wireless stations (STA) are considered as logically external entities to an enterprise network. Radio frequency (RF) waves in most deployment scenarios do not have physical boundaries and thus STAs should be allowed to
access the corporate network only after going through a similar authentication procedure as in the case of remote access. For remote access, enterprises typically use
IPsec for general purpose access to their intranets, and SSL for access to email and
other similar applications. In both cases, remote access servers and clients mutually
authenticate each other, and arrive at a common security association (SA). Use of
keys within that SA is proof of authentication for accessing the enterprise intranet
via the remote access server.

STAs establish a robust security network association (RSNA) with an AP
using IEEE 802.1X and EAP for authentication and key distribution. From the
resulting master key, the AP and the STA engage in a 4-way exchange to derive
session keys. STAs can only communicate to other entities in the wired or wireless
network via an authenticated secure channel (using CCMP or TKIP described in
Chapters 7 and 8 as the security protocols). Thus, an AP enforces access control
to the wired network and provides a means for authenticated and confidential
communication between the STA and other entities in the network.

In this chapter we define the goals and motivation behind the design of RSNAs
and briefly describe the 802.1X and EAP-based authentication protocol and the
process of establishing a master key. We also discuss the 4-way exchange to derive
unicast session keys and the protocols for delivering group keys and keys for direct
secure communication between two STAs associated with the same AP.

6.2 802.11I SECURITY GOALS

802.11 defines three different modes of communication within an ESS, namely:

- Bidirectional one-to-one communication between STAs and wired networks via APs;

- Unidirectional one-to-many communication from an AP to the STAs within the secure group (only STAs associated with the AP qualify as members);

- Bidirectional one-to-one direct communication between two STAs associated with the same AP.

The first case, by which STAs get access to the wired network and thus to the Internet is by far the most popular method of communication. The other two cases have significant use as well, where an AP can efficiently communicate to all the STAs within its BSS, or where two STAs can communicate efficiently without consuming the AP's resources. The latter mode of communication is especially useful for latency-sensitive applications such as voice over IP.

STA and AP authentication procedures are common for all three modes of communication, as are the mechanics of access control. A 4-way exchange between the STA and AP is used to establish the session keys for unicast communication between the STA and the wired network.

6.2.1 Enforcing Authorized Access to a Wired Network

It is desirable that only authorized entities are allowed access to a WLAN and especially to the wired network via an AP.

An RSNA relies on 802.1X port access control to enforce authorized access to the wired network. IEEE 802.11 TGi defines two methods of host authentication. In the first, a preshared key configured on the AP and the STA is used for mutual authentication. The second approach depends on network infrastructure support; a backend authentication server (AS) authenticates the STA and delivers the resultant keys to the AP via an external secure channel. The STA receives or computes the keys as part of the authentication protocol. The resulting key is known as the pairwise master key (PMK). Proof of possession of the PMK by the STA and the AP mutually authenticates them. The AP may provide the AS functionality, in which case the mutual authentication is direct.

6.2.1.1 EAP Method Requirements

The preferred mode of AS authentication is via certificates, supported by EAP-TLS [1], TTLS [2], and PEAP [3] protocols. Client or STA authentication can also be done using certificates, as in EAP-TLS. The downside is that this method provides no privacy to the client's credentials. Alternatively, client's credentials may be sent via a TLS tunnel using PEAP or TTLS protocols. Examples of client authentication methods include EAP-PSK [4] and EAP-AKA (see Chapter 4 and also [5]).

Additional guidance on overall EAP method selection is available in [6]. Specifically, the following requirements are mandatory for a strong EAP method for use in 802 networks:

- The EAP method must be able to support strong symmetric key generation of at least 128 bits in length, and must not be vulnerable to dictionary attacks.

- The EAP method(s) must allow the 802 client and the authentication server to mutually authenticate to each other. In case of EAP-TLS, that protocol itself supports mutual authentication, using certificates. Tunneled methods such as PEAPv2 and TTLS support server authentication using certificates and client authentication using (inner) EAP methods employing symmetric-key based authentication.

- When tunneled authentication protocols are used, key material from the inner and the outer or the tunneled method must be bound together to protect against man-in-the-middle attacks [7]. This is also known as "compound binding" or "cryptographic binding" of EAP methods.

6.2.2 Protection Against Downgrade Attacks

RSN parameter negotiation uses unsecured legacy 802.11 protocols. Consequently, an adversary can trick the negotiating parties to settle for lower security than they support together. For example, an adversary can change probe response messages to reflect that an AP supports only WEP. Thus, RSN protocols must provide cryptographic protection to the negotiation process.

An RSNA requires that the negotiating entities authenticate the parameters in the form of RSN Information Element (IE) during the 4-way exchange. The same RSN IE must be sent in the probe as well during the 4-way exchange so that the AP and the STAs can positively verify them. The STA is allowed to propose a second RSN IE during the 4-way exchange, however. Considering that part of the exchange is cryptograpically protected, there is no scope for a downgrade attack in that context.

6.2.3   Data Protection

Enforcing access control to wireless networks entails authenticating the STA requesting access, and requires that all communications from the STA use the authenticated channel. RSNs support mutual authentication in that the STA also authenticates the authenticating entity, which might be the AP or a backend AS. The AS then transfers the security association to the AP, and the AP allows network access to the STA thereafter. In 802 RSNs, the authenticated channel has the following properties:

Confidentiality. Wireless communications do not enjoy the physical protection of wired media. Anyone with an RF device can read the data without being detected easily. Thus confidentiality of wireless communications is a requirement even if it were not a requirement within the wired media (as is the case generally for intranet communications within an enterprise).

Data integrity protection. It is also not difficult to modify data being sent via a wireless medium. Wireless jamming and transmission equipment can be easily hidden in a van parked outside the physical boundaries of a home or office building that houses the network under attack. Thus 802.11 WLANs need strong, cryptographic integrity protection of data.

Data origin authentication. Data origin authentication is a property that allows a WLAN device to verify the origin of a 802.11 frame. Data origin authenticity only requires that two communicating parties share a common integrity key. Thus, cryptographic integrity protection generally provides this service as well. Symmetric keys fail to provide this service for group communication, however. Digitally signatures are required to provide this service in that case; it is efficient to amortize the cost of the digital signature over multiple data units.

Replay Protection. A WLAN device should be able to filter out old frames being repeatedly sent by an adversary to confuse the device to accept the old data as legitimate new data. A sequence number is typically used for this purpose.

An RSNA provides cryptographic protection to wireless LAN communications. A strong 802.1X and EAP-based mutual authentication mechanism ensures that only authenticated entities can establish a PMK with the AP. The ensuing 4-way exchange authenticates security parameter negotiation and supports key derivation for traffic protection. The combination of TKIP and Michael, or AES-based CCMP, is used to encrypt and integrity-protect the traffic. The AP forwards traffic encrypted with the PTK only, thus enforcing controlled access. A sequence counter initialized during the 4-way exchange provides replay protection.

6.3   COMPONENTS OF AN RSNA

RSNA enables secure communication within WLANs. Depending on the type of communication (unicast or group), it means different things. In the context of an ESS, RSNA supports secure access for a STA to the DS via an AP; this includes protection of data frames in the wireless medium. RSNA also includes support for one-way group communication from an AP to two or more STAs. Finally, in an RSN, an AP enables direct secure communication between two associated STAs.

6.3.1   Security Associations Within an RSNA

RSNA defines four different security associations (SA): a PMKSA, a PTKSA, and optionally, a GTKSA, and a STAkeySA. A SA defines the means — namely secure data transforms, keys, encryption and authentication algorithms, sequence counters, security enforcement, and exception handling policies — to enable secure communication. In the latter two types of SAs (GTKSA and STAkeySA) the AP downloads keys to the STAs, whereas the first two SAs (PMKSA and PTKSA) are established using contributory methods to compute keys.

SA parameter negotiation is the first step in establishing the RSNA. An AP may announce its security capabilities using beacon or probe response messages. STAs negotiate the security parameters, such as encryption and authentication transforms during association or reassociation, and also during the process of establishing the PTKSA, also known as the 4-way exchange.

A PMK known to an AP and a STA proves mutual authentication of the two entities. There are mainly two methods to establish a PMKSA. In the first the AP and STA are configured with a PSK, and the PSK serves as the PMK. Proof of possession of the PSK during the 4-way exchange mutually authenticates the AP and the STA. The desirable method of establishing a PMKSA is for the STA to participate in a 802.1X EAP mutual authentication procedure with an AS. An AS may be a RADIUS or Diameter server; it could be collocated with the AP in some cases. When an AS is a separate entity, it must use a secure channel (for example using IPsec, SSL) to deliver the PMK to the AP. The STA and the AP use the PMK during the 4-way exchange for mutual authentication.

The PTKSA protects the most popular type of communication — between the STA and the distribution system (DS) and beyond, via the AP — within wireless networks. Upon successful completion of an 802.1X authentication of a STA, the AP receives the PMK from the AS. After receiving the PMK, the AP initiates a 4-way exchange with the STA to establish a PTKSA. When a PSK is used for authentication, the AP initiates a 4-way exchange following successful (re)association. The 4-way exchange involves exchange of nonces in the clear, followed by integrity protected RSN IEs for SA parameter negotiation, and encrypted delivery of a GTK where applicable. Once the PTKSA is established, the AP allows the STA to send (encrypted) data to the DS.

GTKSA establishment is part of either the 4-way exchange or a separate group key handshake. The same group key is sent to all the member STAs associated to the AP. Not all the associated STAs need be members of the secure group. There is no relationship between the PMK and the GMK, since each PMK is a one-to-one secret between a STA and the AP. Thus derivation of the GTK is solely in the control of the AP.

The STAkeySA protects direct communication between two STAs associated to a given AP. A STA requests the AP to set up a STAkeySA with another STA in an RSNA with the AP. The AP sends the same key (this is similar in notion to the group key delivery in establishing a GTKSA) to both STAs. The result is a mutually authenticated relationship between the STAs for direct secure communication. This feature serves latency sensitive applications (voice calls) between STAs in an overloaded BSS.

6.3.2 RSN IE

STAs and APs negotiate RSNA parameters using an RSN information element (IE). APs announce their security capabilities in beacon messages or in probe response messages using RSN IEs. STAs and APs negotiate security association parameters during 802.11 association, and may change them during the 4-way exchange. The parameter negotiation process is in the clear during association, but retroactively protected during the 4-way exchange. An RSN IE contains an element ID, length and version fields, and the following optional fields:

Group key cipher suite. The group key cipher suite field indicates the encryption and integrity algorithms used to protect multicast traffic within a BSS. This field is 4 octets in length.

Pairwise key cipher suite count (PKSC). An AP may advertise or a STA may propose multiple pairwise cipher suites (e.g., CCMP and TKIP). The PKSC field holds the number of pairwise key cipher suites advertised or proposed, and is 2 octets in length.

Pairwise key cipher suite list. This field is PKSC × 4 octets in length.

Authentication and key management suite count (AKMC). There are mainly two options for AKM in RSNs: 802.1X authentication, including PMK caching, and preshared key (PSK). Additionally, there is a provision to add vendor-specific AKM mechanisms. The AKMC field holds the number of AKM proposals and is 2 octets in length.

Authentication and key management suite list. This field is AKMC × 4 octets in length.

RSN capabilities. This field is 2 octets in length and contains the following subfields:

  Preauthentication. The preauthentication field is relevant in messages originating from an AP. When set this field indicates that the AP supports preauthentication. This subfield is 1 bit in length.

  Replay counters. This field defines number of replay counters supported per PTKSA. The values 0, 1, 2, and 3 imply that the PTKSA can be used for 1, 2, 4, and 16 replay counters, respectively. This field is 2 bits in length.

PMKID count (PMKC). This field holds the number of PMKIDs in the RSN IE and is 2 octets in length.

PMKID list. A STA can list PMKSAs that it believes are cached at a particular AP. PMKs can be cached during a previous association with the AP, or due to preauthentication with the AP. An AP or STA may flush a PMK from its cache for any reason. A STA can choose to not include a PMKID in the RSN IE to indicate that a particular PMKSA is no longer valid. The PMKID list field is PMKC × 16 octets in length.

6.4 STEPS IN ESTABLISHING AN RSN ASSOCIATION

Several types of messages and protocols are used to establish an RSN association. Recall that an RSNA contains a PMKSA and a PTKSA and optionally a GTKSA and a STAkeySA. The following protocols assist in security parameter negotiation and SA and key management. Figure 6.1 depicts the steps in RSN parameter negotiation.

  • *Beacons and probe messages.* APs announce their RSN capabilities via RSN IEs included in beacon messages. Alternatively, a STA may send a probe request message to an AP. The AP responds with a probe response message containing an RSN IE. In most cases, an AP announces the same RSN IE (i.e., same security parameters) in beacons and probe response messages. If beacon and probe response messages differ, the STA uses the probe response message as the correct version of the AP's capabilities. Beacons are single messages from APs, whereas probing is a 2-way exchange initiated by a STA.

- *Open-system authentication.* After learning an AP's RSN capabilities, a STA uses open-system authentication to assert its identity to an AP. There is no cryptographic protection on these messages and therefore the AP validates any open system authentication request. Open-system authentication is a 2-way exchange.

- *802.11 association.* Security parameter negotiation occurs during 802.11 association or reassociation. The STA selects security parameters that it implements from the target AP's RSN IE in the beacon or probe response message; it selects one pairwise cipher suite and one authentication mechanism, and the group cipher suite, if specified. The STA then constructs an RSN IE with the selected parameters, adds any PMKIDs it believes to have with the target AP, and includes the constructed RSN IE as part of the association request. The AP may include the RSN IE in the association request message or choose to send another RSN IE in the third message of the 4-way handshake for SA establishment. Note that some security parameters cannot be changed during the 4-way exchange; for example, AKM method is no longer negotiable.

- *Mutual authentication.* PSKs or 802.1X and EAP-based authentication are two methods specified in 802.11i for mutual authentication. In 802.1X EAP-based authentication, the AP prompts the STA to start the authentication process; the AP then forwards all the 802.1X EAP messages to a backend AS. After successful authentication, the STA and AS derive a PMK, which the AS delivers to the AP. Proof of possession of the PMK or PSK during the 4-way exchange is proof of authentication.

- *4-way exchange.* The ensuing 4-way exchange to derive a PTK for traffic protection and to authenticate the RSN parameter negotiation during the association phase completes the RSNA establishment process. The AP initiates the 4-way exchange, during which the AP and STA exchange nonces used to generate a PTK from the PMK. Some of the key material generated in this process is used to protect the 4-way exchange itself. Specifically, Messages 2–4 are integrity protected, thus the nonces themselves and the RSN IE sent earlier cannot be altered in transit without detection.

    The AP may send a GTK as part of the 4-way exchange; in that case, the GTK is encrypted with the key encryption key derived during the earlier phase of the 4-way exchange.

- *Group key exchange.* The AP may also send the encrypted GTK as part of a separate 2-way group key exchange. The GTK is accompanied by a sequence number for replay protection of multicast data from the AP to the member STAs. This exchange and GTKSA establishment itself are optional.

- *STAkeySA establishment.* Following the 4-way exchange — irrespective of a group key exchange — a STA may request the AP to establish a STAkeySA with another STA associated with the AP. If the AP has already completed a 4-way exchange with the other STA, it will download the STAkeySA to the peer first, and then to the requester.

AP   STA

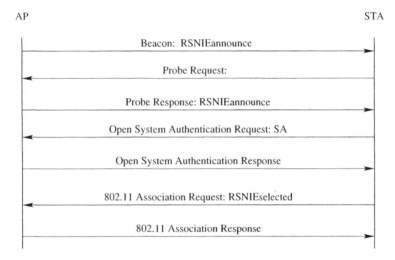

Figure 6.1   Steps in RSN security parameter negotiation.

6.5 MUTUAL AUTHENTICATION IN RSNAS

Once parameter negotiation is complete, and if 802.1X is the agreed upon authentication mechanism, the STA and AS engage in 802.1X EAP exchange via the AP.

6.5.1   802.1X and EAP-Based Authentication

AS-supported mutual authentication is the recommended method to establishing a PMK in RSNs. When the AS is a third-party entity, that creates a vulnerability in enforcing authorized access to the wired network. The vulnerability is mitigated by securing the AS to AP PMK delivery (e.g., using an IPsec or SSL protected channel for secure delivery), and by the 4-way exchange between the AP and STAs. The STA engages in a 802.1X/EAP supported authentication with the AS. 802.11 recommends that asymmetrical EAP methods be used. Note that if the same secret is used to authenticate the server and client, that method reduces in effect to PSK-based authentication. It is recommended that a tunneled EAP method (e.g., PEAP, TTLS) where the server is authenticated using certificates be used and that client authentication be carried out under the protection of the secure tunnel. A less preferred method of client and server authentication using certificates may also be used. Note, however, that in this approach the client identity is exposed to eavesdropping.

6.5.2 PMK Caching

802.1X and EAP-based authentication typically involves SSL/TLS tunnel establishment between the STA and AS and potential use of an IPsec SSL/TLS tunnel between the AS and the AP for PMK delivery. For an actively roaming STA, repeating this computationally intensive procedure frequently may be prohibitively expensive. Recall that PDAs and low-end STAs have computational and power resource constraints. Thus, it is beneficial to cache and reuse a PMKSA. Each PMKSA has an ID, which the STA would include in Message 1 of the 4-way exchange to establish a PTKSA. There are several restrictions to PMK caching, however. A cached PMKSA's parameters (e.g., pairwise cipher, group cipher) cannot be changed. Furthermore, the AP can flush a PMK from its cache for any reason; in that case the STA has to reengage in full authentication using 802.1X/EAP authentication, followed by the 4-way exchange. Each cached PMKSA is identified by a PMKID, a random value derived using the following formula:
PMKID = HMAC-SHA1-128(PMK, "PMK Name" || AA || SA),
where AA is the AP's MAC address and SA is the STA's MAC address.

6.5.3 PSK-Based Authentication

For small-scale deployments such as small-office or home-office (commonly known as SOHO) environments, there is an alternative to the infrastructure supported 802.1X and EAP-based mutual authentication procedure. First, the AS-based method itself may be used, with the AP serving as an AS. If that is infeasible due to economical or other constraints, a preconfigured shared secret may be used for authentication. A preshared key (PSK), similar to WEP keys, may be configured on the AP and the STAs that are likely to associate with the AP. In this case, the PSK serves as the PMK.

Note that PSK-based methods have some inherent and practical security risks. The PSK is a 256-bit random value and if generated from a genuine random source, would be sufficiently strong for a SOHO deployment. However, it is difficult for end users to remember a 64-bit hexadecimal value. Instead, in most cases a password or passphrase is used to generate the PSK. This opens a door for fairly straightforward dictionary attacks on the PSK.

The other problem with PSKs is that in many cases several users tend to share a PSK for authentication with an AP. This is understandable partly because it might be administratively prohibitive to enter a large number of PSKs in an AP. However, such practices of PSK sharing allow STAs to decrypt each other's traffic.

6.5.4   Preauthentication in RSNs

RSNs also support preauthentication to reduce roaming delay. Before roaming, a STA may decide to preauthenticate with an AP it plans to associate with in the near future; this enables faster connection establishment upon roaming. Preauthentication establishes a new PMKSA between the STA and the new AP. The STA sends the 802.1X EAP authentication request to the current AP, with the final destination MAC address in the frame set to the new AP. The STA's current AP acts as a relay for the mutual authentication process. Thus the new AP need not be within the STA's radio range; all communication occurs via the DS. After successful authentication, the STA and the new AP cache the PMK. After roaming, the STA associates with the new AP, and directly proceeds to the 4-way exchange using the cached PMK.

6.6   SA AND KEY MANAGEMENT IN RSNS

An RSNA supports three types of data protection SAs, namely, PTKSA to provide secure network access for the STA via the AP, GTKSA for multicast transmission from the AP to the STAs in the secure group, and finally STAkeySA for direct STA to STA communication. In this section, we discuss SA management, key establishment, and key distribution in RSNs. A 4-way exchange establishes the PTKSA and optionally downloads the GTKSA. If a STA requests the AP to establish a STAkeySA with a peer STA, the AP downloads a common key to both the STAs.

RSNA key management messages are sent encapsulated in 802.1X EAPOL-key frames. Within the EAPOL-key frame format the following subfields are of significance for our discussion:

Key descriptor version. Version 1 indicates that TKIP is the data encryption protocol, Michael is the MIC algorithm, HMAC-MD5 is the EAPOL-key MIC, and RC4 is the EAPOL-key encryption key to protect the GTK, if any.

Version 2 specifies AES-CCMP as the data encryption and integrity protocol, HMAC-SHA1-128 as the EAPOL-key MIC, and AES key wrap algorithm as the EAPOL-key encryption key for encrypting the GTK. This field is 3 bits in length.

Key type. Key type indicates whether the message is for key derivation or download. This field is 1 bit in length.

Key Ack flag. When set, this flag indicates that the message requires a response. This is also a 1 bit flag.

Key MIC flag. When set, this flag indicates that the message is protected by a MIC. This flag is 1 bit in length.

Secure flag. This bit indicates that the link is secure from the sender's perspective. At the beginning of the 4-way exchange, this is cleared; once the negotiating parties can derive the PTK and verify the liveness of the exchange, this bit is set. This is also a 1 bit flag.

Encrypted key data flag. This flag indicates that the key included in the EAPOL-key message (e.g., GTK or STAkey) is encrypted. This flag is 1 bit in length.

Key replay counter. This counter offers replay protection to EAPOL-key frames. The authenticator (typically the AP) initializes the counter to 0 when a new PMK is received from the AS, and increments the counter by 1 each time it sends an EAPOL-key frame within the context of that association. The supplicant (typically the STA) uses the same counter value in the response EAPOL-key frame as the received EAPOL-key frame. This flag is 8 octets in length.

Key nonce. Nonces are used to guarantee freshness of a 4-way exchange, and to generate a fresh PTK. The nonce field is 32 octets in length.

EAPOL-key IV. This IV is used with the KEK and may be derived from the last 16 octets of the key counter. This field is relevant only in message 3. The IV field is 16 octets in length.

Key RSC. The receive sequence counter (RSC) is used for replay protection of secure group communication in WLANs. The RSC is the current PN from the GTKSA. This field is 8 octets in length.

Key MIC. If the Key descriptor version is 1, Key MIC serves as the MD5 key for integrity protection of EAPOL-key frames, and if the Key descriptor version is 2, Key MIC is the SHA1-128 key. The MIC field is 16 octets in length.

Key data length. This represents the length of the (encrypted) key data in octets. This field itself is 2 octets in length.

Key data. This field carries all variable length data required for the key exchange that cannot be accommodated in the EAPOL-key fixed-length fields. Thus, in addition to the encrypted keys (e.g., GTK), this field may hold RSN IEs, MAC IEs (used in STAkeySA establishment), PMKIDs and/or vendor-specific data.

We use the following simplified EAPOL-key message notation to describe the key management messages in RSNs.

EAPOL-key({Ack flag, MIC flag, Secure flag}, EAPOL-key replay counter, ANonce/SNonce, IV, KeyRSC, MIC, {RSN IE, {GID, GTK}})

In RSNs, APs allow only data traffic encrypted with a valid PTK to pass via the controlled port from and to the STAs. A 4-way exchange between an AP and the STA is used to verify the possession of the PMK by the two parties and to establish the PTK. Note that when PSK is used for host authentication, it serves as the PMK, and is used as such in the PTK derivation. The 4-way exchange follows successful association or reassociation (when PSK = PMK), or successful 802.1X/EAP authentication (and after the AS delivers the PMK to the AP). A 4-way exchange could also be the result of an expired PTK. When the replay counter (or packet number) becomes 0, the PTK is no longer secure and must be refreshed using a new 4-way exchange.

The 4-way exchange is similar to other authenticated key exchange protocols such as the Bellare-Rogaway 3-way entity authentication and key distribution protocol [8]. Specifically, nonces are used to prove the liveness of the exchange to the two parties involved, and proof of possession of the PMK is used for mutual authentication of the parties.

6.6.1 4-Way Handshake

RSNs use a key and SA management protocol called 4-way exchange to generate fresh session keys bound to the parties involved in the exchange, authenticate security parameter negotiation in the association exchange, and to deliver group keys where applicable.

6.6.1.1 Message 1

AP $\longrightarrow$ STA: EAPOL-key({Ack, noMIC, nonSecure}, ctr, ANonce, 0, 0, 0, {PMKID})

Message 1 goes from an AP to a STA. After successful association (in the case of PSK = PMK), or after successful 802.1X/EAP mutual authentication, a STA waits for a finite time for the AP to initiate the 4-way exchange, and disassociates and tries another AP.

Message 1 mainly contains the EAPOL-key message counter, the AP's nonce, and the PMKID. The entire message is in the clear and there is no integrity protection. Note that neither party has all the information to derive the EAPOL-key encryption and integrity keys, yet. The EAPOL-key replay counter must contain a value greater than the counter corresponding to the PMKID at the STA; otherwise, the STA considers the message a replay, and sends an error message. Since message 1 is not cryptographically protected, there is no way for the STA to verify whether the message has been modified en route.

In response to message 1, the STA creates a new nonce called SNonce, derives the PTK and thus the EAPOL-key protection keys, and sends message 2 to the AP. Unlike message 1, this message is integrity protected.

6.6.1.2   Message 2

STA $\longrightarrow$ AP: EAPOL-key({noAck, MIC, nonSecure}, ctr, SNonce, 0, 0, MIC(KCK, Message2), {RSNIE})

After processing a message 1, the STA computes the PTKSA (still unverified for liveness and so forth), generates a new nonce called SNonce, and builds and sends message 2. This message is also entirely in the clear, but integrity protected. The message mainly contains the EAPOL-key ctr (same as received), SNonce, and the RSN IE (containing the security parameters) sent by the STA as part of the association request message. The RSN IE must be exactly identical to the one sent earlier, otherwise, the exchange fails.

MIC computation in the 4-way exchange. The last three messages of the 4-way exchange are integrity protected: after constructing the EAPOL-key frame, the WLAN device zeroes out the MIC field (not the MIC flag) and computes the MIC using the EAPOL-key confirmation key and using MD5 or SHA1-128, as indicated in the version field. The 16-octet MIC value replaces the MIC field zeroed out earlier. Notice that authentication follows encryption in this case [9].

Processing message 2. Upon reception of message 2, the AP first checks whether it is expecting a message 2 with the specified EAPOL-key frame counter value; if not, it silently discards the message. Note that while this process makes it easy for an attacker to disrupt service to a STA, it allows efficient operation at the AP. The AP does not need to make any expensive MIC computations to check the message. When the counter value is incorrect, it obviates MIC computation. Furthermore, the same attacker can also modify the SNonce value to make the AP arrive at a different KCK than that derived by the STA.

If the counter value is correct, the AP derives the PTK, extracts the KCK, and computes and verifies the MIC. If the MIC is valid, the AP verifies the enclosed RSN IE with the RSN IE received during association. This verification protects the 802.11 association process from security parameter downgrade attacks.

An adversary engages in a downgrade attack by making two WLAN entities agree upon a data security protocol inferior to the one that they are capable of. For example, a STA and AP that are capable of supporting CCMP can be made to settle for the weaker TKIP as the data security protocol.

The AP continues the 4-way exchange by sending message 3 to the AP. It increments the EAPOL-key frame counter by 1. If the current STA is part of a secure group that the AP manages, the AP includes the GTK in message 3 for efficient operation. The ANonce is also included in message 3 for efficient message processing.

6.6.1.3   Message 3

AP ⟶ STA: EAPOL-key({Ack, MIC, Secure}, Ctr+1, ANonce, IVval, GTK-RSC, MIC(KCK, Message 3), Encr(KEK, {RSNIE, RSNIEnew, {GID, GTK} }))

The AP sends message 3 to the STA in response to a valid message 2. The EAPOL-key replay counter is incremented by 1 compared to message 1. ANonce is the same as in message 1. If the key descriptor version is 1, the IV value is a random number; otherwise, it is 0. If group security was negotiated during association, the AP includes the encrypted GTK and the corresponding sequence number. The AP should only accept group MPDUs with a sequence number larger than the GTK-RSC.

MIC computation is similar to that in message 2. The key data field contains one or more RSN IEs and the GTK IE. The first RSN IE must be exactly the same as the one sent in AP beacon or probe messages. If both messages are sent, the RSN IE in the probe message is included in message 3. The entire key data field is encrypted using the EAPOL-key encryption key (KEK); if a GTK is not part of the key data field, it may remain in the clear. The GTK IE contains a 2-bit GID, Tx bit, and the GTK itself. The AP is now ready to accept encrypted MPDUs from the STA.

Processing message 3. Upon reception of message 3 (the MIC bit and Secure bit are set compared to message 1), a STA first checks whether the Ctr value is larger than that in message 1 and that ANonce is the same as that in message 1. After successful verification of the replay counter and nonce, it verifies the RSN IE, followed by the MIC. Note that this in the order of increasing computational complexity.

The RSN IE must match the one received as part of the probe response message (if available) or that in a beacon message from the AP. If RSNIEnew is part of message 3, the STA evaluates whether it can support the pairwise cipher suite specified. If either of these verifications fails, the STA disassociates.

Next, the STA calculates the MIC using the KCK it already computed when sending message 2. If the computed and received MIC values match, the AP concludes that the 4-way exchange is live and that there is no man in the middle, accepts message 3 and updates the replay counter to $Ctr + 1$, and constructs message 4.

Message 4 serves as an acknowledgment to message 3 and for the AP to update the EAPOL-key sequence counter.

6.6.1.4   Message 4

STA $\longrightarrow$ AP: EAPOL-key({noAck, MIC, Secure}, Ctr+1, 0, 0, 0, MIC(KCK, Message4))

After successfully verifying message 3, the STA sends message 4 as an acknowledgment to the AP. The EAPOL-key sequence counter is the only significant information sent and this message is also protected by a MIC. The secure bit is set to indicate that from the STA's perspective the association is secure. The key data field is empty.

After sending message 4, the STA is ready to send/receive unicast MPDUs using the PTKSA and receive encrypted multicast MPDUs using the GTKSA.

Processing message 4. The AP distinguishes message 4 from message 2 by verifying that the secure bit is set and that the nonce field is 0; there is also no key data field in message 4. It then checks the sequence counter to verify whether it is the same as the one in message 3; if not, it discards the received message. Next, the AP computes the MIC and verifies whether it is identical to the received MIC. If so, it increments the EAPOL-key sequence counter for future key management within the context of the given PMKSA or PTKSA: rekeying the PTKSA, GTKSA, or to establish a STAkeySA.

Figure 6.2 illustrates the 4-way exchange.

6.6.2   Summary of the Security Properties of the 4-Way Exchange

In the following, we discuss security properties of the 4-way exchange, including the algorithms used and protections for various types of common attacks on network protocols, and provide notes on what might not be protected.

Encryption and authentication algorithms. RSNA uses two sets of encryption and authentication algorithms to protect the key management messages. In legacy devices where TKIP and Michael are used for data protection, RC4 and MD5 are used for key management, and in RSN devices, AES key wrap algorithm and SHA1-128 are used. Only the key data, when it contains a GTK, needs to be encrypted. Thus if GTK establishment is not part of an 802.11 association, no encryption is necessary. Messages 2, 3, and 4 of the 4-way exchange are integrity protected.

Liveness of the exchange. RSNs use nonces and sequence numbers to ensure the liveness of the exchange. The nonces themselves are sufficient, however

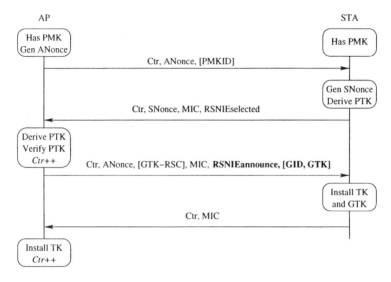

Figure 6.2 4-way exchange for PTK derivation.

the sequence numbers support efficient verification. RSNs use an indirect method to support liveness. Specifically, the nonces are included as part of the computation of the keying material, including the KCK. Verification of the MIC, computed using the KCK, proves liveness of the exchange, and that there is no man-in-the-middle attack in progress.

SA negotiation. The 4-way exchange allows SA negotiation in addition to negotiation during the 802.11 association process. The STA can specify the new security parameters using an optional RSN IE as part of the key data field in message 2. This does not preclude inclusion of the original RSN IE sent as part of the 802.11 association request, however. The original RSN IE is used to protect against downgrade attacks on the negotiation process. The AP can specify a new RSN IE (which can only be a subset of what it sends as part of beacons and probe responses, however) in message 3 to supersede its preference announced earlier, to reflect a change in policy.

Protection against downgrade attacks. RSN parameter negotiation, during 802.11 association, is in the clear and thus susceptible to downgrade attacks. An adversary can modify the RSN IEs in beacons, probe responses, and 802.11 association messages to trick an AP and a STA to negotiate an inferior set of security parameters, whereas they can both support stronger algorithms. This is easily detected by the 4-way exchange, by the requirement that RSN IEs be included as part of messages 2 and 3 by the STA and the AP, respectively, where they are protected by a MIC.

What is in the clear? Only the key data field is encrypted in the 4-way exchange. Contrast this to entire messages 3 and 4 being encrypted in IKEv2. When a GTK is part of the key data field in message 3, that entire field is encrypted; if a GTK is not included in message 3, the key data field can be in the clear. There is no advantage to encrypting the already public RSN IEs included in message 3.

Mutual authentication of the parties involved. Proof of possession of the PMK mutually authenticates the parties. Similar to the liveness verification, this is also indirectly verified as part of the MIC verification process.

6.6.3   Security Assumptions Inherent to the 4-Way Exchange

The 4-way exchange depends on several security assumptions. If any of the following assumptions do not hold, the 4-way exchange fails to serve its purpose.

Secure PMK delivery. Only the AP and STA can hold the PMK. In most deployments, it is efficient to delegate client authentication to an AS, which already plays that role for other applications such as remote access. The AS must deliver the PMK securely to the AP, using an IPsec or SSL connection between the AP and the AS.

Strong PSKs. When a PSK is used for authentication of WLAN devices, it is appropriate to use machine generated 256-bit random keys. If a passphrase must be used, the 802.11i specification suggests using the PBKDF2 method from the PKCS #5 v2.0 standard: PSK = PBKDF2(PassPhrase, ssid, ssidLength, 4096, 256), where passphrase is an 8-63 ASCII character string, 4096 is the number of times it is hashed, and 256 is the number of bits in the output. The passphrase must not be a dictionary word, proper name, or a commonly known catch phrase or sentence, all of which make it easy for a precomputation attack.

Random nonces. The nonces must be cryptographically strong random numbers [10]. Note that the nonces themselves are in the clear and therefore not a substitute for a strong PSK or a PMK.

Correct implementation. As with any cryptographic key exchange, correct implementation cannot be stressed enough. Note that correct operation does not necessarily imply strong implementation. For example, note that the PTK generation process exists to change the data encryption key periodically (before the PN rotates). If strong random numbers are not used, nonces may be reused often (which an adversary can verify easily, as they are in the clear), resulting effectively in using a given PTK for a longer period of time than intended. Similarly, sequence counter verification is not a substitute for MIC verification, and RSN IE comparison as specified in the spec must be implemented.

For a detailed security analysis of the 802.11i RSN design, readers are referred to [11].

6.6.4   PTK Derivation

The PTK used to protect the 4-way exchange and the data MPDUs is derived from the PMK, nonces exchanged during the 4-way exchange, and the AP's and STA's MAC addresses. The nonces ensure a fresh PTK and the MAC addresses ensure that a different PTK is used for communication between an AP, STA pair even if a PSK is used by multiple STAs within the BSS. Note that it is a prudent practice not to use the same PSK for more than one STA. All STAs that have a given PSK can snoop on each others' traffic.

To protect the key management messages (e.g., 4-way exchange, group key exchange) MD5 and RC4 are used in legacy devices and SHA1-128 and AES key wrap in RSN devices. In both cases, a 128-bit key is used for encryption and another 128-bit key is used for message integrity. When TKIP and Michael are used for data protection, a separate key is used for encryption and authentication. A 128-bit key is used for encryption using TKIP and two 64-bit keys — one in each direction, one from AP to STA and another from STA to AP — are used with Michael to compute the MIC. When AES-CCMP is used a single 128-bit is used for both encryption and authentication. In summary, we need to generate a 384-bit key for use with AES hardware and 512-bit key for use with RC4 hardware.

PTK = (KCK-128 || KEK-128 || TK-128/256)
PTK = PRF-384/512(PMK, "Pairwise key expansion",
Min(AA,SPA) || Max(AA,SPA) || Min(ANonce, SNonce) || Max(ANonce, SNonce)
    = PRF-384/512(PMK, string, value)
    = HMAC-SHA1(PMK, string || 0 || value || 0)
    || HMAC-SHA1(PMK, string || 0 || value || 1)
    || HMAC-SHA1(PMK, string || 0 || value || 2)
    || HMAC-SHA1(PMK, string || 0 || value || 3)

HMAC-SHA1 outputs 160 bits, and thus we need three iterations for PRF-384 and four iterations for PRF-512.

6.7 KEY DOWNLOAD PROTOCOLS IN 802.11I

RSNs support group communication and direct STA-to-STA communication. In each case, data protection keys are not negotiated; instead, they are downloaded from the AP to the STAs involved. This is akin to key download in GDOI, MIKEY, and GSAKMP. In the following, we describe the key download protocols in 802.11i.

6.7.1 Group Key Exchange

GTKSA establishment is part of the 4-way exchange. In message 3, the AP sends the encrypted GTK to the STA, which is also indicated in the RSN IE. The GTK may be rekeyed independent of the PTKSA. For example, when MIC failure occurs on a group MPDU, or when the group RSC rotates, the AP rekeys the GTK using the group key exchange. There is a provision for an AP to trigger a group key exchange using EAPOL-key frame with the request flag set and key type flag cleared (indicates group).

Group Key Exchange Message 1.

AP $\longrightarrow$ STA: EAPOL-key({Ack, MIC, Secure}, Ctr, 0, IVval, GTK-RSC, MIC(KCK, Group Key Message1), Encr(KEK, {GID, GTK}))
        This message requires an acknowledgment, contains a MIC, and is secure (EAPOL-key protection keys are already installed). The *Ctr* value is the updated value after the previous key exchange message. IVval is relevant to TKIP only, and is a 16-octet random number. The KCK and KEK are from the latest PTK derivation.

Processing group key exchange message 1. The STA can distinguish group key exchange messages from the cleared type flag (not shown). Message 1 contains an RSC whereas message 2 does not. The STA then verifies the MIC; if the MIC is valid, it uses the GTK-RSC and the GTK to decrypt and verify future group MPDUs.

Group Key Exchange Message 2.

STA $\longrightarrow$ AP: EAPOL-key({noAck, MIC, Secure}, Ctr, 0, 0, 0, MIC(KCK, Group Key Message2))
        This message mainly serves as an acknowledgment to group key exchange message 1. It contains a MIC and little else. The *Ctr* is the same as the one in the received message 1.

Processing group key exchange message 2. The AP verifies the ctr value in Message 2 first, and if it is the same as the one sent to the STA in question, the AP computes and verifies the MIC. After successfully verifying the MIC, the AP increments the Ctr by 1 for future use. Once it receives acknowledgments from all STAs in the group, the AP configures and uses the new GTK to encrypt group MPDUs.

6.7.1.1 GTK Computation

The GTK computation method is similar to PTK computation, but has no implication on interoperability. The AP may compute the GTK using the following method. A PRF-128 is required for CCMP and PRF-256 is required for TKIP.

GTK = PRF-128/256(GMK, "Group key expansion", AA ‖ GNonce).

The PRF computation is the same as in PTK computation. GMK is a local secret to the AP, and the GNonce is derived once again locally by the AP when a new GTK is required. The GTK is rekeyed entirely upon the AP's discretion. A STA may request for GTK rekeying, but the AP does not need to comply.

6.7.2 STAkey Exchange

STAkeySAs protect direct communication between two STAs that are associated with the same AP. Generally speaking communication between two such STAs is via the AP. But, for better quality of service, it is more efficient to use direct link layer communication between the two STAs. This feature is especially useful when an AP is busy forwarding other traffic, or in case of latency-sensitive applications such as voice over IP.

The initiating STA controls security parameter selection in this case. It sends an EAPOL-key request message with the request flag set and with a MAC address IE (containing the target STA's address) in the key data field. The key description version field indicates the pairwise cipher: 1 for TKIP and 2 for CCMP.

The AP sends a STAkey message 1 containing the initiator's MAC address and the STAkey to the target STA. The target STA responds with STAkey message 2 as an acknowledgment. The AP then sends another STAkey message 1 to the initiator STA with the target's MAC address and the STAkey as part of the Data field of the EAPOL-key frame. The initiator STA acknowledges the message.

The AP derives the STAkey in a similar fashion as the GTK. The two keys must be cryptographically different, however. Thus, STAMK must be generated independent of the GMK. The EAPOL-key frames are protected using the EAPOL KEK and KCK derived as part of the PTK.

6.8 SUMMARY

RSNAs consist of strong security parameter negotiation SA establishment to support secure STA-to-DS communication via the AP, STA-to-STA communication independent of the AP, and AP-to-STA group communication. After security parameter negotiation, the STA authenticates itself to an AS using 802.1X/EAP protocol. After successful authentication, the STA and AS agree on a PMK, which the AS delivers to the AP. Proof of possession of the PMK is proof of mutual authentication.

A 4-way key management exchange is used to derive a PTKSA to protect the key management frames, authenticate the security parameter negotiation, and to protect data MPDUs between the STA and the DS. The PTKSA also protects downloading GTK as well as STAkeys.

This chapter provides a high-level summary of the RSNA protocols and SAs for a quick review of the security properties and the protocol details. It is not a substitute for the 802.11i specification.

References

[1] B. Aboba and D. Simon, "PPP EAP TLS Authentication Protocol," RFC 2716 (Experimental), Oct. 1999.

[2] P. Funk and S. Blake-Wilson, "EAP Tunneled TLS Authentication Protocol (EAP-TTLS)," draft-ietf-pppext-eap-ttls-00 (work in progress), Internet Engineering Task Force, Aug. 2001.

[3] A. Palekar, D. Simon, G. Zorn, J. Salowey, H. Zhou, and S. Josefsson, "Protected EAP Protocol (PEAP) Version 2," draft-josefsson-pppext-eap-tls-eap-07 (work in progress), Internet Engineering Task Force, Oct. 2003.

[4] F. Bersani and T. Tschofenig, "The EAP-PSK Protocol: a Pre-Shared Key EAP Method," draft-bersani-eap-psk-01 (work in progress), Internet Engineering Task Force, Feb. 2004.

[5] F. Bersani, "EAP Shared Key Methods: A Tentative Synthesis of Those Proposed So Far," draft-bersani-eap-psk-01 (work in progress), Internet Engineering Task Force, Apr. 2004.

[6] D. Stanley, J. Walker, and B. Aboba, "EAP Method Requirements for Wireless LANs," draft-walker-ieee802-req-04 (work in progress), Internet Engineering Task Force, Aug. 2004.

[7] N. Asokan, V. Niemi, and K. Nyberg, "Man-in-the-Middle in Tunnelled Authentication Protocols," Cryptology ePrint Archive, Report 2002/163, 2002, http://eprint.iacr.org.

[8] M. Bellare and P. Rogaway, "Entity Authentication and Key Distribution," *Advances in Cryptology — Crypto,* Springer-Verlag, Aug. 1994. LNCS 773.

[9] H. Krawczyk, "The Order of Encryption and Authentication for Protecting Communications (or: How Secure Is SSL?)," *Advances in Cryptology — Crypto,* (Santa Barbara, CA), pp. 310–331, Springer-Verlag, Aug. 2001. LNCS 2139.

[10] D. Eastlake III, S. Crocker, and J. Schiller, "Randomness Recommendations for Security," RFC 1750 (Informational), Dec. 1994.

[11] C. He and J. C. Mitchell, "Security Analysis and Improvements for IEEE 802.11i," *Proceedings of Network and Distributed System Security Symposium (NDSS),* (San Diego, CA), Feb. 2005.

Chapter 7

CCMP

7.1 INTRODUCTION

RSNs provide data protection and enforce network access control. An RSNA consists of a PTKSA and optionally a GTKSA, and zero or more STAkeySAs. Each SA contains one or more secret keys for data encapsulation, and policy that specifies the encapsulation protocol, SA endpoints' addresses, and so forth (see Chapter 6). The 802.11i [1] specification lists WEP, TKIP, and CCMP as the data encapsulation protocols with a requirement that RSN devices implement CCMP.

CCMP includes the use of AES counter mode (CTR) for encryption and AES cipher block chaining (CBC) based message integrity code (MIC) for the integrity protection of MPDUs, with a single 128-bit key. Another new data encapsulation protocol known as the temporal key integrity protocol (TKIP), with RC4 as the encryption protocol and Michael as the message integrity algorithm, is to be implemented for legacy hardware based transition security networks (TSN) (see Chapter 8).

Counter mode for encryption, in conjunction with CBC-MAC for message integrity, developed first for use in WLANs and proposed to NIST as a general mode for data protection, is generally known by its short form, CCM (Counter mode with CBC-MAC) [2] mode. CCM is an authenticated encryption mode and can be used in a wide variety of networks including 802.11 RSNs, 802.16 [3, 4] networks (see Chapter 12), and with IPsec [5] in IP networks.

In RSNs, the CCM protocol (CCMP) provides cryptographic protection for MPDUs being transmitted via shared WLANs. In addition to the confidentiality and integrity protection provided by CCM, the protocol provides replay protection, and in summary, supports controlled access to the wired network.

Since CCM is common to 802.11 RSNs as well as 802.16 networks (discussed in Chapters 11 and 12), we separate the discussion on CCMP into two parts. First,

131

in Section 7.2 we discuss AES CCM mode in detail. Section 7.4 discusses CCM parameter selection for 802.11 RSNs and other pertinent protocol specific details.

7.2   AES CCM MODE

CCM is an authenticated encryption mode using a 128-bit key with AES as the underlying block cipher. Other block lengths are possible, but they are not part of the current description. CCM belongs to a class of modes known as combined modes where the same key is used for encryption as well as authentication.

In the rest of this section we describe the CCM mode in detail and explain how it gets around various potential pitfalls. CCMP is an instantiation of the CCM mode that builds on CCM, making the best design choices for WLAN environments; it includes additional techniques to strengthen the mode, and provides more security properties. CCM uses AES-CTR mode for encryption and CBC-MAC for message integrity. It first computes the message integrity code (MIC) using CBC-MAC, and encrypts the message and the MIC using CTR mode encryption.

7.2.1   CCM Parameters

We first describe some terminology that helps us understand the CCM mode.

- A single 128-bit key, K, is used for message integrity as well as encryption.

- There is a provision to authenticate message headers, if any. While this is desirable, some of the fields in message headers may need to be changed in transit or during retransmission. CCM mode is flexible enough to allow selective authentication of the headers. In general terms, the CCM mode includes *additional authentication data (AAD)* in computing the integrity checksum. In the balance of this chapter, we use AAD to indicate portions of message headers to be authenticated, and $l(AAD)$ to indicate the length of AAD in octets; $0 \leq l(AAD) < 2^{64}$.

- L denotes the number of octets in the length of the message, m, to be encapsulated using CCM; $l(m)$ denotes the number of octets in the message to be encapsulated, where, $0 \leq l(m) < 2^{8L}$. The length field may occupy 2 to 8 octets in CCM.

- The CTR mode encryption requires a nonce. CCM mode uses a nonce of length $15 - L$. The nonce, length of the message protected with a given nonce, and flags encoding the nonce length and length of the message length fit in a single 16-octet block (size of the block in the underlying cipher).

- M is the number of octets in the MIC. M is encoded as $(M-2)/2$, and authenticated by being included in the MIC computation.

7.2.2 MIC Computation Using AES-CBC-MAC

CCM supports MICs of length in even numbers between 4 and 16 octets. A 4-octet MIC is too small for most applications, although SRTP [6] allows use of a 4-octet MIC for packet transmission over low bandwidth links, with the caveat that the integrity protection thus afforded is suspect at best. IPsec ESP [7] specifies the use of a 12-octet MIC and TLS [8], a 16-octet MIC. While a short MIC provides little or no integrity protection, a longer MIC would result in excessive per packet/frame overhead.

CCM MIC is computed over a sequence of blocks $B_i, 0 \leq i \leq n$, where

- B_0 contains the nonce, message length, and a flag indicating the presence of additional authentication data, nonce length, and the length of the message length.

- $B_i, i > 0$ contains the length of AAD, if present, followed by the AAD itself.

- The message m divided into 16-octet blocks follows the AAD.

7.2.2.1 Components of B_0

The first octet of B_0 consists of a flag named Adata, which indicates whether AAD is present or not; bit 6 if set, indicates that an AAD is part of the MIC computation. Bit 7 is reserved and must be zero. Bits 5, 4, and 3 contain the length of the MIC encoded as $(M-2)/2$, where M is the length of the MIC in octets. The value of $(M-2)/2$ must not be zero, for it has two implications: a MIC of length 2 octets is not allowed, and more importantly the nonzero value is a precondition for the security of the CCM mode. The final three bits, 2, 1, and 0, represent the number of octets in the length of the message, encoded as $L-1$.

The next octets, from 1 to $15-L$ contain the nonce. The last L octets contain the message length in octets. Figure 7.1 illustrates the composition of B_0.

7.2.2.2 Composition of $B_i, i > 0$

If the Adata flag is set, B_is contain $l(AAD)$ followed by the AAD. Depending on the length of the AAD, $l(AAD)$ is encoded as follows [2]:

- If $0 < l(AAD) < (2^{16} - 2^8)$, $l(AAD)$ occupies two octets with values 0x0001 to 0xFEFF.

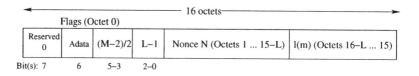

M: Length of MIC, 4, 6, 8, 10, 12, 14, 16

L: Number of octets in the length field, 2–8

l(m): length of message; $0 <= l(m) < 2^{8L}$

Figure 7.1 Contents of B_0 in CCM MIC computation.

- If $2^{16} - 2^8 \leq l(AAD) < 2^{32}$, $l(AAD)$ is encoded as 0xFFFE in the first two octets, and the the value $l(AAD)$ in the next four octets.

- If $2^{32} \leq l(AAD) < 2^{64}$, $l(AAD)$ is encoded as 0xFFFF in the first two octets, and the the value $l(AAD)$ in the next eight octets.

In summary, $l(AAD)$ occupies two, six, or eight octets. The $l(AAD)$ thus formed is prepended to AAD to form one or more 16-octet blocks, B_i, $i > 0$, padding the excess bits of the last block with zeros if necessary.

The final step in forming the B_i blocks is to split the message m into 16-octet blocks, once again padding the excess bits of the last block with zero as necessary. Recall that $l(m)$ is part of block B_0.

7.2.2.3   MIC Computation

The 16-octet blocks, B_i, are used in the following expression to compute the MIC.
$X_1 = E_{AES-CBC-128}(K, B_0)$
$X_i = E_{AES-CBC-128}(K, X_i \text{ XOR } B_i) \ 1 \leq i \leq n$
MIC = first-M-octets-of(X_{n+1})

7.2.3   AES-CTR Mode Encryption in CCM

For encryption, the CCM specification defines a different set of blocks A_i, $i \geq 0$. Considering that CCM uses the same key for both integrity protection as well as encryption, A_0 and B_0 must be different for this mode to be secure. Thus, A_0 is different from B_0 by design; specifically bits 7 through 3 in the first octet of A_0 must be zero. Contrast this to the first octet in B_0, where the combined value represented by bits 5 through 3 cannot be zero. Bits 2, 1, 0 in A_0 are identical to those in B_0. Similarly, A_0 also contains the nonce in octets 1 through $15 - L$; however, the last L octets contain the value of a counter starting at 0, instead of $l(m)$ as in B_0. Thus, in

A_0, the counter value is 0, since $i = 0$. The first $16 - L$ octets of A_i, $i > 0$ are identical to those in A_0, whereas the last L octets contain a counter equal to i, occupying L octets. Figure 7.2 illustrates the composition of A_i, $i \geq 0$.

				16 octets	
Flags (Octet 0)					
Reserved 0	Reserved 0	0	L–1	Nonce N (Octets 1 ... 15–L)	Counter i (Octets 16–L ... 15) i = 0, 1, 2, ...
Bit(s): 7	6	5–3	2–0		

L: Number of octets in the length field, 2–8

Figure 7.2 Components of blocks A_i for AES counter mode encryption in CCM.

Using the 16-octet blocks A_i, CTR mode message and MIC encryption in CCM are defined as follows:

$S_i = E_{AES-128}(K, A_i)$, $i \geq 0$

Encrypted-MIC = MIC XOR first-M-octets-of(S_0)

cipher-text $c = m$ XOR $(S_1 \parallel S_2 \parallel \ldots \parallel S_{2^{l(m)/16}})$

The output of the CCM encapsulation of a message m would be the cipher text c obtained following the CTR mode encryption, appended by the encrypted MIC calculated following the procedure described above.

7.2.4 CCM Decapsulation

For CCM decapsulation, the recipient needs the secret key K, AAD, and the nonce. The recipient first computes A_i, $i > 0$ to recover the message m, and uses A_0 to recover the MIC. It then proceeds to generate B_i, $i > 0$ to compute the MIC by itself. The computed MIC must be identical to the decrypted MIC. If not, the recipient, at most, notes that the MIC verification failed. It must not reveal the final or intermediate values computed in this process to the purported sender or any other entity for that matter. Note that the AES decryption functionality is not required for the decapsulation process. This is an intended feature of the CCM mode whereby implementations, especially hardware implementations, can concentrate on designing an efficient AES encryption module.

7.3 SECURITY ANALYSIS OF THE CCM MODE

CCM requires rekeying before the total number of underlying block cipher operations exceeds 2^{61} [2]. This includes the block cipher operations in computing the CBC-MAC as well as for the CTR mode encryption operations. The communicating entities are responsible for tearing down the connection once the number of block cipher applications exceeds 2^{61}, if rekeying fails.

There are mainly two caveats in the design of CCM. It uses the same key for integrity protection as well as encryption. In most applications of cryptography, using the same key for different purposes is not a good idea. A common technique to get around this problem is to transform the key in different ways for different purposes. That rule applies here as well. The construction of A_i and B_0 so that they all differ from each other follows this rule.

CCM is an authenticated encryption mode. It first calculates the cryptographic checksum (or MIC) of the message, and then encrypts the message as well as the authentication tag. The CCM construction has been formally proven to be secure in [9].

7.3.1 Vulnerability to Precomputation Attacks

In simple terms, CTR mode encrypts a nonce and XORs the result with the plaintext message to obtain ciphertext. Given a secret key K, the nonce must not repeat; otherwise, the mode is easily broken. However, as long as the key is different, the same nonce may be used.

CTR mode is susceptible to precomputation attacks [10]. An adversary with vast amounts of resources may compute $E(K, A_i)$ for a large number of values of K, and a given nonce N. The attacker then waits for an encrypted message to be sent with the nonce N. It is generally assumed that an adversary can easily obtain the nonce. In most cases, the nonce is sent in the clear with the ciphertext, whereas in others it can be derived (e.g., sequence number in reliable transport protocols). The attacker XORs the precomputed value with the ciphertext to obtain the plaintext. To verify the validity of the plaintext, it may choose to attack blocks of the ciphertext corresponding to well-known blocks of the plaintext (e.g., MAC header).

There are at least two solutions to make precomputation attacks difficult for an adversary. The first is to use a longer key. With a longer key, the adversary needs to build a larger table of the values $E(K, A_i)$. Furthermore, note that precomputation attacks require a large amount of storage and mechanisms for fast lookups on the stored values. The larger the key, the more the effort required by the adversary.

Another defense is to add a sender-specific parameter to the nonce. For example, the nonce may be formed using the Ethernet address of the sender and a counter. In this case, the adversary needs to compute a table per sender to facilitate a precomputation attack. Conversely, in the absence of this technique to compute the nonce, an adversary need only to build a single table to attack communications between any two parties.

7.4 802.11I CCMP

CCMP [1] is a secure data encapsulation protocol designed for use in 802 wireless LANs. It uses the CCM mode to provide confidentiality and message integrity and supports a few security properties of its own. First, CCMP removes some of the complexity in CCM by choosing fixed values for the MIC and nonce lengths. Recall that in CCM, the MIC length can be an even value between 4 and 16 octets. Similarly, the nonce length is dependent on the parameter L (i.e., length of the message size in octets). While it is possible for two peers to agree on these parameters as part of the key and security association negotiation process, such flexibility is not necessarily a good idea for all applications. The 802.11i specification requires a length field of 2 octets, a nonce of length 13 octets, and the MIC length to be truncated to 8 octets; the specification also defines a mechanism to construct the nonces. The length parameter selection is based on the largest possible MPDU size, which requires at most 2 octets.

Wireless devices may split MSDUs into MPDUs before transmission. Such fragmentation may be done by a transmitter to ensure reliability in a noisy channel. When there is no fragmentation, each MPDU consists of an MSDU. Forming MPDUs from an MSDU results in a small amount of packet expansion: specifically, a MAC header (as large as 30 octets) and a 4-octet frame check sequence (FCS) using CRC-32. See Figure 7.3 for an illustration.

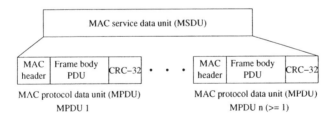

Figure 7.3 MSDU fragmentation to form MPDUs.

7.4.1 Key Derivation for CCMP

CCM uses a single 128-bit key for encryption and authentication. During the 4-way exchange, the STA and the AP derive a 384-bit key when CCMP is the negotiated secure data encapsulation protocol. The first 256 bits are used for protecting the 4-way exchange itself, and the final 128 bits are used as the AES-CCM key for unicast communication between the STA and the AP. For group communication and direct communication between two STAs, the originating entity — an AP in the group case and a STA in the direct communication case — is responsible for generating a 16-octet key and delivering to the other party(ies).

CCMP uses the same 128-bit key for secure unicast communication from the AP to the STA and vice versa. Recall that from the definition of CCM, using the same key with the same nonce would void the security guarantees of the authenticated encryption mode. Thus, CCMP needs a mechanism to ensure that the same nonce is not going to be used by the two parties involved. Note that neither randomly choosing a nonce, nor employing a more popular practice of choosing a sequence number for the nonce work well in this case. Section 7.4.3 describes the nonce construction for CCMP.

7.4.2 Additional Authentication Data in CCMP

It is desirable to integrity protect the MAC header to avoid having an adversary modify information within the header; for example, the receiving station address. Conversely, some of the fields within the MAC header must be changeable as required. Thus, the 802.11i specification defines the formation of the AAD field as follows:

- Frame control field, with the subtype bits, retry bit, power management bit, and more data bit set to zero. The protected frame bit is set to one. The last bit indicates that the frame is cryptographically encapsulated, in this case with CCMP.

- Destination address (i.e., final destination of the MPDU).

- Source address (i.e., original source address of the MPDU).

- Receiving station address.

- MPDU sequence control field, with the sequence number cleared. The sequence number is a modulo-4096 counter that provides MSDU sequencing.

- Transmitter address, if present in the MPDU.

- Optionally, the quality of service control field containing the priority bits. This field is currently being defined by the 802.11e Task Group within the IEEE.

In the absence of the two optional fields — transmitter address, and the quality of service control field — the AAD is 22 octets in length; with both of them present, it is 30 octets in length. Figure 7.4 serves as a quick reference to the AAD construction in CCMP. Following the conventions described in Section 7.2.2.2, the AAD in CCMP is encoded in two octets in computing the MIC.

MAC hdr   30 octets

Frame control 2 octets	Duration/ID 2 octets	Addr 1 6 octets	Addr 2 6 octets	Addr 3 6 octets	Seq control 2 octets	Addr 4 6 octets	Body	CRC–32 4 octets

Additional authentication data: 22–30 octets

Frame control bits 4–6, 11–13 = 0 bit 14 = 1	Addr 1 6 octets	Addr 2 6 octets	Addr 3 6 octets	Seq control bit 4–15 = 0	Addr 4 6 octets	QC 2 octets

Priority; rest is reserved

Figure 7.4   Additional authentication data in CCMP.

7.4.3   Nonce Construction in CCMP

Figure 7.5 illustrates the nonce construction in CCMP. The nonce has mainly two parts: the first is a 6-octet packet number starting at 0 and counting up to $2^{48} - 1$, and the second is the 6-octet source MAC address. The nonce also contains a 1-octet flags field, where the first 4 bits represent the priority of the frame and the next 4 bits are reserved. This octet is currently set to zero. In CCMP, the nonce is the result of concatenation of the flags field, source MAC address, and the packet number, in that order.

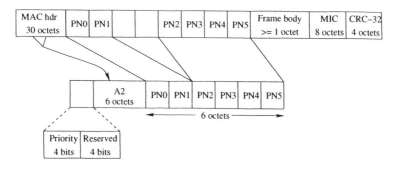

Figure 7.5   Nonce construction in CCMP and its encoding in the CCMP header.

The packet number is the only unique entity between two nonces calculated following this method. This limits the number of MPDUs that can be encapsulated with a given key to 2^{48}. The MAC address as part of the nonce makes it difficult for precomputation attacks. The presence of the MAC address makes it necessary for an adversary to precompute the intermediate values in CTR mode (encrypted nonce with all possible keys) separately for each wireless entity (or more accurately, interface).

7.4.4   Replay Protection

The packet number (PN) in CCMP serves a dual purpose: in addition to being the unique portion of the nonce, it provides replay protection for the MPDUs. The PN is monotonically increasing for each successive MPDU; if it must rotate at some point in transmission, the secret key K must be changed.

There may be more than one replay counter between a given set of entities with an RSN. More specifically, the replay counter is associated with an SA. Thus, when a STA has a PTKSA, GTKSA, and one or more STAkeySAs, it will have as many independent replay counters as the number of SAs it is party to.

The priority field in the MAC header, when used, will require as many replay counters as there are priorities. When an MPDU is received, only the corresponding PN is used for replay detection, and if the received MPDU is legitimate, that PN is incremented.

Finally, the number of replay counters supported by a STA can be negotiated using RSN IEs (see Chapter 6). A STA is responsible for cross checking the number of replay counters it can manage versus the number of SAs and MPDU priorities that it wants to use.

7.4.5   MPDU Encapsulation and Decapsulation

We conclude Section 7.4 with a discussion on CCMP encapsulation and decapsulation of 802.11 MPDUs. CCMP transforms MPDUs to provide confidentiality of the frame body, and integrity and replay protection for the MAC header as well as the frame body itself. The FCS within each MPDU is left intact by the encapsulation protocol. The AAD is derived entirely from the MAC header. The nonce is constructed using the second address field from the MAC header, the priority field, and a monotonically increasing counter. Recall that the counter also serves as a PN for MPDU replay protection.

The 6-octet PN is included in the transformed MPDU (see Figure 7.6). The encrypted MIC derived using the CCM mode is also included to add 8 more octets to the MPDU. In addition to these 14 octets, 2 more octets — one octet containing 0 and reserved for future use, and another containing 5 reserved bits, an extIV flag occupying 1 bit, and a key ID field requiring 2 bits — are also added, to result in a total MPDU expansion of 16 octets due to CCMP encapsulation. The extIV bit is always set for CCMP and the key ID identifies the PSK used.

CCMP decapsulation follows the encapsulation process in constructing the AAD, nonce, and PN fields. First, the AAD can be constructed exclusively from the

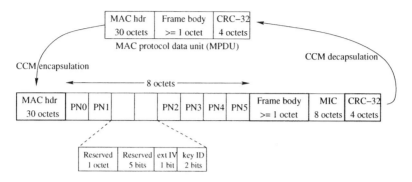

Figure 7.6 CCMP headers.

received MAC header. Next, the nonce is built using fields from the received MAC header and the received PN. Finally, the PN field is part of the CCMP header. The recipient uses the AAD and the nonce to compute the MIC of the received message and compares it to the received MIC. If the MICs are identical, it then verifies that the PN is greater than or equal to the expected PN corresponding to the SA and the MPDU priority. After that the recipient proceeds to decrypt the entire MPDU.

7.5 SUMMARY

This chapter provided a brief description of the CCMP protocol and its base AES mode known as the CCM mode. The underlying block cipher uses a 128-bit key, which is used for both integrity protection as well as encryption by the CCM mode. In addition to the security properties of the CCM mode, CCMP provides MPDU replay protection. Furthermore, CCMP fortifies some of the weaker points of the CCM mode by using a strong nonce construction mechanism, and appropriate parameter selection such as nonce length and MIC size.

References

[1] IEEE, "IEEE Std 802.11i-2004. Amendment to IEEE Std 802.11. 1999 Edition (Reaff 2003)," Amendment 6: Medium Access Control (MAC) Security Enhancements Part 11, IEEE Press, New York, Apr. 2004.

[2] D. Whiting, R. Housley, and N. Ferguson, "Counter with CBC-MAC." RFC 3610 (Informational), Aug. 2003.

[3] IEEE, "Draft IEEE Standard for Local and Metropolitan Area Networks; IEEE802.16-Revd/D5-2004," Tech. Rep. Part 16, IEEE Press, New York, 2004.

[4] "Draft IEEE Standard for Local and Metropolitan Area Networks; IEEE802.16e/D5a," Tech. Rep. Part 16, IEEE Press, New York, Dec. 2004.

[5] R. Housley, "Using AES CCM Mode with IPsec ESP," draft-ietf-ipsec-ciph-aes-ccm-05 (work in progress), Internet Engineering Task Force, Nov. 2003.

[6] M. Baugher, D. McGrew, M. Naslund, E. Carrara, and K. Norrman, "The Secure Real-Time Transport Protocol (SRTP)." RFC 3711 (Standards Track), Mar. 2004.

[7] S. Kent and R. Atkinson, "Security Architecture for the Internet Protocol," RFC 2401 (Proposed Standard), Internet Engineering Task Force, Nov. 1998.

[8] B. Aboba and D. Simon, "PPP EAP TLS Authentication Protocol." RFC 2716 (Experimental), Oct. 1999.

[9] J. Jonsson, "On the Security of CTR + CBC-MAC," *Proceedings of the Ninth Annual Workshop on Selected Areas of Cryptography SAC 2002; LNCS,* (St. John's, NF, Canada), Springer, Aug. 2002.

[10] D. McGrew, "Counter Mode Security: Analysis and Recommendations." http://www.mindspring.com/dmcgrew/ctr-security.pdf, Nov. 2002.

Chapter 8

TKIP

8.1 INTRODUCTION

TKIP is a stop-gap protocol for secure encapsulation of 802.11 frames in legacy 802.11 devices. In brief, TKIP attempts to patch the many vulnerabilities of WEP using an assortment of techniques. TKIP design includes a per-MSDU fresh key generation scheme required to properly use RC4, a longer IV, a new lightweight integrity protection scheme known as Michael, and a counter-based replay protection mechanism. Design choices favor legacy hardware support and thus this is not a long-term solution. For instance, Michael as a MIC is limited in the protection it offers, requiring attack throttling mechanisms as an integral part of the solution. The advantage of the design is that TKIP can be implemented with only a firmware upgrade to allow enterprise and home networks to gradually phase out the legacy WLAN devices in favor of CCMP (see Chapter 7) capable devices. Thus, legacy WLANs implementing TKIP are known as transition security networks (TSN).

The rest of this chapter is organized as follows. In the first section, we will discuss TKIP design — including motivation, design goals, constraints, and choices — in detail. Next, we will discuss each of the TKIP design components. Section 8.3 describes the first component, the specially designed MIC algorithm, Michael, and its application to WLAN MSDUs. The second component — the design of temporal key computation and WEP encapsulation and decapsulation processes — is the topic of Section 8.6. The third component of TKIP design is the per-MPDU sequence counter for replay protection, discussed in Section 8.5. TKIP design constraints translate to use of less than perfect encryption and integrity algorithms. Thus, TKIP employs noncryptographic countermeasures to throttle such attacks. TKIP countermeasures are the topic of discussion of Section 8.6.1. We conclude the chapter with a summary of TKIP in Section 8.7.

8.2   TKIP DESIGN

The IEEE 802.11i [1] standard consists of two solutions: TKIP for legacy devices, and AES-CCMP for new devices. The various problems with the original WEP protocol are well documented (see Chapter 5). The best way to address those issues is to design a protocol based on strong encryption and integrity algorithms. However, there is also a very large installed base of WEP-based WLAN hardware, and it might take a few years before all that equipment is replaced. Software implementation of better encryption algorithms is not feasible in legacy devices since many of them use low-end CPUs (e.g., ARM7), and only a small percentage of the CPU is available for extra computation at peak bandwidths. TKIP is the solution for such devices and designed to require only a firmware upgrade to APs or device driver installation in case of STAs. In the rest of this section, we will discuss TKIP design goals, constraints, and components.

8.2.1   TKIP Design Goals and Constraints

The TKIP design goal is to provide confidentiality, message integrity, and replay protection of 802.11 frames, with the constraint to reuse existing WEP encapsulation hardware in WLAN devices already deployed. First, let us examine the constraints in detail.

- *Limited processing power.* There are two aspects to this constraint. First, for low power consumption many WLAN devices are equipped with low-end CPUs. For instance, PDAs as STAs have limited computing power (approximately 100–200 Mips) and many APs are equipped with very low-end processors (approximately 20–50 Mips).

  Next, most of such devices already operate at high CPU load (e.g., 90%) at peak bandwidth transmissions. Thus, implementing a strong encryption algorithm, such as AES, or message integrity algorithm, such as HMAC, is infeasible.

- *Reuse existing WEP encapsulation engines.* Legacy WLAN devices would have the best chance to maintain their encapsulation bandwidth if we reuse the WEP encapsulation engine. As a result of this constraint, the new design also includes the per-MPDU ICV.

- *MIC computation.* Ideally MIC computation should be at the MPDU level. However, in some cases, for instance in the case of a PC with a WLAN card, MPDUs may not be available at the PC level. Thus, software-based MIC computation can only be at the MSDU level. This has implications in protecting against replay attacks.

Thus, the limited processing power in the low-end devices dictates that WEP hardware be used in designing TKIP to maintain the 802.11 bandwidths. As a result, TKIP addresses the various flaws in WEP by "patching" them with an assortment of techniques, including design of algorithms, introduction of a new MPDU format, and finally preprocessing of the keying material.

Before we review the design components, let us summarize the various weaknesses of WEP encapsulation (also see Chapter 5).

- *Weakness in RC4 KSA.* Fluhrer, Martin, and Shamir prove that the RC4 KSA has two major weaknesses that an adversary can exploit to extract the RC4 key from WEP encrypted traffic. First, there are several weak keys, and second there is a related key vulnerability. The related key vulnerability needs some discussion. When the secret part of the input to the KSA is reused, an adversary can use statistical analysis on the first few bytes of the RC4 KSA output, to derive the secret key. This attack requires access to millions of encrypted MPDUs with the same key, but requires only about a day's work [2] on a general purpose computer.

    This attack can be made ineffective by changing the key frequently or by discarding the first several bytes (256 is the recommended number of bytes to be discarded) of the RC4 KSA's output.

- *Short IV.* WEP uses a 24-bit IV and offers no guidance on IV selection. If random IVs were to be used, there is a good chance of collision after a few thousand packets, due to the Birthday paradox [3].

    If monotonically increasing IVs are used, the IV space will rotate after 2^{24} MPDUs. Unfortunately, in many cases, the WEP key is shared by several devices, increasing the chance of a collision.

    The solution here is rather simple: increase the IV length.

- *Lack of integrity protection.* WEP uses a noncryptographic mechanism, CRC-32, for integrity protection. CRC-32 is linear and its use combined with RC4 allows an attacker to modify WEP encrypted data and include the correct checksum without the communicating parties being able to realize it. We need a cryptographic integrity algorithm to protect 802.11 data.

- *Key reuse.* WEP typically uses the same key for traffic from the AP to the STA and the STA to the AP. Furthermore, in many instances the WEP key is static, which makes it easy for an adversary to derive the key, or deduce cleartext.

- *No replay protection.* WEP does not support replay protection. With a monotonically increasing IV, a replay protection mechanism could be put in place, but that would be ineffective considering all the other weaknesses in the protocol's design.

The solution is to use a monotonically increasing IV with a proper integrity algorithm to protect the IV.

- *Short keys.* As per the original design, WEP uses a 40-bit key (in conjunction with the 24-bit IV, this amounts to a 64-bit RC4 encapsulation key), which makes it very easy for brute force attacks. The enhanced version, commonly known as WEP2, uses a 104-bit key (or 128-bit RC4 key). However, due to the other problems with the WEP design, the longer key only makes attacks linearly difficult, as opposed to being exponentially effective.

    The solution is to not only use a longer key, but also fix the other design problems of WEP.

8.2.2 TKIP Design Components

The TKIP design contains the following components:

1. TKIP uses fresh keys from the 4-way exchange (see Chapter 6) to establish a PTKSA or the 2-way exchange to establish a GTKSA. For TKIP, we derive 256 bits from the key derivation process after the key exchange, and use the first 128 bits as the encryption key (temporal key or TK) and a 64-bit integrity key in each direction of the traffic.

2. TKIP uses a monotonically increasing 48-bit TKIP sequence counter (TSC) per MPDU for replay protection. The TSC contains a 4-octet extended IV, and 2 octets from the WEP IV. The other octet of the WEP IV is derived as a function of least significant bit of the WEP IV.

    There is a unique TSC per MPDU per TK; when the TSC value rotates (to zero), a new key exchange (4-way or 2-way) is initiated to generate a fresh TK.

3. TKIP defines a two-stage cryptographic mixing process to generate a fresh key to encrypt each MPDU and a different key in different directions of the traffic (i.e., from a STA to the AP and the AP to the STA).

    In the first phase, the TK, the transmitter's address (TA) and the extended IV are inputs to a cryptographic function that generates a TKIP mixed transmitter address and key (TTAK). In the second phase, a different cryptographic function mixes the TTAK, TK, and the two least significant octets of the TSC to generate the WEP seed. The key generation process ensures a unique key in each direction of traffic and a unique key per MPDU.

4. A specially designed, lightweight integrity algorithm known as Michael is used for integrity protection of MSDUs, the source and destination MAC addresses, and the priority field.

8.3 MESSAGE INTEGRITY PROTECTION USING MICHAEL

There are two issues to supporting message integrity in existing WEP hardware. First, the computing constraints make it impossible to use a strong integrity algorithm such as HMAC-SHA-1. Next, the design must take into account that the MIC implementation might be in the host CPU and that the host CPU might not have access to MPDUs.

To address the first constraint, a new lightweight integrity algorithm called Michael was designed by Niels Ferguson [4] for the specific purpose of providing acceptable integrity protection to TKIP traffic. The second constraint dictates that the MIC protection is at the MSDU level, and not at the MPDU level (integrity protection is on an MPDU basis in case of WEP and CCMP, and is more efficient).

Thus, TKIP MIC computation works as follows. First, there are two 8-octet MIC keys, one in each direction of the traffic: one from the AP to the STA and another from the STA to the AP. The MIC keys are generated at the end of the 4-way exchange (or a 2-way exchange in case of a GTK SA), similar to the TKIP keys themselves.

The MIC is computed over the SA, DA, 3 reserved octets, priority, and the MSDU data. The 8-octet MIC itself is appended to the MSDU data and may be fragmented into multiple MPDUs as necessary before TKIP encapsulation. Thus the MIC will be RC4 encrypted with a TKIP key. Finally, note that the MIC does not cover the TSC.

The Michael algorithm itself is fairly simple, using modulo addition, 32-bit shift operations, 16-bit word swap, and XOR operations. It takes only a few (< 10) clock cycles per octet on the low end CPUs such as ARM7.

8.3.1 Michael Protocol Limitations

A typical MIC or message authentication tag is more than 10 octets in length: for instance SRTP suggests a 10-octet authentication tag and IPsec, a 12-octet MIC. Michael, at 8 octets, is a shorter ICV. More importantly, the Michael algorithm being fairly simple does not even afford 64-bit security. In fact, Michael was designed with a goal of 20-bit security, and the best-known theoretical limitation on the construction is 29 bits [4].

Michael is a relatively new construction and therefore has not been through as much analysis as more popular integrity protection algorithms such as HMAC. Michael security properties are valid only when the MIC is encrypted and in this case that implies that the TKIP key mixing is secure. In addition, the 29-bit security afforded by Michael is not sufficient in case of active attacks. Thus, for effective integrity protection, Michael needs to be deployed with countermeasures to throttle active attacks.

8.4   CONFIDENTIALITY

TKIP uses an assortment of techniques to use WEP encapsulation hardware to effectively encrypt 802.11 frames.

First, it uses the 4-way exchange (or the 2-way exchange in case of GTKSA) to derive a per-session key. Recall that the 4-way exchange starts out with a PMK, which could be either a PSK or a key derived/shared after 802.1X/EAP authentication. The STA and the AP exchange nonces and use them to derive the TK, thus ensuring that even if the PSK does not change, the TK is fresh and random.

Next, a 48-bit monotonically increasing sequence counter ensures that the IV does not repeat for a long time (the 48-bit IV space translates to several years of communication at peak 802.11 rates without rekeying). Notice that since the IV is a sequence number, there is no chance for collision.

Third, the TKIP design contains a cryptographic mixing function that in part mixes the TA to derive the WEP key. This ensures that even though the STA and the AP use the same TK and the same IV, an adversary gains no advantage in having access to the two MPDUs encapsulated with the keys derived.

Finally, TKIP uses two mixing functions to ensure use of a different key in each direction of the traffic and a different key per MPDU to mitigate the WEP design flaws.

8.4.1   TKIP Key Mixing

TKIP uses two separate cryptographic mixing functions to generate a different per-MPDU key in each direction of the traffic to correctly use RC4 encryption in WEP hardware for secure encapsulation of 802.11 frames. In other words, key mixing is a crucial part of the TKIP design that contributes to the security of the encapsulation. TKIP uses a two-stage process to mix a 16-octet PTK or GTK, a 6-octet TSC, and the 6-octet TA to generate a 13-octet key to serve as the RC4 key. The phases are designed so that the result of the first phase can be cached and reused for several MPDUs — 2^{16} to be precise.

TKIP ensures that a different key is derived in each direction by cryptographically mixing the TA with the TK to derive an intermediate key, called TTAK, 10 octets in length. The cryptographic function is fairly lightweight comprising XORs, logical AND, the addition operation, and finally a nonlinear S-box substitution defined in the 802.11i specification [1]. The most significant 4 octets of the TSC (the extended IV portion; see Figure 8.1) are also used in the derivation of TTAK. The most significant 4 octets of the TSC only change every 2^{16} MPDUs, and thus the TTAK value can be cached for that duration for efficient operation.

TTAK derivation comprises the first phase of the TKIP per-MPDU key derivation process. In the second phase, the TTAK is mixed with the least significant

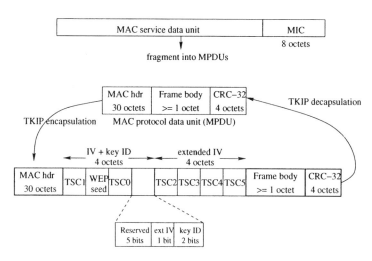

Figure 8.1 TKIP MPDU format before and after encapsulation.

2 octets of the TSC (this is part of the WEP IV) and the TK itself. This phase is also lightweight employing XOR, OR, and AND logical operations, and the addition, and right-shift operations, in conjunction with the S-box substitutions. This phase cryptographically mixes the IV into the per-MPDU key and also ensures that the IV is decorrelated from the secret key. Phase 2 results in 13 octets of per-MPDU RC4 key and a 3-octet WEP IV. The WEP seed is readily usable by a WEP encapsulation engine.

The algorithms for TKIP mixing are specified in the 802.11i specification [1].

8.4.2 Security Limitations of TKIP Key Mixing

The goals of the key mixing process are to eliminate the design flaws in WEP. Two separate but somewhat similar mixing functions are used to ensure that there is a separate key per MPDU and in each direction. The second phase of the mixing function ensures that the publicly transmitted WEP IV is decorrelated from the secret key.

There is unfortunately no quantifiable cryptographic strength to the TKIP mixing functions. The mixing functions use nonlinear S-box substitutions and some simple logical and shift operations to decorrelate the public IV, extended IV (the WEP IV and the extended IV constitute the TSC), and the TA from the per-MPDU key. Note that upto 2^{48} per-MPDU WEP keys can be generated from a TK derived after the 4-way exchange.

The mixing functions got a wide review by the cryptographic community and there are no known flaws or weaknesses in the design. TKIP is certainly more effective than WEP encapsulation and thus should be used on all legacy hardware for better protection. It is important to note however that TKIP is a stop-gap solution and designed with several computational constraints in mind. It must not be used as a long-term solution.

8.5   REPLAY PROTECTION

TKIP uses a 48-bit TSC for replay protection of the 802.11 MPDUs. Ideally, the replay counter must be integrity protected. However, as discussed in Section 8.3, TKIP design does not allow MIC computation on a per MPDU basis. Thus, TKIP only supports indirect integrity protection of the TSC. This still provides an acceptable level of security due to the TSC use in TKIP key mixing.

TKIP uses a 48-bit monotonically increasing sequence number per MPDU within the context of every SA (e.g., PTKSA, GTKSA, or STAkeySA). Each sender within the SA maintains its own TSC. If the priority field is in use for QoS considerations, there could be a separate TSC per priority class. The TSC also serves as the IV for the TKIP key mixing and for WEP encapsulation; specifically, the least significant two octets directly form two octets of the WEP IV, with the second least significant octet contributing to the third octet. The four most significant octets of the TSC are also known as the extended IV (see Figure 8.1). Due to the inclusion of the TSC in TKIP key mixing, any modification of the TSC in transit would result in a failure to derive the correct per-MPDU key, which in turn may result in ICV verification failure. Even if that succeeds, the MIC verification will fail at the MSDU level. TKIP replay protection, although applied at the MPDU level, can only be assuredly verified at the MSDU level. TKIP replay protection can be summarized into the following steps:

- The TSC is initialized to 1 when the TK is established either to begin a TKIP protected session or to reinitialize a TKIP protected session after rekeying and regeneration of the TK. The first MPDU from the sender uses and carries the TSC value of 1.

- For each successive MPDU within the protection of the same TK, the TSC is incremented by 1.

- When the TSC reaches $2^{48} - 1$ or if an exception occurs due to a perceived attack or due to other external input (e.g., user/administrator may prompt rekeying), the TK is rekeyed and the TSC is set to 1.

- The receiver maintains a TSC per SA. If the TSC was seen before, the MPDU is dropped. Otherwise, the receiver decrypts the MPDU and verifies the ICV. If the ICV verification fails, the frame is dropped. The MPDU retransmission mechanism will ensure that the receiver will eventually have the MPDUs required to recover the MSDU and the MIC.

- The receiver then proceeds to compute the MIC and verifies it against the received MIC.

    If the MIC comparison fails, the receiver assumes that it might be under an active attack and throttles the attack using the Michael countermeasures mechanism (described in Section 8.6.1).

    If the MIC comparison succeeds, the receiver can update the TKIP counter to the last received TSC from an MPDU included in the MSDU.

8.6   TKIP ENCAPSULATION AND DECAPSULATION

Figure 8.2 illustrates the TKIP encapsulation process. As shown in the figure, the following steps constitute the TKIP encapsulation algorithm. We assume that the TK SA has been established already and the 802.11 device is ready to transmit data.

- The first step is for the sender to compute the MIC over the SA, DA, priority, the three reserved octets, and finally the MSDU data itself. Next, the sender appends the MIC to the MSDU and hands it to the MAC level for additional processing.

- The MAC level processing might first fragment the MSDU plus the MIC into several MPDUs and sends the MPDUs for TKIP processing.

- A monotonically increasing TSC is used for each MPDU. The TSC supports replay protection and is used to derive a per-MPDU key.

- TKIP uses a two-stage mixing process to derive a per-MPDU key for WEP encapsulation. The result of the first phase, TTAK, can be cached and needs to be repeated only every 2^{16} MPDUs. Thus, in most cases, the second stage needs to be computed as an MPDU is encapsulated.

- The result of the mixing process is a WEP seed that can be readily supplied to WEP encapsulation hardware along with the MPDU.

- WEP encapsulation proceeds normally in that there is a per-MPDU ICV in addition to the per-MSDU MIC.

- The TSC is incremented for the next MPDU.

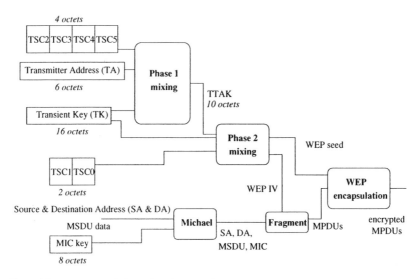

Figure 8.2   TKIP encapsulation and MIC computation.

TKIP decapsulation (illustrated in Figure 8.3) involves the following steps:

- A receiver first verifies that the MPDU is not a replay by checking whether the received TSC matches the expected replay counter corresponding to the SA.

- If the TSC indicates that the MPDU is fresh, the receiver proceeds to use the TSC from the packet to compute the per-MPDU key. The receiver then proceeds to decrypt the MPDU using WEP.

- If the WEP ICV check succeeds the cleartext MPDU is ready for defragmentation, otherwise, the MPDU is dropped.

- After defragmentation, the receiver computes the MIC over the MSDU, SA, DA, priority, and the reserved octets to derive the MIC. If the received and computed MICs match, the MSDU is passed to the higher layer.

- The receiver increments the replay counter to reflect the last correctly received TSC.

- If the MIC verification fails, then we are dealing with an MSDU with correct ICV in all MPDUs. The chance of all ICVs being correct and the MIC being incorrect due to errors at the physical layer is very small.

Recall that Michael is a weak integrity algorithm. Thus, in the event of a MIC failure, the receiver must assume that it is under an active attack and implement countermeasures.

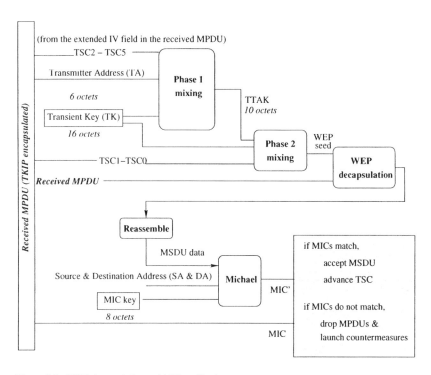

Figure 8.3 TKIP decapsulation and MIC verification.

8.6.1 TKIP Countermeasures

Michael is a weak integrity algorithm due to the design constraints. The design goal was only 20 bits of protection and the best estimate of the strength is at 30 bits of protection [4]. In other words, an adversary may be able to successfully subvert the MIC protection in 2^{-29} packets. Since it is plausible that an adversary can send about that many small MPDUs within a few minutes, TKIP assumes that a MIC failure indicates a potential active attack and throttles the adversary to two tries within a minute. This throttling effectively increases the amount of time it takes to attempt 2^{29} fake packets to about 1 year or so [4].

The TKIP countermeasures mechanism works as follows. The receiver logs each MIC failure as a potential active attack. If there is another MIC failure within one minute of the previous failure, the receiver must disassociate, delete the corresponding SAs, and wait another minute before reassociating.

8.7 SUMMARY

WEP encapsulation is flawed at many levels and TKIP is designed to patch all the vulnerabilities while reusing existing hardware. This is quite a challenge as the design is to take into account the least common denominator of all the constraining factors of the deployed hardware.

The solution, as one would expect, is also a patchwork of clever designs, larger key or IV sizes, and new algorithms tied together with attack throttling techniques. Specifically TKIP adds 4 more octets to 802.11 MPDUs, expanding the IV by 4 octets. TKIP also uses 2 octets of the old IV and the expanded IV to serve as a 6-octet sequence number for replay protection. There is a new per-MPDU key derivation algorithm that mixes the TSC, TA and TK. This algorithm works in two phases, with the possibility of caching the result of the first phase to ease the computational burden on low-end devices. A newly designed lightweight MIC algorithm along with attack limiting guidelines protects the MSDUs from frame modification in transit. In sum, TKIP design is a stop-gap solution that provides an acceptable level of security in legacy WLAN devices. TKIP only requires firmware or device driver updates and is fairly easy to implement and deploy.

References

[1] IEEE, "IEEE Std 802.11i-2004, Amendment to IEEE Std 802.11, 1999 Edition (Reaff 2003)," Amendment 6: Medium Access Control (MAC) Security Enhancements Part 11, IEEE Press, New York, Apr. 2004.

[2] A. Stubblefield, J. Ioannidis, and A. D. Rubin, "Using the Fluhrer, Mantin, and Shamir Attack to Break WEP," *Proceedings of Network and Distributed System Security Symposium (NDSS)*, (San Diego, CA), Feb. 2002.

[3] "Birthday Paradox." Wikipedia entry, http://en.wikipedia.org/wiki/Birthday_paradox.

[4] N. Ferguson, "Michael: An Improved MIC for 802.11 WEP." IEEE TGi doc 802.11-02/020r0, Jan. 2002, http://www.ieee802.org.

Part III

Wireless Roaming Security

Chapter 9

Security in WiFi Roaming

9.1 INTRODUCTION

The primary reason WLANs were developed was to allow untethered connections between a client and an 802.11 access point (AP), as a basis for further access to resources and services on the Internet. The next step in this process is wireless roaming, in which a client can move across multiple APs in one administrative domain and across multiple APs across differing administrative domains. Currently, the most prevalent model for wired roaming consists of a dial-up connection from a client (e.g., a laptop) through an ISP, to a home domain (e.g., corporate network). This model presumes the prior existence of a business relationship between the client (or its corporation) and one or more Internet service providers (ISPs).

The term *WiFi roaming* can be loosely defined as the set of services supporting the deployment and management of 802.11 WLAN access at public venues or public *hotspots*, where the customer of one service provider can obtain services (e.g., IP connectivity) from a different (visited) service provider. The term *service provider* (SP) here is intentionally left abstract since in today's Internet a number of entities can take the role of providing one or more services relating to WiFi roaming. It is important to note that WiFi roaming involves the crossing of both network-administrative boundaries and security-administrative boundaries. Therefore, on-campus WLAN access at different remote locations (e.g., offices, buildings) under the same administrative jurisdiction is not considered here as WiFi roaming.[1]

The business case for WiFi roaming is self-evident: consumers with laptops or handheld devices are willing to pay for IP connectivity through WiFi hotspots located throughout the world, provided that WiFi access is easy to use and secure.

---

[1] This chapter intentionally uses the term "WiFi roaming" specifically for 802.11 WLAN access at public venues, which is different from access to a LAN or WLAN through separate 802.11 APs connected to the same LAN or WLAN. The term is also used to distinguish it from aspects of fast handoff between two APs connected to the same LAN or WLAN.

This desire is already true today, as seen in the case of dial-up IP services. Many traditional ISPs see WiFi roaming as providing a new business opportunity, by extending their edge services to a new kind of access point, namely, the public hotspot, while retaining as much as possible their investment in their existing backend authentication, authorization, and accounting (AAA) infrastructure.

For some *mobile network operators* (MNO) and carriers, the case for WiFi roaming can even be considered imperative, as they are seeking to augment and extend existing mobile-related services to their customers at affordable prices. Mobile handsets that can make use of WiFi hotspots — with speeds of 11 to 50 Mbps — could generate new business opportunities by providing users with higher-quality content and a higher level of interactivity. The case for WiFi roaming is of particular interest to MNOs that have invested heavily in the recent acquisition of 3G licenses.

Given the increasing mobility of the workforce, providing *secure* WiFi roaming is an important challenge today. Corporations see remote access as a given fact of life and expect services from their ISPs supporting remote access. This is true in dial-up today, and it is something expected of WiFi roaming in the near future.

In this chapter we look at the growing area of WiFi roaming. First, we review briefly the existing dial-up services, which are provided by many "traditional" ISPs. The dial-up AAA model provides a background for understanding the view of many ISPs and WISPs in providing WiFi hotspot services. This chapter then looks into the WISPr architecture for WiFi roaming, which is a proposal from a group of vendors and ISPs within the WiFi Alliance (WFA).

9.2   ROAMING IN DIAL-UP IP SERVICES: BACKGROUND

In the last decade, the combination of advances in portable computing technology (e.g., stronger laptops, PDAs), the finalization of the IPsec RFCs in the late 1990s, and the proliferation of dial-up services together promoted user mobility and the corporate acceptance of the notion the "road warrior" (traveling worker) and telecommuters. Thus, the three aspects of user mobility technologies, namely end-user devices, secure end-to-end communications, and IP-supporting services, combined to form much of what we understand — and take for granted — of the "mobile" Internet today.

From the perspective of IP communications mobility, the two most important developments in the last decade have been the establishment of dial-up services and the development of security protocols that protect IP communications end-to-end. These two areas of technology are important in the context of WiFi roaming because many of the concepts underlying WiFi roaming have been derived from the dial-up world. Indeed, existing ISPs and carriers want to retain as much as possible the dial-up infrastructures in the WiFi world in order to maintain their decade-long investments in these infrastructures. The public hotspot phenomenon has so far affected only the "edges" of the Internet. The core of the Internet has largely remained unaffected directly by WiFi-related technologies. Finally, the maturity of the IPsec (ESP) [1] and IKE [2] protocols has allowed IPsec-VPNs to be used over dial-up connections for remote access users. The same protocols continue to be used today over IP connections established at WiFi hotspots.

9.2.1 The Dial-Up Access Model

In the traditional dial-up access, a user uses a modem device to establish a connection to a *network services provider* (NSP), over the *public switched telephone network* (PSTN). The NSP, which is typically also an ISP, hosts a termination device for the PSTN connection (e.g., dial-up concentrators), which usually has IP switch/routing functionality. This is shown in Figure 9.1.

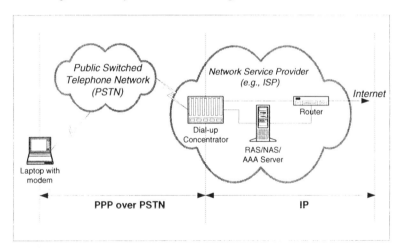

Figure 9.1 The traditional dial-up model.

In terms of IP connectivity, the connection between the user's laptop/modem and the NSP is IP over the *Point-to-Point Protocol* (PPP) [3], which runs over the PSTN network. From the NSP onwards, the connection is IP over whichever medium the NSP uses with the ISP upstream (e.g., T1, leased lines, and so forth). The point here is that the PPP protocol is crucial for the dial-up connection from the user to the NSP.

Note that many dial-up NSPs provide a list of local telephone numbers and toll-free numbers to which the user can dial according to the user's current location.

This approach is common today since most — if not all — PSTN networks in North America provide unlimited calls when they are made within the same area code. For traveling users, often a toll-free number is provided so that users need not pay for either local or long-distance calls.

From the security perspective, the dial-up connection over the PSTN provides better — though not much better — physical security compared to the broadcast nature of 802.11. In either case, an IPsec-VPN or SSL-VPN needs to be deployed to provide true end-to-end communications security.

9.2.2   Authentication in Dial-Up IP Services

In order to support authentication and authorization in dial-up connections, the PPP-Extensions Working Group in the IETF developed the *extensible authentication protocol* (EAP) in RFC2284 [4], with the most recent version of the protocol defined in RFC3748 [5]. For user authentication, typically a password-based protocol is used (e.g., CHAP [6] or MS-CHAP [7]), though EAP itself supports other protocols (e.g., EAP-TLS [8]) which use other forms of credentials (e.g., digital certificates).

When a user seeks IP connectivity over dial-up using PPP, as part of the setup a *PPP authentication* phase must be completed. Typically, the user dials against a *network access server* (NAS), which may or may not be collocated with the dial-up concentrator device (see Figure 9.1). The authentication of the user is done using EAP together with a specific authentication method chosen by the ISP.

Most ISPs prefer to use passwords as the basis for user authentication. Specific protocols implementing the challenge-response authentication model based on a (hashed) password include CHAP [6] and MS-CHAP [7]. This choice is driven by the fact that most ISPs use a simple database (e.g., LDAP) containing a table correlating user IDs, passwords, accounts, e-mail addresses, and other user/employer information.

9.2.3   The Network Access Identifier (NAI)

In the dial-up world, the identity of the user is known at the *network access identifier* (NAI) [9]. The NAI is the user identifier submitted by the client during the PPP authentication phase. Thus, the typical information submitted to an ISP from the client consists of the NAI and password pair. Depending on the specific password-based authentication protocol used, it is usually the hash of the password that is transmitted from the client to the ISP (i.e., NAS device at the ISP). This is to prevent snooping of the plaintext password when it is in transit to the ISP.

The NAI format is similar to the e-mail address, namely user@realm where the realm portion has the usual organizational domain ending. Although the NAI need not be an e-mail address, often ISPs prefer to use either actual e-mail addresses or some other information identifying the user's affiliation. Thus, for example, an NAI could be the e-mail address johndoe@employer.com where employer is the company employing the user and is the entity that established a business agreement with the ISP. Also, often a similar substitute may be used for the organizational name. For example, instead of using the employer realm, the ISP could use any other similar realm, such as employerdial or employernetaccess for example, where it is clear that the NAI refers to the same organization or company called "employer."

Although less secure, often ISPs assign an organization-shared password that is shared for all users of that organization. Rather than storing and managing a unique password per-employee or per-user, an ISP would simply assign a password to the entire organization, providing it only to the authorized IT administrators of that organization. It is then up to the IT administrator of the organization to set up the password and NAI correctly on the employee's dial-up application software. This approach is more practical, particularly from an identity-management perspective, bearing in mind that many dial-up ISPs employ the rudimentary LDAP database with RADIUS [10].

9.2.4 The NAI for Dial-Up Remote Access

In dial-up remote access, which has similarities to WiFi roaming, the purpose of the NAI is to identify the user as well as to assist in the routing of the authentication request. Typically, ISPs provide their customers with a list of numbers to dial in each country in the world where that ISP has a "presence," namely, a relationship with either a local PSTN or ISP (or both). This list is usually incorporated into the software dialer on the user's computer. The visited ISP needs the NAI to identify if the user is a customer of one of its business partners (another ISP) and it needs the realm information of the NAI in order to route an authorization request to that partner.

To illustrate the importance of the NAI, Figure 9.2 shows a simplified fictitious example of two users from the United States who are in France and dialing French ISP numbers.

Without going into details, user1 is an employee of Corporate1 whose provider happens also to be a mediator/broker. The second user, user2, is an employee of Company2, which obtains Internet services from a regular ISP. Both users are visiting Paris, France, and are dialing a telephone number that is served by the local PSTN, namely, France Telecom. In this example, Corporate1 uses GRIC as their service provider in the United States, while Company2 uses UUnet as their ISP in the United States. Coincidentally, both GRIC and UUnet have peering agreements with the same French ISP. Thus, although each user may dial a different number in Paris, their PPP connection is served by the same French ISP.

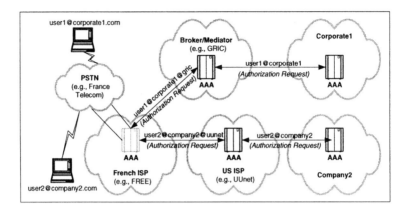

Figure 9.2   Example of NAI use in dial-up roaming.

In the case of `user1`, whose NAI is of the form `user1@corporate1.com`, the French ISP uses the realm information to forward the authorization request to GRIC since `Corporate1` is listed as a customer of GRIC. For `user2` with NAI `user2@company.com`, the French ISP forwards the authorization request to UUnet since the French ISP has a direct bilateral agreement with UUnet.

Note that the above example represents a fictitious example based on fictitious relationships. The aim is to illustrate the use of NAI by service providers for routing AAA-related parameters.

Furthermore, note that in order for service providers to provide WiFi roaming while retaining their AAA infrastructure (as shown in Figure 9.2), the only entity that essentially needs to be replaced in Figure 9.2 is that of the PSTN (replaced with a WiFi hotspot). Thus, instead of dialing a telephone number, the user would obtain 802.11 access at the hotspot, who would forward the authorization requests the same way as in our previous example of Figure 9.2.

9.3   WIFI ROAMING: ENTITIES AND MODELS

Roaming is about relationships among service providers. In order to carry over the roaming model from the dial-up world to the WiFi world, it is useful to understand the entities involved in both types or roaming and the roaming models that may apply to the WiFi world.

9.3.1 WiFi Roaming Entities

In order to analyze the issues and requirements relating to WiFi roaming, it is useful to understand the entities involved in WiFi roaming today (see Figure 9.3):

- *Hotspot wireless Internet service provider (WISP)*: This is the entity that actually manages and operates the 802.11 equipment and other network functions at a hotspot and has the relationship with an upstream ISP that provides basic high-speed IP connectivity out of that hotspot.

  For simplicity, and to avoid confusion, we identify these entities as WISPs, though today many traditional (wired) ISPs are also venturing into providing WISP functions. Thus, many ISPs can also be called WISPs.

  The term "wireless ISP" originated from the earlier days of hotspot footprint expansion and deployment. A handful of (start-up) companies adopted this business model at the outset of the WiFi revolution. However, the revenues coming from this business model proved to be so slim that these businesses were not sustainable. As a consequence, only established traditional (wired) ISPs, carriers, and MNOs could afford the initial rollout costs to enlarge the WiFi footprint to the point of being cost-effective and only such large players have remained today. Thus, it is not surprising today to find that traditional ISPs are providing WiFi hotspot services as extensions of the core ISP business.

- *ISP, carrier, or MNOs*: The ISP, carrier, or MNO is the entity that typically has a direct relationship with either the individual subscriber or the corporate customer (having many roaming employees). From an authorization point of view, all WiFi roaming access must obtain authorization from (or through) this entity, either in real-time or through some predefined (preapproved) service agreement.

- *Broker or aggregator*: A broker or aggregator is an entity whose role is to mediate among as many service providers as possible. It makes its revenue out of providing as large a number as possible of connections among its customers (ISPs, carriers, MNOs). Note that in recent years, some aggregators have begun to also own corporate customers directly, as a way to enhance their business model.

- *Corporate network*: This entity reflects corporate customers. Many enterprises in the past have required that dial-up authorization be obtained from the corporate network (i.e., the corporate AAA server). Thus, the same authorization model is also being adopted for WiFi roaming by some service providers.

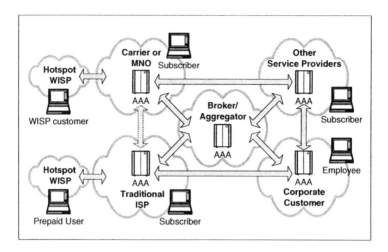

Figure 9.3 WiFi roaming entities and relationships.

It is important to note that although Figure 9.3 identifies three roles that provide services, in practice multiple roles (or all three roles) can be assumed by a single organization. Thus, for example, a traditional ISP could take on the first two roles by extending its services through additional hotspot footprints. Another example would be the case of the traditional carrier (Telco) who converts its public telephone booths into WiFi hotspots by adding an 802.11 access point and DSL modem atop (or instead of) its public telephone booths. Here, if the carrier is not an Internet ISP then the carrier would in fact be adopting the first role (hotspot provider) and the third role (WISP for billing and accounting). Finally, an entity could take up all three roles such as the case of an MNO who may already possess an ISP business unit and who now wishes to roll out WiFi hotspots with WiFi roaming capability for their customers.

9.3.2 Roaming Models

From a business perspective, three general roaming models are applicable to WiFi roaming. Which of these models are adopted in a given case is dependent on a number of factors, including existing business agreements, existing infrastructures and services, geographic locations, available software/hardware, and others.

In the following, we use the term *service provider* (SP) loosely, as it can refer to a new WISP, a traditional ISP, a carrier, MNO, or combinations of these. The three roaming models are as follows:

- *Bilateral model.* Here, a relationship between two SPs is assumed to exist where they enter into bilateral contractual agreement, allowing one SP's customer to use another's hotspots.

  In this model, each SP would need to maintain a list of originating domains, allowable users, and even some kind of routing table. In general, for a large number of SPs this model does not scale as each SP would need to enter into $n * (n - 1)$ bilateral agreements with every other SP, where n equals the total number of roaming partners.

- *Roaming consortium model.* Here, a collection of SPs establish a roaming consortium that sets contractual roaming agreements for all its members. The consortium may also act as a clearinghouse that stores the routing table, list of member domains, and possibly a list of customers. Once set up, such a body can easily add new members who agree to participate in the pricing and billing structure established by the consortium organization.

- *Broker/aggregator model.* Here, an organization acts as a broker or intermediary between multiple SPs. In contrast to the consortium model, an SP may buy services from the broker on a more flexible and varied basis (e.g., on a per-use only basis). As such, this model may be more attractive to SPs compared to the consortium model.

  In this model, the broker maintains a relationship with each SP, negotiating pricing and other roaming support details independently and confidentially. An SP that signs up a relationship with the broker agrees to allow the broker to use other SPs, according to an acceptable *service level agreement* (SLA). Thus, for example, when a user roams into a visited hotspot, that hotspot provider (WISP) will forward the AAA session to the broker. If the broker is unable to authorize this session, it may forward it to the appropriate SP who can authorize it (e.g., the SP who actually owns the user).

The first two models represent the traditional model for (wired) ISPs, extended for WISPs. These models carry over much of the inherent operational difficulties of legacy authentication/authorization systems. Furthermore, they presume that business relationships exist among the concerned SPs, in order to manage and pass billing information among the roaming partners.

9.3.3 WiFi Roaming Security Requirements: A Classification

Aside from the security issues surrounding 802.11 technology, WiFi roaming has brought additional security issues that need to be addressed. In this section we briefly attempt to classify these issues according to a basic network topology that spans from the client (supplicant) to the corporate network. In looking at the criteria for classification, it is important to realize that in reality there are a number of ways the entities are involved and services are provisioned. Thus, a single solution to cover all these situations is impractical, if not impossible. Furthermore, the classification ignores the fact that business relationships exist between the entities and that the end-user can be a consumer (subscriber) that is "owned" by differing entities.

To simplify the discussion, we employ the notion of an *AAA session*, which can involve differing end points. For example, authentication could be against an ISP, while authorization is actually obtained from a corporate server (i.e., the user's employer) and accounting/billing is handled by yet another entity.

Figure 9.4 shows a simplified classification or grouping of security requirements in WiFi roaming, where again the term "service provider" (SP) is used to mean ISPs, WISPs, carriers, and MNOs. The basic idea here is that a client needs to be authenticated against a AAA server before the client can obtain IP connectivity at the WiFi hotspot. Typically, service providers only provide connectivity to the "open Internet" at the IP layer, beyond which the user/client needs to provide additional protection for traffic flowing over the IP connection (e.g., through IPsec-VPNs). The classification is as follows:

- *WLAN hotspot security requirements.* The segment of the AAA session between the client and first-hop AAA server or AAA proxy needs to be protected against various possible attacks, both at the IP layer and the 802.11 MAC packet layer. Both the IEEE and IETF communities today are working toward solving and standardizing solutions.

- *Inter-SP security requirements.* If an authentication session traverses SP boundaries, then protection needs to be provided for that session. This includes cases where a broker/aggregator is involved in the AAA session. This means that security mechanisms and policies governing provider-to-provider interaction needs to be deployed. Often, this interaction is dependent on the roaming model underlying the business relationship of the providers.

- *Intra-SP security requirements.* Several ISPs, carriers, and MNOs are large enough that they run dozens to hundreds of AAA servers and proxies within their own network. Thus, a AAA session must be protected even within the internal networks of SPs. Some SPs today use a permanent or semi-permanent IPsec-VPN or SSL-VPN between pairs of AAA servers in a fully connected graph fashion.

- *SP-to-corporate security requirements.* The last segment of the AAA session is often between a service provider with an enterprise, in the case of the roaming employee. In such cases, the final authorizer is the corporate AAA server. Note that in many instances, the authorization request (for the employee to obtain IP connectivity at a WiFi hotspot) need not go all the way to the corporate AAA server. Depending on the business agreement between the service provider and the corporation, the corporation may simply trust the service provider for all authorizations (e.g., up to a certain threshold or cost, based on some metric).

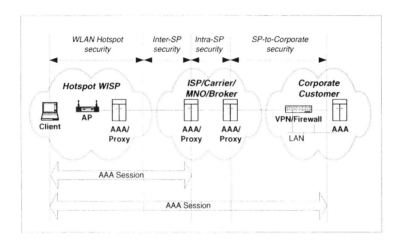

Figure 9.4 A classification of security requirements in WiFi roaming.

9.4 WISPR: THE WIRELESS ISP ROAMING ARCHITECTURE

As mentioned previously in Chapter 2, a small group of networking hardware vendors and ISPs inside the *Wireless Ethernet Compatibility Alliance* (WECA), called the *Wireless ISP roaming* (WISPr) group [11], began developing a framework for AAA function in the context of WiFi roaming. The WiFi Alliance is a nonprofit international association formed in 1999 to certify interoperability of wireless LAN products based on IEEE 802.11 specifications. The WISPr group was chartered by WFA to describe the recommended operational practices, technical architecture, and authentication, authorization, and accounting (AAA) framework needed to enable subscriber roaming among WiFi-based WISPs [11].

In this section we briefly look at the WISPr example as an illustration of WiFi roaming in practice. The WISPr architecture is shown in Figure 2.2 in Chapter 2, while its topology is similar to that shown in Figure 9.4. A roaming user obtains WiFi services at a hotspot run by a hotspot operator (or WISP, in our current terminology). The hotspot operator runs the access points, one or more *public access control* (PAC) gateways, and one or more AAA servers (e.g.,

RADIUS [10] or Diameter [12]). A given AAA session may traverse through a "roaming intermediary" (which is optional), terminating at a *home entity*, which in practice could be the user's corporate AAA server or a AAA server at a home ISP. As mentioned in Chapter 2, for user authentication WISPr uses the Web-based password approach, called *universal access method* (UAM).

9.4.1 Hotspot Operational Aspects

The PAC gateway is used by hotspot operators to provide the access and services control in their WiFi network. The PAC gateway performs several key functions for the hotspot operator in order to support the UAM authentication method. Besides user authentication, the primary PAC gateway functions include the following [11]:

- *IP address management.* The hotspot operator or WISP needs to manage the user's IP address allocation, before authentication (over an IP connection) can occur. Note that this in contrast to the 802.1X authentication approach where IP address allocation is subject to a successful authentication.

    Several methods may be used for providing IP layer connectivity to the user. These include a DHCP lease to the user, or address translation for those users who already posses a static IP address. The PAC gateway may support DHCP server functions (and/or DHCP relay functions) to provide the user with a public or private IP address obtained from the pool of addresses belonging to the WISP. Note that if a private address is allocated, then in order to support a user's VPN, the PAC gateway has to perform address translation and support VPN protocols.

- *Home page redirection.* Crucial to the UAM approach is home page redirection, which provides the ability of the PAC gateway to intercept the initial HTTP request (destined to an *origin server*) of the user's browser. The user is then redirected to the WISP's welcome page. In order to prevent a man-in-the-middle attack on the user's username/password while in transit, an SSL layer must underlie the HTTP connection to the WISP's page. The PAC gateway needs to also include the ability to detect and adapt for browser proxy configuration, such as being configured to use a private proxy server. This assures that users are able to access the WISP's welcome page without having to reconfigure their browsers proxy settings.

- *Authorization.* The WISPr group has specified a number of *WISPr attributes* (for RADIUS) which must be supported by WISPs that participate in the WISPr initiative. Thus, during a given AAA session, a PAC gateway should enforce the services each user is authorized for as specified by the WISPr attributes (as returned by the home entity during the RADIUS authentication process). Examples of these attributes include service time periods and service bandwidth levels.

- *Accounting.* The PAC gateway must provide accurate and timely RADIUS accounting records for billing purposes. These accounting records must identify the location, duration, and service level of the call.

- *RADIUS client functionality.* In order to perform AAA functions, the PAC gateway must implement RADIUS-client functionality (as the PAC gateway will be a RADIUS client when interacting with the RADIUS server at the home entity). The PAC gateway must also provide for both explicit (active) and implicit (passive) logoff capabilities. In order to support explicit logoff, it should deliver a logoff pop-up to the user's browser. In either case, the event must trigger a RADIUS *accounting stop record*, containing information about the session duration and bytes transferred. The PAC gateway should also support RADIUS challenge-response using the RADIUS *access-challenge* messages.

9.4.2   AAA Sessions in WISPr

An example of an AAA session in the context of WISPr is shown in Figure 9.5. Here, the entities involved are similar to those mentioned in Section 9.3.1. The hotspot operator is the WISP, while the roaming intermediary in WISPr could be an ISP, carrier, MNO, or a broker/aggregator. The home entity can either be a corporation running (its own AAA server) or a "home ISP" with whom the corporate customer or the individual subscriber has a business relationship.

Figure 9.5 shows a number of events that reveal the importance of the PAC gateway in the WISPr architecture. In event 1 and event 2, the initial network connectivity (i.e., 802.11 association) between the client and the WISP occurs. Once the user opens his or her browser (event 3), an SSL session is opened between the client and the PAC gateway. The user's name/ID and password is then delivered protected by this SSL session (events 4, 5, and 6). The PAC gateway converts the user's name and password from the HTTPS connection to a RADIUS authentication message (event 7) and triggers the authentication process at the RADIUS server at the home entity. If the user is successfully authenticated by the RADIUS server and a RADIUS authentication-accept message has been received by the PAC gateway from the RADIUS server (event 8), the PAC gateway signals an accounting-start message to the RADIUS server (event 9). The accounting-start message indicates the beginning of the billable session and the user is automatically redirected to the start page of the WISP (as specified in the *vendor-specific attributes* list coming from the home entity in event 10).

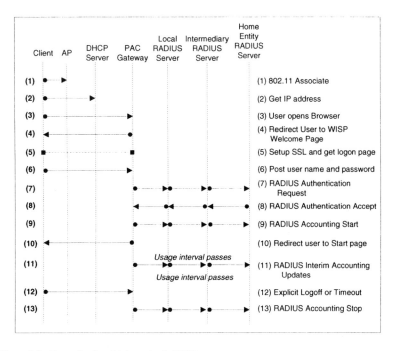

Figure 9.5   Example of an AAA session in WISPr.

Throughout the connection session, periodic interim accounting updates are sent from the PAC gateway to the home entity (event 11). This is done periodically to limit the loss of accounting information should one or more of these entities crash or if some RADIUS messages are lost. The accounting update information is specified by the home entity in its RADIUS attributes list. Once the user is finished with the session and issues an explicit logoff (event 12), or if a timeout occurs, the PAC gateway sends a RADIUS accounting-stop message to the home entity, indicating the end of the user's connection session.

Note that the above basic events are not particularly new or unique to the WISPr approach and most of these steps are used today in dial-up RADIUS accounting. This reflects the conscious decision on the part of WISPr to provide a solution that interoperates with existing legacy authentication infrastructures that are found in many ISPs today, most of which are RADIUS-based.

9.4.3 Alternative Authentication Methods in WISPr

The deficiencies of the Web-based UAM approach for authentication has been described in Chapter 2. Among others, the UAM approach was not integrated into the key management function in the AP and the client and thus could not trigger the establishment of the appropriate keys for use by the encryption algorithm (i.e., TKIP) at the MAC packet layer.

Some members of the WISPr community, however, were aware of this problem and understood the longer-term need for better authentication. As such, the 802.1X authentication framework was proposed as an alternative to the UAM, with the authentication protocols suggested being PEAP and EAP-TLS. The PEAP approach was promising to many ISPs since it was compatible with the user-password approach with which many ISPs were familiar. In addition, since PEAP was an EAP method, the protocol was integrated into the key management aspects of 802.1X. Finally, from a deployment aspect in WISPr, PEAP was being supported by a major networking hardware vendor and thus provided the most promising avenue for a more secure WISPr solution going forward.

9.5 SUMMARY

The WISPr initiative presented one of the earliest efforts toward providing interoperability of WiFi roaming functions across WISPs, guided by a best practices document (BCP) that defined a standard Web-based user interface, a common network architecture, and a common set of RADIUS attributes for AAA requirements. Although WISPr itself was relevant toward providing a framework for all WISPs in the new field of WiFi roaming, the WISPr group itself was initiated within WECA (now WiFi Alliance), which is essentially a vendor compatibility and certification body. Hence, the primary interest of the vendors participating in WECA was to ensure that their products — hardware and software — correctly implemented the IEEE 802.11 and 802.1X specifications and were interoperable. Hence, although chartered within WECA, the WISPr group remained more or less a small unofficial group inside WECA.

Efforts to bring major carriers and MNOs to WISPr were unsuccessful at that time largely because these large companies were unsure about the future of 802.11 WiFi roaming (despite tremendous uptake of 802.11 gear by the home consumer market). They were also unclear about how to integrate WiFi roaming into their existing networks and unsure about the WiFi roaming business model. In addition, in North America many were in the process of migrating their networks to 2G and/or 2.5G technologies. Other similar efforts, such as *Pass-One* [13] in 2002, also met with difficulties in both the definition of their business model and in the uptake by vendors and operators in North America.

References

[1] S. Kent and R. Atkinson, "IP Encapsulating Security Payload (ESP)," RFC 2406 (Proposed Standard), Internet Engineering Task Force, Nov. 1998.

[2] D. Harkins and D. Carrel, "The Internet Key Exchange (IKE)," RFC 2409 (Proposed Standard), Internet Engineering Task Force, Nov. 1998.

[3] W. Simpson, "The Point-to-Point Protocol (PPP)." RFC 1661 (Standards Track), July 1994.

[4] L. Blunk and J. Vollbrecht, "PPP Extensible Authentication Protocol (EAP)." RFC 2284 (Standards Track), Mar. 1998.

[5] B. Aboba, "Extensible Authentication Protocol (EAP)." RFC 3748 (Standards Track), June 2004.

[6] W. Simpson, "PPP Challenge Handshake Authentication Protocol (CHAP)." RFC 1994 (Standards Track), Aug. 1996.

[7] G. Zorn and S. Cobb, "Microsoft PPP CHAP Extensions." RFC 2433 (Standards Track), Oct. 1998.

[8] B. Aboba and D. Simon, "PPP EAP TLS Authentication Protocol." RFC 2716 (Experimental), Oct. 1999.

[9] B. Aboba and M. Beadles, "The Network Access Identifier (NAI)." RFC 2486 (Standards Track), Jan. 1999.

[10] C. Rigney, S. Willens, A. Rubens, and W. Simpson, "Remote Authentication Dial In User Service (RADIUS)." RFC 2865 (Standards Track), June 2000.

[11] B. Anton, B. Bullock, and J. Short, "Best Current Practices for Wireless Internet Service Provider (WISP) Roaming," Best Practices Document, Wireless Ethernet Compatibility Alliance (WECA), Wireless ISP Roaming (WISPr) Initiative, Mar. 2002.

[12] P. Calhoun, J. Loughney, E. Guttman, G. Zorn, and J. Arkko, "Diameter Base Protocol." RFC 3588 (Proposed Standard), Sept. 2003.

[13] Pass-One, "Pass-One Global Roaming Specification — General Description of WISP-provided Roaming Services." Technical Specifications, Pass-One Consortium, May 2002, Draft 1.0.

Chapter 10

3G-WLAN Roaming

10.1 INTRODUCTION

WiFi roaming has recently taken an interesting direction in North America due to the entrance of a number of *mobile network operators* (MNO) into this space. These MNOs want to enhance their 2G and 2.5G (and later their 3G) offerings with WiFi-related services. Many MNOs already perceive that in practice UMTS may not reach its theoretical data rates of 2 Mbps. Thus, WiFi at hotspots — with speeds of up to 11 Mbps in 802.11b and up to 54 Mbps in 802.11a — may provide a solution for the need for higher data rates complementing their 2.5G and 3G offerings. From a content perspective, the marriage of GSM/UMTS and WiFi roaming makes very good sense. The ability of 802.11 WiFi hotspots to provide high-speed connectivity to the Internet makes it attractive for downloading richer content for mobile devices (e.g., PDAs and GSM phones) beyond the ring tones of today. Such content may include MP3 music files, interactive online games, and MPEG4 video clips, depending on the capabilities of the device.

10.2 A BRIEF HISTORY OF GSM AND 3G

Currently in North America a number of wireless telecommunications providers are introducing the *global system for mobile communications* (GSM), which could be called second generation or 2G (with the old analog system being first generation or 1G). In both Europe and Asia GSM is the dominant approach for wireless voice communications, using *time division multiple access* (TDMA) as the radio transmission technology. In North America 2G GSM systems are either based on TDMA (IS-136) or based on CDMA (IS-95A). Typically, 2G phones today have a data transmission rate of only 9.6 Kbps.

Since the cost of 3G network development has been made expensive due to the 3G license costs, many carriers are developing 2.5G systems and networks as the next generation offering (or "upgrade") from GSM, serving also as a transition network to true 3G systems. The radio transmission technology used in 2.5G uses packet-switching based on the *general packet radio service* (GPRS) standard, which is also dominant in Europe. Here, data transfer rates can reach up to 50 Kbps. GPRS puts an overlay packet-switched architecture onto the GSM circuit-switched architecture, thereby allowing operators to retain as much as possible their investments in GSM, while obtaining some experience with running packet networks in preparation for 3G in the future.

For North American carriers and operators using TDMA (IS-136) and those using GSM, another possible avenue toward providing packet-switching is to move to *enhanced data for global evolution* (EDGE), referred to also as UWC-136. The UWC-136 standard was developed by the Universal Wireless Communications Consortium and was one of the 3G candidates submitted to the International Telecommunication Union (ITU) by the United States. From the perspective of preserving infrastructure investments and subscribers, EDGE has the advantage that it uses the same TDMA logic channel, frame structure, and the same 200-kHz carrier bandwidth as GSM networks. EDGE is supposed to be able to reach data rates three times that of GPRS, though in practice it may be around 150 Kbps.

10.3   3G-WLAN INTERWORKING: THE 3GPP PERSPECTIVE

The primary technology and standards development community for WiFi roaming in the 3G context has been the *3rd Generation Partnership Project* (3GPP), which is a joint initiative by a number of telecommunications standards bodies in Europe, the United State, Japan and Korea. These bodies have been working together in 3GPP to produce the world wide specifications for the *universal mobile telecommunications system* (UMTS), which is the next generation or 3G system. Since the WLAN technology adoption and the WiFi roaming phenomenon occurred during the development of the next release of the 3GPP specifications (namely, 3GPP Release 6), it was natural for the MNOs to also want to add WLAN interoperability with 3G for the coming release. The term used by the 3GPP community is *interworking*, namely, that of WLAN hotspots and services with the 3G networks.[1]

Figure 10.1 shows the 3GPP perspective on WiFi hotspots and their interworking with the rest of the 3GPP architecture. The first important concept in Figure 10.1 is that of the *home network* and *visited network*, which are architecture entities derived from the GSM world. Users and *user equipment* (UE) are typically

---

1   The current work describes version 2.4.0 (2004-01) of the 3GPP to WLAN interworking specifications [1].

assigned a home network where the user's profile and other parameters are maintained. A GSM operator typically owns all the users assigned to its home network. In GSM and 3G terminology, the home network is referred to as the *home public land mobile network* (HPLMN) while the visited network is the *visited public land mobile network* (VPLMN)

The second important concept is that the 3GPP views WiFi hotspots as an extension of the visited network because from a control perspective the WiFi hotspot may not be under the administration of the home network operator. Finally, viewing WiFi hotspots as a *WLAN access network* allows the development of the specifications for 3G (in 3GPP) and for WiFi (in IEEE and IETF) to proceed more or less on parallel tracks, with as little interdependency as possible. Note that in Figure 10.1 the user is assumed to possess either a *subscriber identity module* (SIM) card for GSM networks or UMTS SIM (USIM) card used for 3G/UMTS networks.

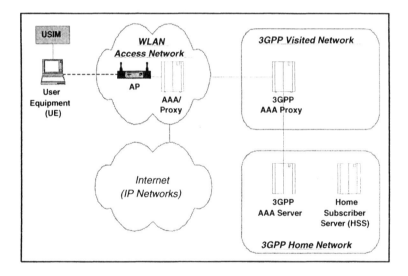

Figure 10.1 The 3GPP view of WiFi hotspots.

In looking at the basic topology of Figure 10.1, it is important to note that the WLAN access network (i.e., WiFi hotspot) may belong to a traditional ISP/WISP or to an MNO. At least three possible scenarios may occur (Figure 10.2):

- Case (a): An MNO owns and operates the WiFi hotspot. Here the user is essentially not roaming in the GSM sense, but simply using a different radio technology and connection transport to obtain *provided services* (PS) at the home network. The MNO is not relying on any other party for its AAA functions.

- Case (b): An MNO (home network) has a direct relationship with a traditional ISP or WISP. Here the user is indeed roaming into a WiFi hotspot operated by a non-GSM and non-UMTS entity. Any PS would be provided by the home network who owns the user.

- Case (c): An MNO (home network) has a direct relationship with a second MNO — which is a true visited network in the GSM sense — who in turn has a direct relationship with the traditional ISP/WISP operating the WiFi hotspot. Thus, in Figure 10.2, a subscriber (of operator MNO No. 2) can roam to the WiFi hotspot by virtue of the fact that operator MNO No. 2 (owning the subscriber) has a relationship with operator MNO No. 1, who in turn has a direct relationship with the ISP/WISP operating the hotspot.

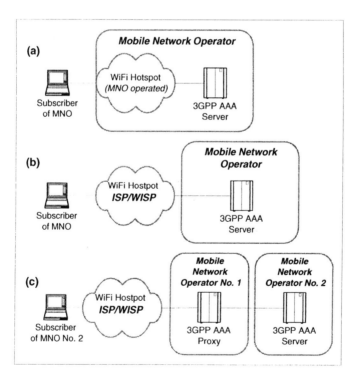

Figure 10.2   3GPP-WLAN possible roaming cases.

10.4 THE 3GPP-WLAN INTERWORKING ARCHITECTURE

The *3GPP-WLAN Interworking* specifications [1] provide a reference model for both roaming and nonroaming. In the nonroaming reference model (Figure 10.3), the 3GPP home network directly interacts with the WLAN access network, without the aid of a visited network. All 3G-specific services are obtained by the user from the home network. In the roaming reference model, 3G-specific provided-services could be obtained either from the home network (Figure 10.4) or from the Visitor Network (Figure 10.5).

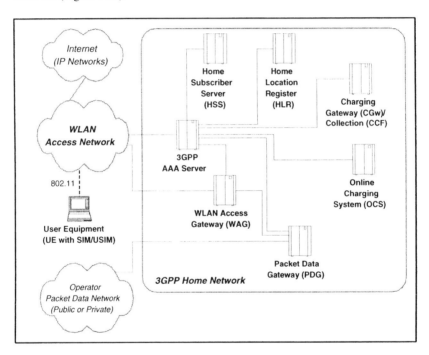

Figure 10.3 3G-WLAN nonroaming reference model.

In looking at the 3GPP-WLAN reference model, it is important to note that a user has two ways to connect to an IP network. It can do so directly from the WiFi hotspot (or WLAN access network) to the open Internet. Alternatively, a tunnel can be setup between the user and the 3GPP home network (more specifically the *Packet Data Gateway* (PDG) at the home network), which carries all of the user's data plane. This second approach is useful and attractive because in many instances both the visited network and the home network operators may want to provide services that are only accessible through the operator's *Packet Data Network* (PDN), which is typically a private IP network (as opposed to the open/public Internet). In 3GPP-WLAN language, these services are referred to as *provided services* (PS) and may include services such as multimedia messaging service (MMS), wireless application protocol (WAP), and 3GPP IP multimedia subsystem (IMS). In the 3GPP-WLAN reference model IP network selection is done using the *WLAN access point name* (W-APN), which is a parameter chosen by the user. Tunnel establishment from the user to the home network PDG (see below) is based on W-APN as the identification parameter.

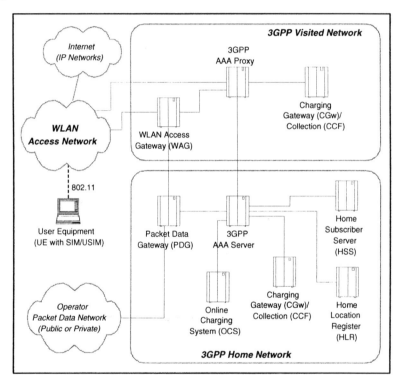

Figure 10.4   3GPP-WLAN roaming reference model — home provided services.

10.4.1   3GPP-WLAN Interworking: Entities

The entities involved in the 3G-WLAN Interworking are as follows [1] (see Figures 10.4 and 10.5):

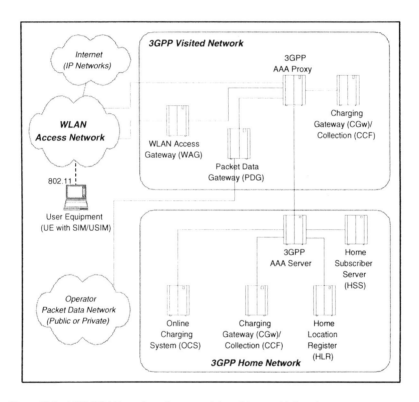

Figure 10.5 3GPP-WLAN roaming reference model — visitor provided services.

- *WLAN user equipment (UE)*. For WLAN use, the UE — namely, the user's laptop, PDA, or other device — is assumed to have either a SIM or USIM card. The WLAN UE functions include the selection of the access point (AP), association with the selected AP, client authentication (using one or more EAP methods for authentication), selection of the visited network (VPLMN) the user is entering, NAI formation, tunnel establishment to the PDG, and accessing services provided in the operator's PS domain.

- *3GPP proxy*. The 3GPP AAA proxy is used in both cases of the roaming reference model (Figures 10.4 and 10.5) and represents proxying and filtering functions that resides in the visited network. Its role includes, among others:

  - Supporting the AAA session between the WiFi hotspot and the 3GPP AAA server at the home network.

  - Enforcement of policy, according to the roaming agreements between 3GPP operators and those between the WISP running the hotspot and the 3GPP operator.

  - Reporting per-user roaming charging/accounting information to the charging gateway/function at the visited network and service termination.

  - Protocol conversion when the AAA session between the WiFi hotspot and the proxy is different from that between the AAA proxy and the AAA server.

  Note that the 3GPP AAA proxy functionality can reside in a separate physical network node, within the 3GPP AAA server, or within any other physical network node.

- *3GPP AAA server*. Typically, the 3GPP AAA server is located within the home network. Among others, its functions include:

  - Retrieving authentication information and subscriber profile from the HLR/HSS of the user's home network.

  - Authenticating the user based on the authentication information retrieved from HLR/HSS and communicating authorization information to the WLAN access network (i.e., WiFi hotspot). This is done possibly through one or more AAA proxies.

  - Registering its own AAA server IP address with the HLR/HSS for each authenticated and authorized user. It also initiates the purge procedure when the 3GPP AAA server deletes the information regarding a user.

- Reporting per-user roaming charging/accounting information to the charging gateway/function at the user's home network.

- Communicating service authorization information to the PDG (see the following).

• *Home location register (HLR) and home subscriber server (HSS).* The HSS/HLR are entities in GSM that are used here also for user authentication in WLAN-3G interworking.

  Traditionally the HLR is a database located in the home network (or more precisely, the home PLMN), which is responsible for the maintenance of user subscription information. In addition, the HLR may provide routing information for mobile terminated calls and *short message service* (SMS), by distributing this information to *visitor location register* (VLR) in a visited network. The HSS is a database of variables and identities for the support, establishment and maintenance of calls and sessions made by subscribers. The HSS can be logically viewed as a single database, though in practice it can be made of several physical databases. The parameters stored include the user's *international mobile subscriber identity* (IMSI), security variables (e.g., SIM/USIM parameters), and location information.

  Together, the HLR/HSS can be viewed as the entity located within the user's 3GPP home network which contains authentication and subscription data required for the 3GPP subscriber to access the WLAN interworking service.

• *WLAN access gateway (WAG).* The WAG is a gateway through which the data to/from the WLAN access network is routed (through a PLMN), in order to provide the user's UE with 3G PS-based services. This is relevant in the 3GPP roaming reference model because tunnels may be established between the user's UE and the PDG (see below), where the PDG acts as a gateway to remote IP networks.

  In the roaming cases (Figures 10.4 and 10.5), the WGA is located in the visited network, while in the nonroaming model (Figure 10.3) it is located in the home network. Among others, its functions include the following:

- In the case of roaming, it supports the visited network in generating charging information for user's obtaining access at a hotspot.

- It enforces routing of packets through the PDG and collects per-tunnel accounting information used later for interoperator settlements. Statistics collected include volume count (byte count) and elapsed time.

- It performs packet filtering, forwarding those that are either part of an existing tunnel (from the UE to the PDG) or are control-messages relating to the tunnel establishment and other service requests. Typically, the WAG drops all packets from unknown IP addresses.

- *Packet data gateway (PDG)*. The PDG is a gateway for the user to connect to remote IP networks through the visited network and the home network. This connection takes the form of a tunnel from the user's UE to the PDG in the user's 3GPP home network, with the PDG being the terminating point of all tunnels. Its function includes the following:

  - It holds routing information for users connected at a hotspot (WLAN access network) and routes packets from/to the user to/from the operator's *Packet Data Network* (PDN), which is typically a private IP network.

  - It supports the allocation of the user's (UE) remote IP address. When an external IP network address allocation is used, the PDG relays to the UE the remote IP address that has been allocated (by an external IP network) for that UE.

  - It performs address translation and mapping. The PDG performs registration of the UE's local IP address and the binding of this address with the UE's remote IP address. The PDG also provides procedures for unbinding.

  - The PDG generates per-user charging information relating to data traffic.

  - It may also function as a policy enforcement point and perform *quality of service* (QoS) on the user's traffic.

Note that in the case where the provided service (PS) is given by the home network operator (Figure 10.4), the PDG is located within the home network, while if the PS is given by a visited network operator (Figure 10.5), then it is located at the visited network.

10.4.2   3G-WLAN Roaming: The NAI

In order to provide roaming compatibility with the existing AAA infrastructures in the IP world, the 3GPP-WLAN interworking specifications [1] have adopted the same NAI realm structure [2] as that for dial-up roaming (see Section 9.2.3). However, for 3G-WLAN roaming, the NAI contents must be derived from the PLMN identifier that is obtained from the IMSI, which is a unique 15-digit number that designates the subscriber. An IMSI identifier consists of the *mobile country code* (MCC) portion, *mobile network code* (MNC) portion, and *mobile station identity number* (MSIN) identifying the unit.

In simple terms, to make up the NAI a period (dot) is placed between the MCC and MNC. The order is reversed and then concatenated to the WLAN realm name. Thus, for example, assuming a home network with the realm

```
HomeNetwork.3GPPnetwork.org
```

for an IMSI value of 234150123456789, with the MCC portion being 234, the MNC portion being 15, and the MSIN portion being 0123456789, the home network NAI will take the form of

```
15.234.HomeNetwork.3GPPnetwork.org
```

The reader is directed to [1] for further developments on the NAI format for 3G-WLAN roaming.

10.4.3 3G-WLAN Roaming: Security Issues and Requirements

As mentioned in Chapter 4 the authentication protocol used in GSM has been the *subscriber identity module* (SIM), while for UMTS it will be *UMTS subscriber identity module* (USIM) [3]. Both take the physical form of a *universal integrated circuit card* (UICC), with the next generation based on tamperproof smartcard technology. In the context of 3G-WLAN roaming, the proposed protocols (EAP methods) for authentication are EAP-SIM [4] for SIM-based users and EAP-AKA [5] for USIM-based users.

The choice of the SIM and AKA methods for authentication has been dictated by the need of the MNOs to keep as much as possible their back-end AAA infrastructure unmodified for WiFi usage. However, since the SIM and AKA protocol were designed for GSM/UMTS networks, they are not transferable to the IP world without introducing some vulnerabilities [6]. Thus, the "naked" SIM or AKA exchange needs protection while in the IP segment of the end-to-end handshake between the SIM/USIM card (in the UE) and the HLR/HSS at the home network. One possible solution around this problem is to wrap the SIM/AKA exchange within a TLS layer, which can be done by layering the SIM or AKA handshake above (wrapped within) PEAP or TTLS (see Chapter 4).

However, in addition to these issues that are specific to EAP-SIM and EAP-AKA, the 3GPP-WLAN interworking security specifications [7] have also outlined a number of other issues and requirements. Some of these are as follows:

- *Mutual authentication.* In addition to the user authenticating itself to the home network, the network must in turn authenticate itself to the user. As mentioned in Section 4.6, the EAP-AKA protocol provides this feature.

- *Signaling and user data protection.* The subscriber should have at least the same security level for WLAN access as for his or her current cellular access subscription. This requirement translates to the need to protect the interfaces or connections between the WiFi hotspot (namely, the WLAN access network) and the 3GPP network, between the 3GPP AAA proxy to the 3GPP AAA server, and between the 3GPP server and the HSS. These interfaces are in general similar to those shown in Figure 9.4.

For the connection between the WiFi hotspot and the 3GPP network, since the specifications of [7] have to accommodate legacy WLAN access networks, most likely the protocol used will be RADIUS [8–10] or Diameter [11].

- *Identity privacy.* The user's privacy while roaming from one WiFi hotspot to another needs to be guarded. That is, when the user is assigned a temporary identifier (or pseudonym), it should be infeasible for an attacker to reverse the process and correlate the pseudonym with the actual user identifier. Naturally, it should also be infeasible for an attacker to generate a valid pseudonym. Note that temporary identifiers can be used within EAP-AKA.

- *Protection of the interface between UIC and WLAN access devices.* Here, the concern relates to the wish of operators to reuse existing UICC and GSM SIM cards in laptops and PDAs, which may have different physical security measures than mobile handsets. Thus, the UE is perceived to possibly have a functional split implemented over several physical devices/components, where one device holds the UICC/SIM card, while another device provides WLAN access.

  The interface across this functional split needs to be protected. There is little point in providing a near tamper-free UICC or SIM card, when the WLAN-access device at the user (e.g., radio circuitry or WLAN software/hardware) can be manipulated by an attacker to obtain Provided Service (PS) from the home network or visited network, as these services are core to the business of MNOs.

  The aim is to provide protection to the level where attacking the PS domain (in UMTS network) by compromising the WLAN access device is at least as difficult as attacking the PS domain by compromising the card-holding device.

  It is for this reason that there is currently interest in providing EAP functionality on board the UICC, thereby achieving true end-to-end EAP-AKA (or EAP-SIM) exchange between the network and the UICC (instead of the laptop hosting the UICC).

The reader is directed to [7,12] for further discussion on other security issues within 3GPP-WLAN interworking. The reader is also directed to [13] for a good overview of 3G-WLAN interworking efforts and to the specifications [1] for further details.

10.5 SUMMARY

With the recent adoption of 2G and 2.5G technology by MNOs in North America, there is a growing momentum toward providing WiFi roaming services for subscribers of the MNOs. The full roll out of WiFi roaming capabilities and services across MNOs may take some time to achieve. However, in itself the interworking between 3G networks and WiFi hotspots is by no means an easy task from a technical perspective. In addition, many North American operators are either completing or have just completed their transition to 2G and 2.5G. Therefore, they are holding back on WiFi roaming services until such time that enough hotspots have been rolled out to make the business viable and until mainstream portable computing devices — such as laptops and PDAs — have SIM or USIM card readers. Security plays an increasingly important role in all the factors and trends affecting 3G-WLAN interworking.

This chapter has looked at interworking between 3G systems and WiFi hotspots. Many MNOs view WiFi hotspots — with their high data rates — as providing a potential for business revenue, complementing their current 2G and 2.5G offerings. The 3G-WLAN interworking is particularly relevant to MNOs since the next generation (3G) networks can only provide data rates below that of 802.11 WLANs. Thus, the combination of 3G, WiFi, voice-over-IP, rich content, and strong digital rights management (DRM) systems promises these MNOs new sources of revenue in the future.

References

[1] 3GPP, "3GPP System to Wireless Local Area Network (WLAN) Interworking — System Description (Release 6)," Technical Specification Group Services and System Aspects TS 23.234 Version 2.4.0, 3rd Generation Partnership Project (3GPP), Jan. 2004.

[2] B. Aboba and M. Beadles, "The Network Access Identifier (NAI)," RFC 2486 (Standards Track), Jan. 1999.

[3] 3GPP, "3GPP TS 33.102 V5.1.0: Technical Specification Group Services and System Aspects; 3G Security; Security Architecture (Release 5)," 3GPP Technical Specification, 3rd Generation Partnership Project (3GPP), Dec. 2002.

[4] H. Haverinen and J. Salowey, "EAP SIM Authentication," draft-haverinen-pppext-eap-sim-12 (work in progress), Internet Engineering Task Force, Oct. 2003.

[5] J. Arkko and H. Haverinen, "EAP AKA Authentication," draft-arkko-pppext-eap-aka-11.txt (work in progress), Internet Engineering Task Force, Oct. 2003.

[6] U. Blumenthal and S. Patel, "EAP-SIM Security Analysis: Keyspace and Mutual Authentication Weaknesses," Proceedings of the 57th IETF, (Vienna, Austria), July 2003.

[7] 3GPP, "Wireless Local Area Network (WLAN) Interworking Security — 3G Security (Release 6)," Technical Specification Group Services and System Aspects TS 33.234 Version 0.8.0, 3rd Generation Partnership Project (3GPP), Dec. 2003.

[8] C. Rigney, S. Willens, A. Rubens, and W. Simpson, "Remote Authentication Dial In User Service (RADIUS)." RFC 2865 (Standards Track), June 2000.

[9] C. Rigney, "RADIUS Accounting." RFC 2866 (Informational), June 2000.

[10] B. Aboba and P. Calhoun, "RADIUS Support for Extensible Authentication Protocol (EAP)." RFC 3579 (Informational), Sept. 2003.

[11] P. Calhoun, J. Loughney, E. Guttman, G. Zorn, and J. Arkko, "Diameter Base Protocol." RFC 3588 (Proposed Standard), Sept. 2003.

[12] G. Koien and T. Haslestad, "Security Aspects of 3G-WLAN Interworking," *IEEE Communications Magazine*, vol. 41, pp. 82–88, Nov. 2003.

[13] K. Ahmavaara, H. Haverinen, and R. Pichna, "Interworking Architecture Between 3GPP and WLAN Systems," *IEEE Communications Magazine*, vol. 41, pp. 74–81, Nov. 2003.

Part IV

WMAN Security

Chapter 11

An Overview of 802.16 WMANs

11.1 INTRODUCTION

The area of broadband Internet has gained a lot of interest in recent years due the exciting business opportunities enabled by high-speed Internet connectivity to homes and businesses. Content owners (e.g., movie studios and record labels) and content providers/distributors (e.g., music and MPEG4 download services) see broadband Internet to the home as crucial to providing the next source of revenue, as it solves the difficult "last mile access" problem. Thus, if "content is king" as the saying goes, last mile access is the "queen" that enables content to flow to the consumer.

Today, only a fraction of U.S. households have broadband Internet, in the form of cable modem services or DSL services. The mid-2004 subscriber numbers indicate that there are just over 18 million subscribers to broadband Internet. This is due, among others, to the difficulty in installing cables for those services in dense areas with old buildings and infrastructures, despite the fact that the two technologies have reached maturity. Furthermore, in many areas in the United States consumers who do have cable modem services available are unable to choose among service providers because a virtual monopoly has been established by one (or two) provider(s). The opportunity to remedy the situation is somewhat better in countries who are still developing their physical infrastructures today since they are able to build in broadband Internet into their infrastructure designs.

It is with this background that *wireless metropolitan area networks* (WMANs) based on the 802.16 technology have recently gained a lot of interest among vendors and ISPs as the possible next development in wireless IP offering and a possible solution for the last mile Access problem. With the theoretical speed of up to 75 Mbps and with a range of several miles, 802.16 broadband wireless offers an alternative to cable modem and DSL, possibly displacing these technologies in the future.

In this chapter we provide an overview of 802.16 WMANs or WiMAX, with particular emphasis on the MAC layer and above, and aspects that are pertinent to the security of 802.16. First we review the basic WMAN network topology and review the general features of 802.16 in Section 11.2. This is followed by a discussion in Section 11.3 on the network entry process used by a subscriber station or client in 802.16. Security discussions begin in Section 11.4 with the PKM protocol that is used in 802.16 for key management and security associations management. Since device certificates are defined by the IEEE 802.16 standard [1], Section 11.5 briefly covers the issue of certificates and certificate hierarchies.

In the following discussions we use the terms *wireless MAN* (WMAN), *broadband wireless access* (BWA), and *WiMAX* interchangeably to mean 802.16-based wireless networks and the technologies underlying these networks. The term broadband wireless access or BWA is the formal title used in the IEEE 802.16 standards documents, while WiMAX is the industry's coined term for the technology (much in the same way that *WiFi* has been used for 802.11). We use the more general wireless MAN to mean both the technology and the industry around the technology.

Note that this chapter is intended to provide only a brief introductory overview of 802.16 in order to focus on security-related issues. Thus, little is provided on the physical and MAC layers of 802.16. As such, the reader is directed to the work of [2] for a good summary of those layers. Those who need further details on the physical and MAC layers of 802.16 — but who find the IEEE 802.16 standard [1] to be difficult to absorb — are directed to the excellent work of [3]. Finally, the reader who seeks broader discussion on the network architecture aspects of 802.16 is directed to the work of [4] for an interesting and useful point-of-view on this topic.

11.2   BACKGROUND ON 802.16 WMANS

In this section we briefly cover some characteristics of 802.16 WMANs. The aim is to provide enough context for the ensuing sections and for discussions regarding security-related issues. As such, much of the technical details regarding the physical and MAC layers are not covered, and the interested reader is directed to the IEEE 802.16 standard documents.

11.2.1   The Basic 802.16 Network Arrangement

The basic arrangement of an 802.16 network or cell consists of one (or more) *base stations* (BSs) and multiple *subscriber stations* (SSs). Depending on the frequency of transmission, the SS may or may not need to be in the line-of-sight of the BS antenna. In addition to base stations and subscriber stations, there might also be other entities within the network, such as *repeater stations* (RSs) and routers, which provide connectivity of the network to one or more core or backbone networks. This is shown in Figure 11.1. The BS has a number of tasks within the cell, including management of medium access by the SS, resource allocation, key management, and other security-related functions.

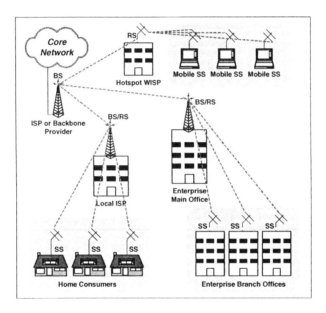

Figure 11.1 The 802.16 WiMAX network topology.

An implementation of an 802.16 network will typically deploy a fixed antenna for the SS, with the BS using either a sectored antenna or omnidirectional antenna. The BS would be installed in a location that can provide the best coverage, which would usually be the rooftops of buildings and other geographically high locations. Although a fixed SS would use a fixed antenna, with the future development of the *mobile subscriber station* (MSS), it is possible that an SS could be using an omnidirectional antenna. In practice, the cell size would be about 5 miles or less in radius. However, given suitable environmental conditions and the use of *orthogonal frequency division multiplexing* (OFDM), the cell radius can reach 20 or even 30 miles. In order to increase the range of a given implementation, a *mesh topology* can also be used instead of the point-to-point topology.

11.2.2   Frequency Bands in 802.16

The 802.16 standard release in December 2001 defines the MAC and PHY layers for 802.16 WMANs. Within the MAC layer, the 802.16 standard specifies the support for multiple physical layer specifications, in answer to the broad frequency range of 802.16 (namely, the 2-GHz to 66-GHz band). Since the electromagnetic propagation in this broad range is not uniform all over, the 802.16 standard splits the range into three different frequency bands, each to be used with a different physical layer implementation as necessary. The three frequency bands are as follows:

- *10 to 66 GHz (licensed bands)*: Transmission in this band requires line-of-sight between a BS and SS. This is due to the fact that within this frequency range the wavelength is very short, and thus fairly susceptible to attenuation (e.g., due the physical geography of the environment or interference). However, the advantage of operating in this frequency band is that higher data rates can be achieved.

- *2 to 11 GHz (licensed bands)*: Transmission in this band does not require line-of-sight. However, if line-of-sight is not available, the signal power may vary significantly between the BS and SS. As such, retransmissions may be necessary to compensate.

- *2 to 11 GHz (unlicensed bands)*: Here, the physical characteristics of the 2 to 11 GHz unlicensed bands are similar to the licensed bands. However, since they are unlicensed there are no guarantees that interference may not occur due to other systems or persons using the same bands.

11.2.3   The 802.16 Protocol Layers

The 802.16 protocol layer consists of the *physical layer*, the *security sublayer* (or *MAC privacy sublayer*), the *MAC common-part sublayer*, and the *MAC convergence sublayer* (also known as *service specific convergence sublayer*). This is shown in Figure 11.2.

The *physical layer* (PHY) supports various functions pertaining to frequency selection, ranging, power control, and others. In the 10- to 66-GHz bands, the BS transmits a TDM signal, while individual SSs are allocated timeslots in a serial manner. Uplink transmission from an SS uses *time division multiple access* (TDMA). In the 2- to 11-GHz bands (both licensed and unlicensed), three air interface specifications have been developed, namely, the *WirelessMAN-SC2* physical layer, the *WirelessMAN-OFDM* physical layer, and the *WirelessMAN-OFDMA* physical layer.

The physical layer provides services to the MAC layer through the PHY *service access point* (SAP). Communication between the two is conducted through primitives for data transfer, management primitives, and other local primitives

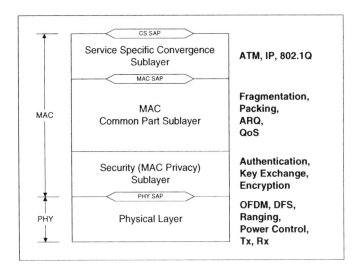

Figure 11.2 The 802.16 protocol layers.

for layer control. As mentioned previously, the 802.16 standard specifies multiple physical layers in order to support the various usage scenarios of the three frequency bands.

11.2.4 The MAC Security Sublayer

The 802.16 MAC security sublayer (also referred to as the MAC privacy sublayer) focuses on the security functions pertaining to the MAC layer frames. It is useful to view this sublayer as consisting of two component protocols [1]:

- *Encapsulation protocol*: This protocol defines the set of "cryptographic suites" that support the encryption of packet data between a BS and SS. The suites include information regarding the pairings of data encryption and authentication algorithms, and the rules for applying the algorithms to a MAC PDU payload.

- *Key management protocol*: This protocol pertains to the management and distribution of keying material from a BS to SS. The protocol of choice here is the *privacy key management* (PKM) protocol already deployed in the DOCSIS-compliant cable modems. The PKM protocol will be discussed further in Section 11.4.

Reminiscent of the ISAKMP, IPsec, and IKE protocols, the MAC security sublayer employs the notion of *security associations* (SAs), which in 802.16 refers to the set of parameters and information shared between a BS and SS to manage secure communications between them. The set of parameters include such things as the traffic encryption keys and initialization vector values for certain ciphers. Each SA in 802.16 is identified by a *security association identifier* (SAID). A BS must ensure that a client SS has access to only the SA which that client SS is authorized to access.

Three different types of SAs are defined in the IEEE 802.16 standard [1]:

- *Primary SA*: Each SS established a unique Primary SA with its BS, and the identifier (SAID) of that primary SA is made equal to the *Basic Connection ID* (CID) of that SS. The Primary SA is established during the SS initialization process (see Section 11.3).

- *Static SA*: The static SA is established within the BS. It is used for internal purpose of the BS.

- *Dynamic SA*: A dynamic SA is created and destroyed as needed in response to the initiation/termination of specific service flows.

The keying material related to a given SA is also assigned a lifetime by the BS, and a given SS is expected to request new keying material from its BS before the current keying material expires. The protocol used to manage keying material — so that there is an overlap in time between expiring and new keying material — is the PKM protocol.

There are some rules with regard to the use of the SA types with the connections between an SS and its BS. Following the BPI+ specifications [5], in 802.16 for a given SS all the upstream traffic from the SS to the BS is protected (encrypted) using the primary SA of the SS. Although typically all downstream unicast traffic is protected using also the primary SA, additionally some selected downstream unicast traffic flows can be protected under static or dynamic SAs. Note that multicast traffic — aimed at multiple SSs — can really only be protected under static or dynamic SAs (as opposed to a primary SA which is unique per SS).

11.3 NETWORK ENTRY AND INITIALIZATION

Before proceeding to discussing the PKM Protocol, which is core to the 802.16 MAC security sublayer, in this section we briefly look at the behavior of a subscriber station in the context of gaining network access and initialization. As we will see, the PKM Protocol is used during the network access and initialization phase, in the authentication and authorization steps.

A subscriber station (SS) must perform a number of tasks before gaining access to a network. These tasks are summarized in the following [2]:

- *Scanning and synchronization*:
  Here the SS must first scan for a downlink signal from the BS and attempt to synchronize with it. If a prior downlink channel existed, the SS will try reusing those operational parameters. Otherwise, the SS must scan all the possible channels in the downlink frequency band. When a channel has been selected, the SS attempts to synchronize with the downlink transmission by detecting the periodic frame preambles.

- *Uplink/downlink channel parameters detection*:
  After synchronization has been established at the physical layer, the SS then proceeds to search for the *downlink channel descriptor* (DCD) and the *uplink channel descriptor* (UCD) messages that are periodically broadcasted by the BS. The DCD and UCD messages carry information regarding the physical layer characteristics of both the downlink and uplink channels. Among others, these messages then allows the SS to learn about the modulation type and forward error correction (FEC) scheme of the carrier. Depending on the PHY specification chosen for a given scenario, the BS also periodically transmits uplink-map (UL-MAP) and downlink-map (DL-MAP) messages that define their burst start times. It is through the DL-MAP and UL-MAP messages that the BS can allocate access to the respective channels.

- *Ranging and SS capabilities negotiation*:
  In this phase, the SS performs *ranging*, which is the process of aligning the SS transmission timing-wise to the start of a slot during contention for access. This process is part of framing and media access in 802.16 and consists of *initial ranging* and *periodic ranging*.

  The initial ranging contention slot is used for network entry. Here, the SS sends a *ranging request* packet (RNG-REQ) in the initial ranging contention slot. If this message is received correctly by the BS, it then responds to the SS with a *ranging response* packet (RNG-RSP) describing the timing and power adjustment information to the SS. This allows the SS to adjust the timing and power of its signal as received by the BS. The response will also tell the SS about the connection IDs (CID) chosen by the BS. The other type of ranging, namely, periodic ranging, provides opportunities for the SS to send ranging-request messages to the BS in order to adjust power levels, time, and frequency offsets.

  After ranging is completed, the SS reports its physical layer capabilities to the BS. This includes the modulation and coding schemes supported by the SS, and whether the SS within the 802.16 *frequency division duplexing* (FDD)

supports half-duplex or full-duplex. The BS has the choice of accepting or rejecting these capabilities of the SS.

- *SS authentication, authorization, and registration*:
  At this stage, the SS must be authenticated by the BS (using the PKM Protocol) and obtain authorization from the BS.

  Each SS device is assigned to an X.509 digital certificate [6], which is physically bound to the device hardware during manufacturing. One possible implementation is to include the device's MAC-address in its certificate. The MAC address in 802.16 is the usual 48-bit address used in other IEEE 802 standards (e.g., Ethernet). It is important to note that just as in DOCSIS-compliant cable modem devices, the digital certificate and the private key are assigned during manufacturing of the SS device. The private key must be embedded in the hardware in such a way that it is difficult or infeasible for the user to access or extract.

  Note that the IEEE 802.16 standard [1] only mandates the SS to be assigned a certificate, and not the BS. This means that authentication is not mutual or symmetric, in that the BS does not authenticate itself to the SS. This is in contrast to the BPI+ specifications [5], which mandates that both endpoints — the CM/client and CMTS/server — be assigned X.509 certificates, respectively.

  After authentication and authorization have been completed, the SS proceeds with the registration phase. Here, the SS sends a *registration request* message to the BS, who responds with a *registration response* message containing among others a secondary management connection ID for the SS and the IP version used for the secondary management connection. The arrival of the registration response message from the BS indicates to the SS that it has been registered in the network and thus allowed to enter the network.

- *IP connectivity*:
  At the completion of registration, the SS can now obtain an IP address through the DHCP protocol, obtain current time information (e.g., through the Internet Time Protocol), and also obtain other parameters from the BS.

- *Service flows setup (optional)*:
  Optionally, if there are service flows that were preprovisioned and were initiated by the BS during SS initialization, then the BS may continue to set up connections for these service flows. Note that, in general, service flows in 802.16 must be preprovisioned. However, service flows can be established in a dynamic fashion by either the BS or SS.

11.4 THE PRIVACY KEY MANAGEMENT (PKM) PROTOCOL

As mentioned previously, the 802.16 MAC security sublayer employs the *Privacy Key Management* (PKM) Protocol to perform key and SA management between the SS (as the client) and the BS (as the server). It is important to note that the PKM protocol employed in 802.16 was borrowed by and large from the DOCSIS specification, which was developed by Cable Laboratories (CableLabs) for the cable television industry and is referred to as the *baseline privacy plus interface specification* or BPI+ [5].

In the following we provide an overview of the PKM Protocol flows in order to provide some context of the behavior of the protocol and provide a summary of message types that are exchanged between the BS and an SS. We then discuss the issue of security associations in 802.16, notably in the PKM protocol. Since the 802.16 MAC security sublayer specification [1] follows very closely the BPI+ specification [5], the reader is directed to the latter for more information about the motivations and design decisions behind the PKM Protocol.

11.4.1 Background to the PKM Protocol

The PKM Protocol is used by an SS to obtain authorization and traffic keying material from the BS, and to support periodic reauthorization and key refresh.

The PKM protocol uses X.509 digital certificates [6, 7], and two-key triple DES to secure key exchanges between a given SS and BS, following the client-server model. Here, the SS as the client requests keying material while the BS as the server responds to those requests, ensuring individual SS clients receive only the keying material for which they are authorized. The PKM protocol first establishes an *authorization key* (AK), which is a secret symmetric key shared between the SS and BS. The AK is then used to secure subsequent PKM exchanges of *traffic encryption keys* (TEK). The use of the AK and a symmetric key cryptosystem (e.g., DES) reduces the overhead due to the computationally expensive public key operations.

The BS authenticates an SS during the initial authorization exchange. As mentioned before, each SS device contains a hardware-bound X.509 device certificate issued by the SS manufacturer. The SS device certificate would contain the RSA public key (whose private half is burned into the device hardware), and other device-specific information, such as its MAC address, serial number, and manufacturer ID. Within the authorization exchange, the SS would then send a copy of this device certificate to the BS. The BS must then verify the syntax and information in the SS certificate, and possibly perform certificate path validation checks. If satisfied, the BS as part of its response to the SS would encrypt the AK (assigned to that SS) using the public key of the SS (found within the received certificate from the SS).

Since only the SS device contains the matching private key, only the SS device can decrypt the message and obtain the AK assigned to it (and begin using the AK).

Note that although the SS device certificate is open to the public (or attacker) to read, only the SS device has access to the matching private key of the public key in the certificate. As such, to prevent a device and its certificate from being cloned, it is paramount that the private key be embedded within the device hardware. That is, the cost of an attacker extracting the private key from the device must be far higher than the possible value obtained from the attacker using the cracked device.

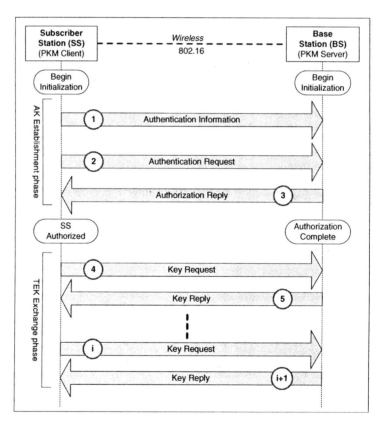

Figure 11.3   Basic PKM protocol flows.

11.4.2 Authorization Key Establishment

The process of an SS obtaining authorization and an *authorization key* (AK) from a BS consists of several flows, beginning with the SS proving its identity to the BS through the authentication flow. The authorization process is summarized as follows (Figure 11.3):

Flow-1: *SS authentication information message*

The SS as the client initiates the authorization request process by the SS sending an *authentication information* message to the BS. This message is optional and may be ignored by the BS (since the next message, namely, the authorization request message, will contain much of the same information). However, this first message allows the BS to be aware of the SS and learn of the capabilities of the SS.

The authentication information message payload contains the following information:

- The MAC address of the SS;

- The RSA public key of the SS;

- The X.509 certificate of the SS (issued by the manufacturer);

- The list of the cryptographic capabilities supported by the SS;

- The identifier (SAID) of the primary SA of the SS;

- The X.509 CA certificate of the manufacturer of the SS device.

Note that this message allows the BS to immediately verify that the SS possesses a valid primary SA, that the certificates of the SS and of the manufacturer are valid (i.e., not expired or revoked), and that the manufacturer is truly the maker of the SS device.

The description of the set of cryptographic capabilities supported by the SS takes the form of a list of cryptographic-suite identifiers. Each suite identifier indicates a particular pairing of packet data encryption and packet data authentication algorithms the SS supports.

Flow-2: *SS authorization request message*

Immediately following the authentication information message, the SS sends the BS an *authorization request* message, which is actually a request for an AK and for the SAIDs of any static SA in which the SS is authorized to participate. The authorization request message includes the following parameters:

- The SS device serial number and manufacturer ID;

- The MAC address of the SS;

- The RSA public key of the SS;

- The X.509 certificate of the SS (issued by the manufacturer);

- The list of the cryptographic capabilities supported by the SS;

- The identifier (SAID) of the primary SA of the SS.

Note that the SAID of the primary SA of the SS is equal to the primary connection ID or CID (static) that the SS obtained from the BS during the network entry and initialization phase (see Section 11.3).

Flow-3: *BS authorization reply message*
Upon receiving an authorization request message from an SS, the BS verifies the certificate of the SS and checks the set of cryptographic capabilities of the SS. If all is well and the BS supports one or more of the cryptographic capabilities of the SS, the BS sends an authorization reply message to the SS. This message contains the following parameters:

- A unique authorization key (AK), encrypted with the RSA public key of the SS;

- A 4-bit key sequence number, used to distinguish between successive generations of AKs;

- A key lifetime value for the AK;

- The SAIDs and properties of the primary SA, plus zero or more additional static SAs for which the SS is authorized to obtain keying information. This tells the SS of all the static SAs that the BS has information about, associated with the SS. As before, the SAID of the primary SA will be equal to the primary CID.

Note that for security reasons no dynamic SA must be identified in the authorization reply message.

A given SS must periodically refresh its AK for security purposes. This is done by the SS resending the BS an authorization request message. Here reauthorization is identical to authorization (flow-2), except that for reauthorization the SS need not begin with sending the authentication information message (flow-1). This is because the BS knows the identity of the SS and has (at least) one live AK.

Note that a given SS and the BS must be able to support up to two simultaneously active AKs in order to correctly support reauthorization. This is because in order to avoid service interruptions during reauthorizations, successive genera-tions of the AKs must have overlapping lifetimes, with the overlap representing the transition period.

In the next section, we continue with the TEK exchanges phase (flow-4), where the SS obtains TEKs from the BS.

11.4.3 The TEK Exchanges Phase

Upon receiving the authorization reply message (containing SAIDs) from the BS signifying that authorization has been granted to the SS, the SS proceeds to obtain TEKs from the BS. As mentioned above, the authorization reply message contains the SAIDs and properties of the primary SA, plus zero or more additional static SAs for which the SS is authorized to obtain keying information. Therefore, the SS proceeds to start a separate *TEK state machine* for each of the SAIDs identified in the authorization reply message.

Each TEK state machine operating within the SS is responsible for managing the keying material associated with its corresponding SAID. This includes refresh-ing the keying material for those SAIDs. To refresh keying material for a given SAID, the corresponding TEK state machine in the SS uses the *key request* message.

Flow-4: *SS key request message*
A given SS sends a key request message to the BS containing the following parameters:

- The SS device serial number and manufacturer ID;

- The MAC address of the SS;

- The RSA public key of the SS;

- The SAID of the SA whose keying material is being requested;

- An HMAC-keyed message digest (authenticating/protecting the key request message payload).

Flow-5: *BS key reply message*
The BS responds to key request message from an SS by sending a *key reply* message to that SS. Prior to sending the key reply message, the BS must verify the SS identity and perform the HMAC digest check on the received key request message in order to detect tampering of the message.

If all is well, the BS sends a key reply message that contains the active keying material of the SAID requested by the SS. It is important to note here that at all times the BS maintains two active sets of keying material per SAID. The lifetimes of the two generations overlap such that each generation becomes active halfway through the life of its predecessor and expires halfway through the life of its successor.

The keying material in the key reply message includes the following parameters:

- The TEK (encrypted under triple DES);
- The CBC initialization vector;
- A key sequence number for the TEK;
- The remaining lifetime of each of the two sets of keying material;
- An HMAC keyed message digest (authenticating/protecting the key reply message payload).

Here the TEK is triple-DES encrypted using a key encryption key (KEK) derived from the authorization key (AK) obtained earlier in the authorization reply message (flow-3).

Note that the key reply message contains information about the remaining lifetime of each of the two sets of keying material. This is needed to help the SS estimate the time when the BS will invalidate (i.e., terminate use) a particular TEK. This in turn tells the SS when to schedule future key requests such that the SS requests and receives new keying material before the BS invalidates the keying material that the SS currently holds.

11.4.4   Key Transitions and Synchronizations

As mentioned previously in Section 11.4.2, an SS uses the authorization request (flow-2) to obtain authorization from the BS, while the BS uses the authorization reply (flow-3) to provide the SS with, among other things, an authorization key (AK). The active lifetime value of the AK (as reported by the BS in the authorization reply message) reflects the remaining lifetime of the AK at the time the authorization reply message is sent by the BS. This means that if the SS fails to reauthorize before the expiration of its current AK, the BS will consider the SS as being unauthorized and remove from its keying tables all TEKs associated with the primary SA of that SS.

11.4.4.1   AK Transitions

In order to provide uninterrupted connectivity, the BS actually supports two simultaneously active AKs for each SS, with overlapping lifetimes. The BS realizes that a transition is needed when it receives an authorization request message from an SS and the BS finds that it only has a single active AK for that SS. This event signals the start of the *AK transition period*. The BS then sends an authorization reply message which contains a (new) second AK to the SS.

Since the existing (first) AK will remain valid until its expiration time, the second AK will have a lifetime (set by the BS) to be equal to the remaining lifetime of the first AK plus its own lifetime. Obviously, the second AK's lifetime must be beyond the expiration time of the first AK to make the transition worthwhile. The new/second AK will be assigned a key sequence number one greater (modulo 16) than that of the old/first AK.

Note that by design, a given BS must always be prepared to respond to a request from an SS and reply with a AK. This means that if the BS receives an authorization request message from an SS in the middle of the BS transitioning to a new AK (thus the BS holding both the old active AK and new active AK), the BS will respond by sending the new active AK to the SS. Once the older key expires, an authorization request will trigger the activation of yet another new AK, and the start of a new key transition period.

11.4.4.2 TEK Transitions

Similar to the use of two AKs, a BS and SS must also share two active TEKs (and their keying material) per SAID at any one time. This is achieved using the key request (flow-4) and key reply (flow-5) messages, as discussed in Section 11.4.3. The newer TEK will be assigned a key sequence number one greater (modulo 4) than that of the older TEK.

Note, however, that unlike AKs that are used to protect TEK-carrying messages (downlink), the TEKs are used to protect data traffic in both directions, uplink and downlink. As such, their transition is more complex than AK transitions. In general, it is the BS that drives the transitions of TEKs, and it is the responsibility of the SS to update its TEKs in an optimal manner.

From the perspective of key transitions, there are a number of rules governing TEK transitions. The BS transitions between the two active TEKs differently depending on whether the TEK is used for downlink or uplink traffic:

- For each of the SAIDs used for encryption purposes, at expiration of the older TEK the BS will immediately transition to using the newer TEK.

- An uplink transition period begins from the time the BS sends a key reply message (containing a new TEK) and the transition is considered completed when the older TEK expires.

This represents a comfortable duration for the SS to react and to transition. Regardless of whether the SS has received the new TEK, at the expiration of the older TEK the BS will transition to that new TEK for downlink traffic encryption.

From the perspective of the actual use or application of the two active TEKs, the BS will use the TEKs differently depending on whether the TEK is used for downlink or uplink traffic:

- For encrypting downlink traffic (to an SS) the BS will use the older of the two active TEKs. This is because the BS knows for certain that the SS will have the older of the two TEKs (but not necessarily have obtained the newer TEK). This is, of course, subject to the older TEK still being unexpired.

- For decrypting uplink traffic (from an SS) the BS will apply either the older TEK or the newer TEK. That is, since the BS is unsure as to which of the two TEKs the SS will use for uplink traffic, the BS will apply either of the two keys, as indicated in the packet header (subject to a TEK still being unexpired).

With regard to the actual duration of use of a TEK, it is important to observe that for downlink traffic (to an SS) the BS will encrypt with a given TEK for only the second half of that TEK's total lifetime. In simple terms, this occurs because for a given active TEK the older/previous TEK will still be active and the SS is sure to possess the older/previous TEK. Hence the BS will opt for this sure (older) TEK. The BS will switch to a new TEK when it sees a key request message from the SS. Whereas in contrast, for uplink traffic (from an SS) the BS will be able to decrypt with a TEK for that TEK's entire lifetime This is because the BS will be in possession of whichever of the two active TEKs the SS decides to choose from for its uplink traffic to the BS. The reader is directed to [1, 5] for further discussion on the PKM protocol, key transitions, and other aspects of 802.16 key management.

11.5 CERTIFICATES IN 802.16

Aside from adopting the PKM protocol from the DOCSIS specification [5], the IEEE 802.16 standard [1] also adopted the use of X.509 certificates for the subscriber station (SS) devices. In the current section we discuss the adoption of device certificates by the cable modem manufacturers and service providers and provide a brief overview of the CableLabs certificate hierarchy.

11.5.1 The Need for Certificates in Subscriber Devices

In the case of cable modems, Cable Laboratories (CableLabs) has been the consortium organization that has developed the cable modem specifications and promoted the broad adoption of cable modem technology and services to the broader community. The original project covering the cable modem specifications is known as *Data Over Cable Service Interface Specification* (DOCSIS). The DOCSIS project defined a number of specifications relating to *cable modem* (CM) devices (typically located within the user's premises) and *cable modem termination system* (CMTS) devices (typically located at the service provider premises). Since the completion of the DOCSIS 1.0 specifications, CableLabs has embarked on a number of broader related projects, including *CableHome* (covering digital home networking), *Packet-Cable* (covering Multimedia and VoIP) and *OpenCable* (covering next generation set-top-box technology).

The DOCSIS project and specifications for certified CMs defines interface requirements for cable modems involved in high-speed data distribution over cable television system networks. The project also provides cable modem equipment suppliers with a fast, market-oriented method for attaining cable industry acknowledgment of DOCSIS compliance and has resulted in high-speed modems being certified for retail sale [8]. Thus, one of the primary objectives was to allow the retail sale of CM devices off-the-shelf to the consumer, while inhibiting or preventing the cloning of those CM devices.

Since the need to prevent CM device cloning also came from the cable modem service providers (referred to as *multisystem operators*, or MSOs), the DOCSIS specification mandated that CM devices contain a unique X.509 certificate that was bound to the hardware of the CM. This would allow the CMTS (head end) to identify validly manufactured CM devices (as opposed to clones) using a mutual authentication protocol (namely, the PKM protocol) during the initialization phase of the CM device, immediately after boot-up.

With the IP-based Internet possibly emerging as being the primary medium for transport of future digital content to the home, it was imperative that only authorized CM devices be allowed connectivity to the cable network. With over 17 million cable modem subscribers (and growing) in the United States, it is clear that the security of CM devices and services represented an important concern for the cable modem industry as a whole.

11.5.2   The CableHome Certificate Hierarchy

Originally having started with only a single root certificate for DOCSIS in 2001, today the CableLabs certificate hierarchy consists of three distinct root CA certificates grouped together under the *CableHome certificate hierarchies* [9].

The CableHome certificate hierarchies are as follows (Figure 11.4):

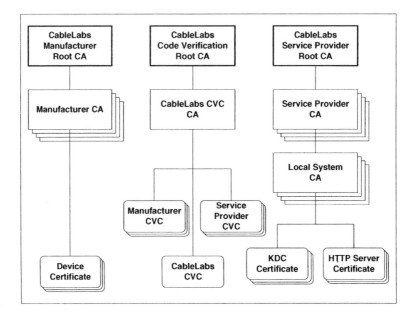

Figure 11.4 The CableLabs CableHome certificate hierarchy.

- *CableLabs manufacturer root CA*: The manufacturer root CA is used to issue manufacturer CA certificates to individual authorized CableLabs manufacturers. A manufacturer who is a member of CableLabs can obtain a manufacturer CA certificate from CableLabs, and use it to issue (sign) individual device certificate for the CM devices which it ships. The manufacturer chain is rooted at the CableLabs manufacturer root CA.

- *CableLabs code verification root CA*: The *code verification certificate* (CVC) root CA is used to issue (sign) code verification certificates to individual manufacturers and service providers. The certificate (i.e., the private key of the public key pair) is used by a manufacturer to provide integrity protection (through digital signatures) for CableLabs compliant software images and firmware updates.

    Thus, for example, this certificate allows them to push downstream (from the CMTS) signed firmware updates to a CM device that is currently in service at a user's home. The CM device will first verify the signature of the firmware update before installing it.

- *CableLabs service provider root CA*: The service provider root CA is used to issue (sign) certificates for a set of authorized CableLabs service providers. This allows a service provider to issue certificates to the system devices within its network.

Note that in order to achieve mutual authentication between a CM as a client and the CMTS as server, certificate path validation must be performed by the CMTS when it is verifying the certificate status of a given CM device. Since all members of CableLabs have access to copies of the manufacturer CA certificates and service provider CA certificates in the CableLabs hierarchy (plus all the root CA certificates in the three respective chains), a CMTS can perform certificate path validation by traversing the chain upwards and verifying the current status of each certificate in the chain (i.e., unexpired and unrevoked).

Typically, besides its own key pair and certificate (issued by its manufacturer), a CM device would also carry a copy of its manufacturer's CVC certificate in order for the CM device to be able to recognize its manufacturer's digital signature (e.g., on firmware update files).

Although CM device certificates have a life time of 10 years or more (depending on the manufacturer), certificate revocation is a function that is required by CableLabs. This function is needed to address cases where a device is found to have been cloned or where more severe security emergencies occur, such as when a manufacturer finds that its root CA certificate has been compromised (e.g., its private key lost or stolen). Although CableLabs began with the use of *certificate revocation lists* (CRL) as the method to perform certificate revocation, it has begun to move towards a more efficient certificate revocation architecture based on the use of real-time certificate status verifications via protocols such as the *online certificate status protocol* (OCSP) [10].

In order to address the issues related to PKI management in the light of manufacturing and operations costs, the CableHome specifications allow for the hosting model for the PKI infrastructure and PKI management. This allows manufacturers or service providers to outsource the management of the PKI relating to the certificates and chains that are relevant to them, thereby reducing operations costs and allowing them to focus on their core business.

11.5.3 A Certificate Hierarchy for the WMAN Industry

The certificate hierarchy employed in CableLabs provides a useful example and possible future direction for manufacturers of 802.16 devices and WMAN service providers. Indeed, such a hierarchy for the 802.16 WMAN industry may be needed if the industry is to develop a strong security infrastructure and thus develop credibility with content owners and content providers/distributors. It is important to note here that a certificate hierarchy is not an end to itself, but must be deployed as part of a larger governance effort of the industry by manufacturers and service providers. The industry may operate fine without one, though having a certificate hierarchy very much helps service providers in the operations of the devices (SS and BS) and in achieving network infrastructure security.

Along similar lines, the work of [11] suggested the use of device certificates for 802.11 WLAN devices (e.g., 802.1X supplicants and authentication servers) and the development of a certificate hierarchy for the WLAN industry, with the WiFi Alliance (WFA) possibly being the WLAN industry's root CA. However, a number of issues have prevented such a hierarchy emerging for the WLAN industry. These include pricing limitations (i.e., commoditization 802.11 technology) and organizational constraints (i.e., WFA chartered differently from CableLabs). In addition, in the context of home networking there is the fundamental difference in the areas of application of 802.11 WLAN and 802.16 WMAN technologies.

First, there is a difference in the service model underlying 802.11 WLANs and 802.16 WMANs, and thus the market for both technologies. In the home consumer market similar to cable modems, the 802.16 WMAN is the "fat pipe" that connects the home to the open Internet and thus to content. A service provider is required to operate a 802.16 WMAN, and the service to the home-user being based on some longer-term contractual agreements. In contrast, 802.11 LANs are perceived to provide short-distance connectivity with limited throughput, with easy setup and tear down by the user. Furthermore, for certain types of contents (e.g., MPEG4 movies) it will be the consumer electronic (CE) end point devices (e.g., TV, set-top-box, or personal video recorder) that will decipher the (encrypted) content and render it to the user. As such, unlike cable modem services and 802.16 WMANs that bring content to the doorstep and thus are crucial to the home entertainment industry, the existence of 802.11 LANs is not presumed by the content provider and is seen merely as a local "thin pipe" that can be replaced by other technologies (e.g., 802.3 Ethernet).

This points to second difference, namely, that of the underlying business model. Although enterprise adoption of 802.11 is growing today, in itself 802.11 deployment has been a grassroots development, with the first adopters being ordinary (nonenterprise) users. Indeed, despite the security issues with WEP — which put off many enterprises — the purchase of 802.11 by individuals continues to grow. This is further evidenced by the continued popularity of (and media attention drawn by) "warchalking," namely, drawing a chalk symbol on a wall or pavement to indicate the presence of a free 802.11 networking node or access point. In addition, WISPs and hotspot providers continue to find difficulties in selling hotspot services because of the lack of a suitable business model for serving pure hotspot services.

Related to the service model and the business model issues is the accessibility of the device internals to the user. Most cable modem devices today are "dumb boxes" to which the user has no user interface to the internal functions of the device.

The user (or the cable modem technician) simply connects the wires to the box and connect its power supply. In contrast, most 802.11 access point products today allow the user to manage the operations box, performing various changes ranging from its MAC address to IP filtering rules. Although having easy user manageability does not translate to device cloning or device-certificate theft, this aspect has a strong impact, if only psychological, on the CE and content industries.

11.6 SUMMARY

It has been the aim of this chapter to provide an introductory overview of 802.16, with special focus on the security aspects of the standard. The basic 802.16 WMAN network topology and 802.16 frequency bands have been discussed in Section 11.2, illustrating the possible configurations of BSs and SSs — both fixed and mobile.

A given SS must go through network entry and initialization, as described in Section 11.3, before it can gain access to the services on the network. This process involves a number of steps, one being the authentication of the SS by the BS using the PKM Protocol, which was derived from the DOCSIS BPI+ specification for cable modems in CableLabs. Although authentication and authorization presumes that the SS has been assigned a device certificate (during its manufacture), currently the BS device is not required to have a similar certificate. Hence, authentication in this phase is not a mutual one. Successful authorization of the SS is signaled by the BS sending it a message containing an AK, which is used to protect the subsequent delivery of TEKs from the BS to the SS. Both the AKs and TEKs are managed by separate state machines, and the older keys are periodically refreshed with newer keys through a number of key transitions.

Finally, in discussing the current certificate hierarchy used in the cable industry (managed by CableLabs), this chapter has also discussed the possibility of 802.16 manufacturers and service providers developing their own certificate hierarchy following the model used in the cable industry.

References

[1] IEEE, "IEEE Standard 802.16-2000 Standard for Local and Metropolitan Area Networks." Air Interface for Fixed Broadband Wireless Access Systems Part 16, IEEE Press, New York, 2001.

[2] C. Eklund, R. B. Marks, K. L. Stanwood, and S. Wang, "IEEE Standard 802.16: A Technical Overview of the WirelessMAN Air Interface for Broadband Wireless Access," *IEEE Communications Magazine*, pp. 98–107, June 2002.

[3] T. Cooklev. *IEEE Wireless Communication Standards: A Study of 802.11, 802.15, and 802.16.* New York: IEEE Press, 2004.

[4] E. Agis, H. Mitchel, S. Ovadia, S. Asisi, S. Bakshi, P. Iyer, M. Kibria, C. Rogers, and J. Tsai. "Global, Interoperable Broadband Wireless Networks: Extending WiMax Technology to Mobility," *Intel Technical Journal*, vol. 8, pp. 173–187, Aug. 2004.

[5] CableLabs, "DOCSIS1.1 Baseline Privacy Plus Interface Specification," Data-Over-Cable Service Interface Specifications SP-BPI+-I11-040407, Cable Television Laboratories, Apr. 2004.

[6] R. Housley, W. Polk, W. Ford, and D. Solo, "Internet X.509 Public Key Infrastructure Certificate and Certificate Revocation List (CRL) Profile." RFC 3280 (Standards Track), Apr. 2002.

[7] ITU, "ITU-T Recommendation X.509 (1997 E): Information Technology — Open Systems Interconnection — The Directory: Authentication Framework." ITU-T Recommendation, June 1997.

[8] "Cable Television Laboratories," 2004, http://www.CableLabs.org.

[9] CableLabs, "CableHome 1.1 Specification," CableHome Issued Specification CH-SP-CH1.1-I05-040806, Cable Television Laboratories, Aug. 2004.

[10] M. Myers, R. Ankney, A. Malpani, S. Galperin, and C. Adams, "X.509 Internet Public Key Infrastructure Online Certificate Status Protocol (OCSP)." RFC 2560 (Standards Track), June 1999.

[11] T. Hardjono, "Certificate Hierarchy for the WLAN Industry." IEEE TGi doc 802.11-02/401r0, July 2002, http://www.ieee802.org.

Chapter 12

Wireless MAN Security

12.1 INTRODUCTION

Wireless MAN security architecture has two main design goals: to provide controlled access to the provider's network, and to provide confidentiality, message integrity protection, and replay protection to the data being transmitted. WMAN communications can be one-to-one or one-to-many. In one-to-one communication, typically users are interested in protecting their data, and service providers in controlling access to their networks. In one-to-many communication, service or content providers encrypt data and provide keys to their subscribers; thus content access control is the only goal in this case.

For access control, one may use asymmetric (digital certificates) or symmetric (e.g., preshared keys, SIM cards) authentication methods; the revised 802.16 [1] specification allows the use of either of these two classes of authentication methods. From a provider's perspective, an SS authenticating itself to a BS is sufficient for enforcing controlled access to the provider's network. However, for user data confidentiality, the one-way authentication is not sufficient. Consider, for example, that SS to BS authentication alone will not help detect an adversary claiming to be a BS and thereby launching a man-in-the-middle attack.

The revised IEEE 802.16 specifications [1, 2] update the cryptographic algorithms used for encryption and integrity protection, increase key lengths, and add replay protection. The revised key management protocol design consists of robust protection again replay attacks.

A few further additions to the 802.16 security architecture facilitate symmetric key-based authentication, and more importantly mobility. Specifically, a key hierarchy is defined for fast keying when a mobile SS (MS) associates with a new BS.

12.2 WMAN THREAT MODEL AND SECURITY REQUIREMENTS

Controlled or metered access to the WMAN or any content disseminated via the WMAN is the foremost requirement of service providers. This basic requirement typically translates into many components.

First, any service provider's BS must be able to uniquely identify an MS that wants to get access to the network. The MS may identify itself to a BS using digital certificates or indirectly to a legacy authentication server (AS, e.g., AAA server) in conjunction with a symmetric authentication method. In the latter case, the MS does not need to perform expensive computations as would be the case with digital certificates. Furthermore, in most cases, the BS only forwards authentication protocol messages to the backend AS for authentication. After verifying the MS's credentials, the AS informs the BS of the result — authentication success or failure — and securely transfers the master session key (MSK).

The second component of enforcing access control is key distribution. The BS must be able to uniquely and easily identify packets from authorized MSs so it can enforce authorized access to the WMAN. Thus, after successfully authenticating an MS, the BS establishes a secret key with the MS. The MS must include a proof of possession of the secret key with each packet. The most common way to achieve this is to compute a cryptographic integrity checksum with each packet, and include it with the packet. In WMANs, the BS and MS may derive the keying material as part of the authentication protocol, or the BS may supply the key(s) to the MS.

Third, the IEEE 802.16 specification defines a multicast and broadcast service (MBS). This allows WMAN service providers to distribute content efficiently via multicast to relevant subscribers. The provider enforces controlled access to the content by distributing a per-group secret key to the subscribers who paid for the additional services.

In addition to covering service providers' requirements, the security sublayer addresses WMAN users' requirements. User requirements are typically to protect the confidentiality and integrity of the data. In simpler terms, users want to ensure that a third party cannot read their communications, their data is not modified en route, and that no one injects or drops packets without being detected. It is quite difficult, if not impossible, to protect against an adversary dropping packets; the other requirements are fairly easy to achieve and the 802.16 standard specifies how to in the WMAN context. Specifically, in addition to encryption, WMAN secure encapsulation provides per-MPDU integrity protection as well as replay protection.

12.2.1 Original Design of the 802.16 Security Sublayer

The 802.16 MAC layer communication between a BS and an MS is connection-oriented. Each connection has a connection ID (CID) and has two slot maps, an uplink map (UL_MAP) and a downlink map (DL_MAP). There are typically three types of connections between a BS and MS pair: there is a primary management connection for broadcasts, initial ranging and general management, a secondary management connection for IP layer management such as DHCP, and finally one or more transport connections for data transmission. Only the secondary management connection and the transport connections are afforded protection.

After network entry (where an MS scans for a signal and establishes channel parameters) and initial ranging (establishment of primary management channel), an MS runs the PKM protocol for secure communication. The PKM protocol consists of two main parts: a secure encapsulation protocol and an authenticated key establishment protocol. The secure encapsulation protocol provides confidentiality and message integrity to MPDUs. The encapsulation SA consists of the TEKs and the cryptographic policy, namely, the encryption algorithm and the use of the SA parameters in the context of encapsulation 802.16 MPDUs. The KM part of the protocol consists of MS identity establishment to the BS, and the BS after verifying MS's credentials to receive the requested services, delivering an AK, and TEKs. Chapter 11 discusses the PKM protocol in detail. In this section, we highlight the shortcomings of that design and motivate the need for redesign of the PKM protocol. Interested readers are also referred to another security analysis [3] of the 802.16 specification.

12.2.1.1   Insufficient Key-Length and Incorrect Use of Cipher Modes

The original choice of encryption algorithm for MPDU confidentiality in WMANs is DES-CBC with a 56-bit key. The per-packet IV is computed using an initial IV sent during TEK establishment and the per-MPDU physical layer synchronization sequence number.

The above encapsulation is flawed in several respects: first, 56-bit key DES does not provide any meaningful confidentiality protection to MPDUs. Next, the CBC mode requires an unpredictable IV for safe operation. A fixed IV XORed with a sequence number does not meet this requirement.

TEK rekeying is protected using 2-key 3DES (EDE mode), which seems to be sufficient for confidentiality, but for the use of ECB mode for encryption, which is not secure.

12.2.1.2   Lack of Integrity Protection of MPDUs

The DES-CBC mode for secure encapsulation of MPDUs does not have associated message integrity protection. The key management traffic is protected by HMAC-SHA-1 as per the 802.16-2004 [2] specification.

12.2.1.3   Lack of Mutual Authentication

The PKM protocol authenticates the MS to the BS, but not vice versa. Specifically, the BS sends the AK encrypted with the MS's public key. Thus only the legitimate MS can decrypt the AK. The MS however has no way of knowing whether the entity sending the AK is a legitimate BS or not. Consider for instance the possibility of an authorized MS, called MS_a as an adversary. MS_a could first establish a connection with a BS, and after that pose as a legitimate BS to an MS that it wants to attack. Since a BS does not have to prove its authorization or authenticity to an MS, this is possible. MS_a can forward traffic for all the MSs it serves, which results in breaking both the goals of the PKM protocol: confidentiality of user data as well network access control. Note that the actual attack might be slightly more complicated in that the adversary's device must act as an MS and a BS simultaneously.

12.2.1.4   Small-Key ID Fields

The AK ID is 4 bits in length and the TEK ID is 2 bits in length. The key IDs are small to save bandwidth. However, this opens the possibility of a key being reused without detection. An adversary may replay old messages to trick the MS to encapsulate PKM messages or data MPDUs with old keys. This may allow the adversary to attack the underlying cipher.

12.2.1.5   Lack of Replay Protection

The PKM protocol does not protect against replay attacks. There is also no chance for liveness verification in PKM authentication and key establishment protocol. The lack of replay protection allows an adversary to trick an MS into accepting an old AK as a fresh AK. Since the AK (indirectly) protects the TEK download from the BS to the MS, it is plausible that an adversary may be able to exploit the replay attack to attack the underlying cipher (3DES-ECB) that protects the TEKs. Note that ECB itself is not a secure mode.

In the rest of this chapter, we discuss PKMv2, the revised privacy and authentication protocol designed to provide stronger MPDU encapsulation, and authenticated key establishment for WMANs with mobile SSs (MS).

12.3   PKMV2

The original security sublayer in the 802.16 specification is somewhat simplistic and does not quite address the threats and satisfy the requirements listed in the previous section. In the revisions of the spec, the security sublayer has been enhanced and the original is now called the *basic* security sublayer. Chapter 11 discusses the basic security sublayer, whereas this chapter focuses on the *extended* security sublayer.

Within the extended security sublayer there are two versions of the PKM protocol: version 1 is quite similar to the basic security sublayer, except that it supports new ciphers including 3DES-ECB and AES-ECB for confidentiality of key material, and AES-CCM for MPDU confidentiality. HMAC-SHA-1 protects the integrity of the key management messages. PKMv2 comparatively has many more desirable properties, including mutual authentication using various combinations of RSA-based and EAP-based authentication protocols, additional message integrity algorithms and key management protocols.

Before we delve into that discussion, a bit of context of the design motivation for PKMv2 is in order. PKMv2 is part of a specification to add mobility extensions to the base 802.16 standard. When MSs are mobile, it may be desirable that they preauthenticate with a BS they plan to associate with, to reduce any potential for interruption in service, be it access to the provider's network, or a·multicast/broadcast content delivery service. Thus preauthentication is one of the additional features in PKMv2. Similarly a key hierarchy is defined to allow an MS to authenticate itself to the backend AAA server once, irrespective of any number of BSs it may associate with. Along with these extensions for mobility, the new specification includes several enhancements to the WMAN security protocols. In the rest of this chapter, we discuss these additional features and their advantages and shortcomings.

12.3.1 Mutual Authentication Between a BS and an MS

Providers want to ensure that only authorized subscribers can connect to their networks. Thus a BS wants to verify the authenticity and authorization of each MS requesting association. Subscribers want to associate with legitimate BSs to protect against man-in-the-middle attacks. In other words, an MS entering a provider's network would like to verify that the BS it is associating with is a provider-authorized device.

PKMv2 supports two different mechanisms for authentication: the BS and the MS may use RSA keys for public-key–based authentication, or EAP for symmetric-key based authentication. EAP is an authentication credential carrier protocol and is an increasingly common protocol for user/device authentication for network entry (e.g., EAP over 802.1X in wired or wireless LANs) or remote access (e.g., using EAP over IKEv2 for authentication and IPsec SA establishment). An EAP method such as EAP-AKA is required for the actual authentication.

12.4   AUTHENTICATION AND ACCESS CONTROL IN PKMV2

PKMv2 [1, 2] fixes most if not all of the flaws in the PKM design. Specifically, AES-CCM [4] is the new MPDU encapsulation algorithm (see Chapter 7 for a summary of AES-CCM). CCM is comprised of counter mode as the encryption mode, and CBC-MAC as the message integrity algorithm. Recall that 802.11i specification [5] also uses CCM, and as such this mode has received a wide review in the cryptographic community. For replay protection of 802.16 MPDUs, there is a monotonically increasing 32-bit sequence number in the security encapsulation header.

The authentication and key establishment protocol portion of PKMv2 has also several new properties and protects again the various attacks that PKM is vulnerable to. First, the basic RSA-based initial exchange supports mutual authentication and authorization. There is also an EAP-based authentication protocol for user authentication using back-end authentication infrastructures, such as the AAA (e.g., RADIUS) architecture. The authenticated key exchanges also contain nonces for liveness verification and to protect against replay attacks. There is a key hierarchy so that the MS and the BS can amortize the cost (computational, latency, and so forth) of the initial authentication and authorization process. Finally, there are new provisions for fast handover under discussion: these include preauthentication of an MS to a BS it might associate with in the future, and also the concept of the backend authentication server or authenticator facilitating key establishment with multiple BSs after only a single authentication exchange with the MS. In the rest of this section, we discuss the new protocols and algorithms in detail.

12.4.1   Public-Key–Based Mutual Authentication in PKMv2

The public-key–based mutual authentication and authorization consists of three messages with an optional announcement message from the MS to the BS (see Chapter 11).

12.4.1.1   Authorization Request Message

The MS initiates the RSA-based mutual authorization process by sending an authorization request message. This message contains a 64-bit MS_RANDOM number, the MS's X.509 certificate, list of cryptographic suites (integrity and encryption algorithms) that the MS supports. The SAID is the MS's primary SAID, and in this case equal to the CID assigned to the MS during initial ranging.

Note that the authorization request message itself is not signed by the MS; therefore the BS has no way of differentiating a bogus request from a legitimate one.

12.4.1.2   Authorization Response Message

The BS sends the authorization response message to the MS requesting access to the network services. In the response message, the BS includes the 64-bit MS_RANDOM number received, includes its own 64-bit random number, BS_RANDOM, RSA encrypted 256-bit pre-PAK (encrypted with the MS's public key), PAK attributes (lifetime and sequence number, and one or more SAIDs); the BS also includes its own certificate and signs the entire authorization response message.

The MS can readily verify that an authorized BS has in fact signed the authorization response message. Note that at this stage in the WMAN authorization process, there is not yet secure network access available to the MS, so it is advisable to have the BS manufacturer certificates or the WiMAX certificate available to the MS.

After the signature verification, the MS verifies liveness by comparing the MS_RANDOM it sent with the MS_RANDOM number in the authorization response message. It then extracts the PAK, the associated attributes, and finally the SAIDs. Note that only the authorized MS can extract the PAK and therefore MS authorization can be verified by proof of possession of the PAK.

The SAIDs are optional in this message, if the RSA authorization exchange is to be followed by an EAP authentication exchange.

12.4.1.3   Authorization Acknowledgment Message

The BS cannot yet verify the liveness of the message, and also cannot determine if an authorized MS has indeed requested access to network services. The authentication acknowledgment message provides these assurances.

In the authorization acknowledgment message, the MS includes the number received in the authorization response message (BS_RANDOM) for liveness proof, and its own MAC address (identity) and includes a cryptographic checksum of the acknowledgment message. The integrity algorithm specified is the OMAC algorithm with AES as the base cipher, and the OMAC key is derived from the PAK with 0 as the packet number in the derivation (see Section 12.4.3 for details on key derivation).

At the end of the RSA authorization exchange, the BS is authenticated to the MS and the MS — the device — is authenticated to the BS.

12.4.2   EAP-Based Mutual Authorization in PKMv2

EAP-based mutual authorization in PKMv2 alone can support mutual authentication (indirect mutual authentication via a proof of possession of a key, if a backend AS is involved). However, a combination of RSA authorization followed by an EAP authentication may also be used in WMAN access. In that case, the RSA authorization is considered to provide device mutual authentication, whereas the EAP authentication is user authentication (which is especially true if a SIM card is involved in authentication).

EAP authentication in PKMv2 is similar to that in the 802.1X/EAP-based authentication of 802.11i STAs: the MS authenticates to an AS via an authenticator. The BS in 802.16 networks serves as the authenticator, although in some architectures the functionality of the authenticator and the BS might be separated (this model of separating the BS and the authenticator needs a further review before being considered secure). EAP authentication follows the steps below:

- The authenticator or the BS initiates the EAP authentication process. Note that in the public-key based authentication protocol, the MS requests authentication. The BS sends an EAP request message to the MS. This is typically an EAP identity request encapsulated in a MAC management PDU (i.e., the secondary management channel carries the EAP messages).

- The MS responds to the request with an EAP response message. The authenticator and the MS continue the EAP exchanges until the authentication server determines whether the exchange is a failure or a success. The exact number of the EAP messages depends on the method used for authentication.

- An EAP success or an EAP failure terminates the EAP authentication and authorization process. At the end of the protocol run, the BS and the MS have the primary master key (PMK).

If the EAP exchange follows and RSA authorization exchange, the EAP messages are protected using the EAP integrity key (EIK) derived as a result of the RSA authorization exchange. The EAP messages contain an AK sequence number (the AK and the EIK are derived from the RSA exchange, see Section 12.4.3) for replay protection and an OMAC digest, computed using the EIK, for integrity protection.

If a backend AS is involved in the EAP authentication process, the AS delivers the PMK to the authenticator or the BS after the EAP exchange is complete. The BS and the MS then engage in a 3-way exchange to prove to each other that they possess the PMK. The 3-way exchange can be run several times under the protection of the PMK to amortize the cost of the EAP authentication exchange.

12.4.2.1 3-Way Exchange Between the BS and the MS

The BS and the MS derive the PMK from the AAA key (this is the result of the EAP authentication exchange) by simply taking the 20 lowest-order octets of the AAA key. The 3-way exchange mainly establishes proof of possession of the PMK between the BS and the MS, and as such this is construed as authorization process for the MS to gain network entry for normal communication. (Compare the 3-way exchange to the 4-way exchange in the 802.11i RSNA specification; see Chapter 6.) The 802.16 specification uses EAP to carry the 3-way exchange messages, which in turn are carried in MAC management PDUs. The end goal in addition to mutual authorization is to establish the TEKs and KEKs necessary for the MS to gain access to the network services. The 3-way exchange consists of the following messages:

- The BS initiates the exchange by sending an EAP establish key request message to the MS. This message contains a 64-bit nonce denoted by RandomBS, the AKID of the AK whose proof of possession is being established, and finally a message integrity checksum on the message. This checksum is computed using an integrity key derived from the PMK.

  The nonce is to prove the liveness of the exchange to the two parties involved, and also protects against replay attacks.

- The MS responds with an EAP establish key response message. The MS creates a 64-bit nonce and calls it RandomMS, and includes the RandomBS in the first message. It also identifies the AKID, which must be the same as that received in the received message. The MS also includes the cryptographic suites it can support in this message.

  Recall that in the public-key based authentication and authorization exchange, the cryptographic suites are in the first message sent by the MS. If the 3-way exchange follows the RSA authorization exchange, the MS is to wait until this message to negotiate cryptosuites.

  The final field is the cryptographic checksum using either the HMAC or OMAC algorithm. This checksum is computed using a MIC key computed to protect messages 2 and 3 of the 3-way exchange. The MIC key is bound to the BSID, MSID, RandomBS, and RandomMS.[1] It is desirable to include the nonces in the key derivation since the PMK derivation includes a third party (or several entities in case of AAA proxying). Inclusion of nonces would place an additional burden on potential adversaries trying to get illegal access to WMAN keying material. Details of the key derivation are in Section 12.4.3.

---

[1] There is an ongoing discussion in the 802.16 Task Group e on whether or not to include the random values in the KEK derivation.

- The final message is an EAP establish key reject or EAP establish key confirm depending on whether the BS can verify the liveness and the integrity of the received message 2 of the 3-way exchange.

    This message contains the RandomMS, RandomBS, and the AKID, and contains an encrypted SA key update attribute in addition to the integrity checksum. The SA key update attribute contains TEKs, and group keys GKEK and GTEK encrypted with AES-keywrap algorithm. The encryption key, unicast KEK, is derived in a similar manner as the MIC key, by mixing the BSID, MSID, and the nonces in the exchange with the AK.

    Upon receipt of message 3, the MS verifies that the BS is indeed live and that the 3-way exchange is not a replay of an old exchange between the BS and the MS. It then proceeds to extract the keys included in the key update attribute, and using the 802.16 channel for data transmission.

12.4.3   PKMv2 Key Hierarchy

The primary motivation behind the PKMv2 key hierarchy is to amortize the cost of exchanges that involve computationally intensive operations or require several round-trips. First, there is an RSA exchange between the BS and MS that requires several exponentiation operations. Alternatively or in addition to the RSA exchange, the BS and MS might use EAP-based authentication, in which the AS is a backend server. The backend server may be several hops away or could even be off-line at times. The EAP exchange itself could also require public-key operations (e.g., EAP-TLS requires the client and the server to mutually authenticate using certificates), but at least involves several exchanges with a potentially far away AS.

    The 802.16 specification uses the result of the the RSA and/or EAP authentication and authorization exchanges to establish an AK. The goal of these exchanges is for the BS to provide one or more TEKs to the MS so that the MS can securely access the network services. The key hierarchy starts from the AK and builds towards how KEKs and TEKs can be generated without having to repeat the authorization exchanges.

    The notion of amortizing the cost of initial authentication is not new in 802.16. WLAN security protocols use the same technique: for instance after the 802.1X/EAP authentication, the STA and AP in an RSNA use the 4-way exchange and the group exchange to establish the TEK and the GTEK, respectively. The STA and the AP may repeat the 4-way exchange under the protection of the PMK (established via the 802.1X/EAP authentication) — until the PMK expires — to refresh the TEKs. Similar key refreshment provisions — commonly known as rekeying mechanisms — are available in IP layer key management protocols such as IKE and GDOI.

12.4.3.1 AK Establishment and Derivation via the RSA Exchange

During the RSA authorization protocol, the BS delivers a 256-bit pre-PAK to the MS encrypted with the MS's public key. The pre-PAK serves two purposes: the first is to derive a message integrity key to authenticate the authorization acknowledgment message in the RSA exchange, and to derive a 160-bit PAK. Figure 12.1 illustrates this extraction. To explain the PAK derivation, we need to first describe the 802.16 key derivation function (also known as dot16KDF). There are two different KDFs defined depending on whether the PRF is an HMAC or an OMAC.

```
dot16KDF(key, keyDerivationString, keyLength)
{
      result = null;
      Kin = Truncate(key, 128);
      (128 is the AES block size; AES is the OMAC cipher)
      for(i = 0; i ≤ (keylength-1)/128; i++)
      {
            result = result || AES-OMAC(Kin, i||keyDerivationString||keyLength);
      }
      return Truncate(result, keyLength);
}

dot16KDF(key, keyDerivationString, keyLength)
{
      result = null;
      Kin = Truncate(key, 160);
      (160 is the SHAN-1 digest length)
      for(i = 0; i ≤ (keylength-1)/160; i++)
      {
            result = result || HMAC-SHA-1(Kin, i||keyDerivationString||keyLength);
      }
      return Truncate(result, keyLength);
}

Truncate(key, keyLength)
{
      return keyLength-most-significant-bits(key);
      (extract the required bits starting at the most significant bit)
}
```

From the pre-PAK, the BS and MS derive the integrity key (IK) — a 128-bit OMAC key to authenticate the authorization acknowledgment message of the RSA exchange (see Section 12.4.1), and a 160-bit PAK. Thus,

IK-128 ∥ PAK-160 = dot16KDF(pre-PAK, MSID∥BSID∥"EIK+PAK", 128+160).

The entire string MSID∥BSID∥"EIK+PAK" is the keyDerivationString in the dot16KDF functions listed above. If RSA is the only authorization protocol (i.e., no EAP authentication follows the RSA exchange), the PAK serves as the AK.

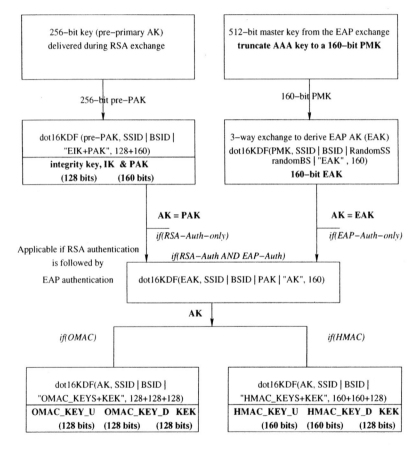

Figure 12.1   The 802.16 PKMv2 key hierarchy.

EAP authorization exchange described in sec:WMAN-EAP-PKMv2 results in a 512-bit AAA key, from which the MS and the BS derive a 160-bit PMK. The PMK derivation is a simple truncation process. This also allows the AAA key to be shorter than 512 bits as might be the case with some authentication methods such EAP-AKA.

The PMK serves the role of the pre-PAK in key derivation, to derive an EAP authorization key (EAK). If EAP is the only authorization exchange, the EAK serves as the AK.

EAK-160 = dot16KDF(pre-PAK, MSID||BSID||"EAK", 160);

If a combination of RSA authentication followed by the EAP authentication is used, the AK derivation is as follows:

AK-160 = dot16KDF(EAK, MSID||BSID||PAK||"AK", 160);

12.4.3.2   KEK Derivation and TEK Delivery

Recall that the TEKs are delivered via a 3-way exchange (see Section 12.4.2.1). The 3-way exchange must be integrity protected and the secret keys (TEK and GTEK) delivered must be encrypted. For these purposes the MS and BS derive two HMAC or OMAC keys, one for downlink communication and another for uplink communication, and a KEK to protect the TEKs included in the TEK update attribute. If the MS is authorized to receive one or more GSAs, the BS sends the corresponding GTEK and GKEK in the key update attribute. The keys protecting the 3-way exchange can be derived before the exchange if the derivation does not include the nonces, namely RandomMS and RandomBS in the 3-way exchange. Thus,

OMAC-KEY-U-128, OMAC-KEY-D-128, KEK = dot16KDF(AK, MSID||BSID|| "OMAC_KEYS+KEK", 384);

HMAC-KEY-U-128, HMAC-KEY-D-128, KEK = dot16KDF(AK, MSID||BSID|| "OMAC_KEYS+KEK", 448);

12.4.4   TEK and GTEK Update

During reauthorization, or when the TEK expires, the MS and BS do not need to engage in full RSA or EAP authentication process. Instead, as long as the AK has not expired (and a counter counting the number of 3-way exchanges does not reach a configured maximum), the MS and BS can use the 3-way exchange to refresh the TEK. If nonces are not used in the key derivation, note that the KEK and the integrity keys do not change.

The 802.16 specification also defines a TEK update message to efficiently update a TEK. The message contains the current AK sequence number, new TEK attributes (remaining lifetime, ciphersuite, IV) and an HMAC/OMAC attribute to protect the TEK update message. The TEK itself is encrypted using the KEK.

To refresh the GTEKs, the BS multicasts a GTEK update message containing the new GTEK. GTEK update message is a single broadcast message from the BS to all the MSs in the secure group. The GTEK is protected by the GKEK. There is a monotonically increasing counter for replay protection. Each MS initializes the counter to zero when the GKEK is first received from the BS. An OMAC or an HMAC digest protects the update message. However, note that symmetric-key based authentication using a group key would only provide limited protection, in that any SS in the group can claim to be the BS and send a bogus update message. The update message must be digitally signed by the BS for message integrity.

The 802.16 specification also allows an MS to request a new GTEK. This is a one-to-one 2-way exchange between the MS and BS. The GSA key request message contains a monotonically increasing GSA message ID, the GSAID, and it is integrity protected using the unicast KEK. The BS replies with the GSA key reply message with the same message ID as in the request message, and returns the GTEK and the associated parameters protected by the KEK. This message is also integrity-protected using the downlink OMAC/HMAC key. The message ID counter protects this exchange against replay protection. The counter is initiated to zero when the KEK is first established.

12.5   CCM ENCAPSULATION OF 802.16 MPDUS

For unicast and multicast data transmission, 802.16 devices use AES-CCM (DES-CBC is also allowed, but it does not provide sufficient protection) encapsulation. The CCM mode of 802.16 uses AES-CTR-128 mode for encryption, a 4-octet packet number for replay protection, and an 8-octet ICV for message integrity protection using AES-CBC-MAC. The CCM encapsulation of 802.16 MPDUs results in a packet expansion of 12 octets. Figure 12.2 illustrates the WMAN CCM payload.

In CCM, the same key is used for encryption as well as integrity protection. The same key is also used for UL as well DL traffic. The following CCM parameters are used in 802.16:

- The 802.16 specification selects 2 octets to hold the number of octets in the payload, thus the parameter L in the NIST CCM specification is 2. Consequently, the nonce must be of length 13 octets.

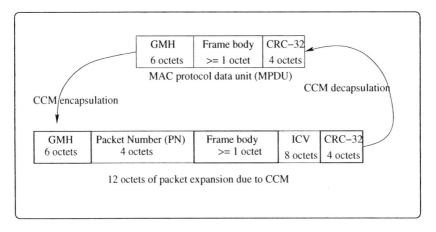

Figure 12.2 WMAN CCM payload.

Generic CCM construction of Block B₀ for MIC computation

←	16 octets				→
Flags (Octet 0)					
Reserved 0	Adata	(M−2)/2	L−1	Nonce N (Octets 1 ... 15−L)	l(m) (Octets 16−L ... 15)

Bit(s): 7   6   5–3   2–0

l(m): length of message; $0 <= l(m) < 2^{8L}$

M: Length of MIC, 4, 6, 8, 10, 12, 14, 16

L: Number of octets in the length field, 2–8

802.16 CCM construction of Block B₀ for MIC computation

L = 2, and M = 8; Adata = 0
Flags = 0 0 011 001 = 0x19   len(Nonce) = 15−L = 13; len(Packet Number) in 802.16 is 4

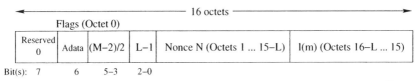

Octets   1   5   4   4   2

Flags 0x19	First 5 octets of 802.16 GMH	Reserved 0x00000000	Packet Number (PN)	Length of data (in octets) not including padding

← Nonce of length 13 octets →

Figure 12.3 WMAN CCM B_0 block construction for ICV construction.

- WMAN MPDUs are protected using an 8-octet ICV, thus M = 8. The value of M determines a portion of the flag field, as illustrated in Figure 12.3.

- The 802.16 specification does not use the additional authentication data provision in the CCM specification. This might be used to protect the GMH. Thus, Adata = 0.

- The CCM specification requires formation of a block B_0 for CBC-MAC computation, and counter blocks A_I for CTR mode encryption. The first octet in these blocks is a flag. The value of the flag in B_0 used for the computation of the CBC-MAC is 0x19 (see Figure 12.3), and the corresponding flag value in counter blocks A_i is 0x01 (see Figure 12.4).

Generic CCM construction of Block A$_i$

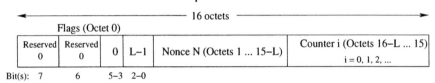

L: Number of octets in the length field, 2–8

802.16 CCM construction of Block A$_i$

L = 2
Flags = 0 0 000 001 = 0x01   len(Nonce) = 15–L = 13; len(PN) in 802.16 is 4

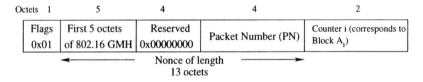

Figure 12.4 WMAN CCM A_i block construction.

12.5.1 Nonce Construction

The 802.16 CCM construction requires a 13-octet nonce. A large counter would allow the communication to continue without rekeying, while incurring a large per-MPDU overhead. For instance using a 13-octet PN would add 21 octets (recall that the ICV length is 8) overhead to each MPDU. A smaller PN would result in frequent rekeying. To optimize the per-MPDU overhead, the 802.16 specification uses the first 5 octets of the GMH and 4 octets of zero to fill 9 octets and uses a 4-octet PN to construct the nonce.

12.5.1.1   Replay Protection

The 4-octet PN allows transmission of 2^{32} MPDUs without requiring TEK rekeying. The PN is a monotonically increasing number starting at 1. It serves as the unique value in the nonce for the AES counter mode encryption, and for replay protection of the 802.16 MPDUs. Since there is no AAD, and the same TEK is used for UL and DL MPDU protection, the PN is split between UL and DL frames. To do so, the PN is XORed with 0x80000000 on UL connections. Thus all PNs with the MSB of 1 are used to protect MPDUs sent by the MS and the PNs with the MSB of 0 are used to protect the MPDUs sent by the BS.

12.6   SECURE ENCAPSULATION OF MULTICAST AND BROADCAST MPDUS

The 802.16 specification also contains a "special" multicast and broadcast service (MBS) to broadcast multimedia to subscribers with protections against potential theft of service. For MBS content protection, the provider is to encrypt the data and provide keys to authorized subscribers.

The primary goal of the MBS security design is to enable content protection with the least possible amount of overhead. AES-CCM encapsulation overhead (see Section 12.5) is considered overly burdensome in this case. Furthermore, integrity protection is deemed unnecessary for the applications that might use MBS security. Note that the 802.16 specification already has a group keying mechanism to protect data in one-to-many communication scenarios. Thus, when integrity and replay protection are required, AES-CCM encapsulation using the GTEK can be used.

With these considerations, MBS security encapsulation uses AES in counter mode for access control. As noted earlier, there is no integrity protection on the data. Note that counter mode is especially vulnerable to integrity attacks and always comes with a strong caveat that integrity protection is required. However, it appears that the 802.16 MBS security protocol designers have considered that and decided that integrity protection is not required for applications such as digital TV distribution that might use MBS security.

Since 802.16 channels are lossy, counter mode would require a nonce to to be included with each MPDU. A 32-bit monotonically increasing counter is used for encrypting each MPDU. For counter mode encryption, the IV is copied three times to form a 128-bit nonce. Normally, the 32-bit counter is sent along with the MPDU.

To further reduce the per-MPDU overhead, the 32-bit counter is formed using a 24-bit physical layer synchronization field and an 8-bit rollover counter (ROC). The 8-bit ROC is included with each MPDU.

12.6.1   802.16 Security Associations

There are several SAs protecting 802.16 communications. The primary SA is the AKSA. It is identified by a 16-bit SAID, which is unique within a BS. Within the AKSA, there is a 128-bit KEK, and the KEK algorithm. Finally, the integrity algorithm is an attribute within the AKSA. It can have the values of HMAC-SHA-1 or OMAC.

The KEKSA protects the delivery of TEKs. The TEK attributes include the TEK encapsulation algorithm, which is generally AES-CCM. Alternatively, 3DES-CBC with HMAC-SHA-1 can be specified. Note that there are two TEKs and two PNs corresponding to the two TEKs.

There is also a GSA containing a GKEK and GTEK and the algorithms used for group security encapsulation. The GKEK or the KEK itself protects GTEK delivery.

In addition to the above SAs, there is an MBSSA to protect MBS services. There is a corresponding MBS AK from the special authorization process for MBS service access, an MBSKEK, MBSTEK, and the corresponding algorithms and lifetimes within this SA.

12.6.1.1   802.16 SA Parameter Negotiation

The 802.16 revised specification allows for security parameter negotiation at various stages in the authorization or key establishment process.

Before initial authorization, the BS and the AS can negotiate the PKM version, authorization mechanisms, message integrity algorithm, and PN window size supported. The PKM version can be 1 or 2. The authorization can be RSA-based or EAP-based or RSA+EAP-based. The integrity algorithm can be HMAC or OMAC.

All other parameter negotiation is during the various exchanges. For instance, as discussed in Sections 12.4.1 and 12.4.2, the MS and the BS negotiate SA parameters during the RSA or EAP authorization exchanges.

12.7   SECURITY ISSUES IN THE 802.16 SPECIFICATION

Several open security issues remain in the 802.16 specification, and at the time of this writing the specification has not been finalized.

First, the initial parameter negotiation is not protected. An adversary may launch a downgrade attack and thus the BS and SS can never be sure that they are using the strongest protocols that they both support. Recall that the 4-way exchange in the 802.11i specification authenticated the security parameters negotiated during association. Unfortunately, the 802.16 specification does not contain such a mechanism.

Next, the specification supports encryption algorithms in the ECB mode, which is not secure. Unfortunately, those algorithms will continue to be supported for backward compatibility purposes.

TEK derivation in the 802.16 specification is still in debate. It is best to use a key derivation function such that a back-end AS cannot derive the TEKs between the BS and the MS.

In 802.16 group communication, data integrity is supported using a group key. This, known as group authentication of data, allows any authorized MS in the group to impersonate the BS.

The MBS service uses encryption to enforce access control of broadcast data. There is no integrity protection on the data, thus applications that need integrity protection must not use MBS.

12.8 SUMMARY

This chapter described the revised IEEE 802.16 security specifications. WMAN security design is motivated by protection against theft of service and eavesdropping; thus the security design is to provide network access control and message confidentiality and integrity protection. The original design fails to achieve these goals. The primary problem is that the design takes the requirements literally and requires only subscribers requesting access to authenticate themselves and provides confidentiality only, and using an ineffective encryption algorithm at that.

The design described in this chapter improves all those aspects. Specifically, it specifies the use of AES-CCM for data encapsulation and HMAC-SHA-1 and OMAC-AES-128 for integrity protection of keying messages. In the new design called the PKMv2, the BS and MS mutually authenticate to each other using public-key technology, and/or EAP to take advantage of authentication infrastructures deployed for other similar purposes. An elaborate key hierarchy and the associated key management/establishment protocols allow amortization of the expensive full authentication exchange.

References

[1] "Draft IEEE Standard for Local and Metropolitan Area Networks: IEEE802.16e/D5a," Tech. Rep. Part 16, IEEE Press, New York, Dec. 2004.

[2] IEEE, "Draft IEEE Standard for Local and Metropolitan Area Networks; IEEE802.16-Revd/D5-2004," Tech. Rep. Part 16, IEEE Press, New York, 2004.

[3] D. Johnston and J. Walker, "Overview of 802.16 Security," *IEEE Privacy & Security Magazine*, pp. 40–48, May 2004.

[4] D. Whiting, R. Housley, and N. Ferguson, "Counter with CBC-MAC." RFC 3610 (Informational), Aug. 2003.

[5] IEEE, "IEEE Std 802.11i-2004, Amendment to IEEE Std 802.11, 1999 Edition (Reaff 2003)," Amendment 6: Medium Access Control (MAC) Security Enhancements Part 11, IEEE Press, New York, Apr. 2004.

Chapter 13

Conclusion and Outlook

This book has attempted to provide the reader with the technological background and a snapshot of developments in the WLAN and WMAN networking industry, which are constantly evolving every day. Judging from the success of WiFi in the last three years, both WLAN and WMAN technologies and services will have a dramatic impact on how the IP-based Internet as we see today will develop and how it will be seen by future generations.

Generally speaking, the entire field of the "wireless Internet" — namely, wireless connectivity to the IP network — is still relatively new and may take a few more years to reach the level of ubiquity comparable to other access technologies such as dial-up over PSTN. What is evident, however, is that user mobility is a crucial aspect of the next generation Internet services where the ordinary user will expect connectivity to be something that is permanently available, much like electricity that is "always on."

There are a number of emerging technological trends today that may influence the future of WLANs and WMANs. We summarize these in the following and describe possible outcomes and developments in this exciting field.

- *The transparent "always on" Internet*
  Increasingly the details of the operations of the IP Internet will become transparent or removed from the ordinary user. In the past, many early-home adopters of WLANs have had to familiarize themselves with important IP networking concepts (such as IP addresses, ports on switches/routers, and so forth) in order to set-up a home WLAN. Today, through improved quality and ease of use of WLAN products, most products are essentially plug-and-play.

  This human aspect is important because it contributes to the user's expectations of an always-on Internet, whether they access it from a home WLAN, a WiFi hotspot, a wireless broadband (WMAN) provider, or from a 3G/GPRS provider. Increasingly, the lay user will not care how connectivity is provided, but will expect high-bandwidth connectivity to be ubiquitous. This expectation will in turn influence how service providers establish seamless services between the IP Internet and the 2G/3G mobile networks.

* *Increased adoption of 802.1X*
The 802.1X approach for WLAN authentication is increasingly being adopted by Enterprises, due in part to its support within the Microsoft Windows family of products. Although various networking vendors have been touting proprietary security products for WLAN authentication, the completion of the revision to the IEEE 802.1X standard together with recent progress in the IETF on EAP-related standards should lead to the strengthening of 802.1X in the market.

  In the context of WiFi roaming, technically 802.1X provides better security than the UAM web-based approach. Thus, one possible development is for MNOs to also begin adopting 802.1X for their WiFi hotspots, possibly reusing their SIM-based authentication with 802.1X (e.g., using an EAP method such as EAP-SIM).

* *Enterprise adoption of "IPsec everywhere"*
Many enterprises who were early adopters of intracampus WLANs solved the 802.11 WEP security problem by running IPsec connections internally within the enterprise network. Although the "IPsec everywhere" approach was initially promoted as a temporary patch over the insecure WLAN segment of the network, increasingly some enterprises have continued to use IPsec for other purposes (e.g., establish virtual LANs). There are a number of possible consequences — intended or unintended — of using IPsec in this manner.

  One possible effect of the widespread use of IPsec within internal corporate networks — both LANs and WLANs — is to bring the connectivity layer one step higher, introducing a new *IPsec layer* in the stack. Thus, here IPsec could be seen as the network layer transport (instead of the plain IP at ISO/OSI layer 3), where the actual IP addresses of the endpoints become less important than the identity and IPsec credentials (e.g., digital certificates or shared secrets) of those endpoints. This deemphasizing of the IP layer and increased focus on the IPsec layer may force networking hardware vendors to introduce richer security functionality into their hardware. Examples would be routers that can route based not only on IP addresses, but also on other characteristics of the IPsec connection (e.g., IKE and IPsec security associations).

* *Endpoint integrity*
One of the topics receiving much attention recently is endpoint integrity, which refers to the "health" level of endpoints (e.g., client and server) that are engaging in a network connection or transaction. The notion is that a

server should verify the health status of a client as part of the authentication and authorization process for network access requests from the client. A client machine is deemed to be healthy if it possesses the correct configuration and integrity status as determined by the network security policy. The client configuration includes the correct antivirus signature updates, the correct operating system patches, correct hardware components, and so on. Three architectures have been proposed for endpoint integrity. These are the *Network Access Protection* (NAP) from Microsoft Corporation, the *Network Admission Control* (NAC) from Cisco Systems, and the *Trusted Network Connect* (TNC) from a group of network vendors working under the auspices of the Trusted Computing Group (TCG).

One possible outcome of the introduction of endpoint integrity concept in 802.1X-based networks is the eventual support of integrity-related features in the network hardware itself. Thus, to take a 802.1X example, if the authentication server is assigned the task of verifying the integrity status of every entity seeking network connectivity, it is likely that the same policy of integrity checking will also apply to network layer entities and elements. That is, the AS will also want to verify the software and firmware versions, device credentials and other component information of hardware such as access points, switches, and routers when they are introduced to a network. This may in turn affect how next generation networking hardware is designed and architected, making the concept of "self-defending networks" a reality through the implementation of integrity protection throughout the network stack.

• *Content as the primary driver of the wired and wireless Internet*
There is little doubt that rich content and interactive content will increasingly be the primary drivers for future technologies that affect the home and mobile user. To that extent, one could conceive the day when network connectivity — be it WLANs for the last 100 feet, WMANs and cable for the last mile, and 3G networks for global roaming — will become a commodity in itself and where market competition will revolve around the type and quality of content.

Thus, although cable operators may initially view WMANs as a competitive technology for the home high-speed Internet market, it is only a matter of time before operators will own and operate unified services based on these two types of physical networks. To the home content consumer, it matters little if the content for their IP-based television is delivered over wired or wireless broadband. Similarly, although 3G operators may initially view WLAN and WMAN services as a threat to 3G services for the mobile content market, it is again a matter of time before carriers and mobile operators see beyond voice services, and incorporate WLAN and WMAN services to enhance the availability of content to their mobile user.

About the Authors

Thomas Hardjono is a principal scientist at Verisign, Inc. His current areas of work covers new technologies in security, including trusted computing, wireless LAN and MAN security, digital rights management, certificates, Web services security, cryptographic protocols, and algorithms. Over the years, he has worked in several roles ranging from software engineer to principal architect at a number of organizations, including NTT, Bay Networks, and Nortel Networks. Dr. Hardjono has also been active in various standards development organizations, including the IETF, IEEE, and TCG, and in various industry forums in different roles ranging from editor to working group chair. He has a Ph.D. in computer science from the University of New South Wales and is a member of the IEEE and ACM.

Lakshminath R. Dondeti is a staff engineer in the standards group at QUAL-COMM, Inc. His current areas of work include multicast and group security, wireless LAN and MAN security, and voice over IP security. He is generally active in the security area standards in the IETF and IEEE. He has been a cochair of the Group Security research group and currently is a cochair of the Multicast Security working group within the IETF. Dr. Dondeti has a Ph.D. in computer science from the University of Nebraska, Lincoln, and is a member of the IEEE 802.16 group, IEEE SA, and ACM.

Index

Recent Titles in the Artech House Computer Security Series

Rolf Oppliger, Series Editor

Bluetooth Security, Christian Gehrmann, Joakim Persson, and Ben Smeets

Computer Forensics and Privacy, Michael A. Caloyannides

Computer and Intrusion Forensics, George Mohay, et al.

Contemporary Cryptography, Rolf Oppliger

Defense and Detection Strategies against Internet Worms, Jose Nazario

Demystifying the IPsec Puzzle, Sheila Frankel

Developing Secure Distributed Systems with CORBA, Ulrich Lang and Rudolf Schreiner

Electric Payment Systems for E-Commerce, Second Edition, Donal O'Mahony, Michael Peirce, and Hitesh Tewari

Evaluating Agile Software Development: Methods for Your Organization, Alan S. Koch

The German Enigma Cipher Machine: Beginnings, Success, and Ultimate Failure, Brian J. Winkel, Cipher A. Deavours, David Kahn, and Louis Kruh

Implementing Electronic Card Payment Systems, Cristian Radu

Implementing Security for ATM Networks, Thomas Tarman and Edward Witzke

Information Hiding Techniques for Steganography and Digital Watermarking, Stefan Katzenbeisser and Fabien A. P. Petitcolas, editors

Internet and Intranet Security, Second Edition, Rolf Oppliger

Java Card for E-Payment Applications, Vesna Hassler, Martin Manninger, Mikail Gordeev, and Christoph Müller

Multicast and Group Security, Thomas Hardjono and Lakshminath R. Dondeti

Non-repudiation in Electronic Commerce, Jianying Zhou

Outsourcing Information Security, C. Warren Axelrod

Privacy Protection and Computer Forensics, Second Edition, Michael A. Caloyannides

Role-Based Access Controls, David F. Ferraiolo, D. Richard Kuhn, and Ramaswamy Chandramouli

Secure Messaging with PGP and S/MIME, Rolf Oppliger

Security Fundamentals for E-Commerce, Vesna Hassler

Security in Wireless LANs and MANs, Thomas Hardjono and Lakshminath R. Dondeti

Security Technologies for the World Wide Web, Second Edition, Rolf Oppliger

Techniques and Applications of Digital Watermarking and Content Protection, Michael Arnold, Martin Schmucker, and Stephen D. Wolthusen

User's Guide to Cryptography and Standards, Alexander W. Dent and Chris J. Mitchell

For further information on these and other Artech House titles, including previously considered out-of-print books now available through our In-Print-Forever® (IPF®) program, contact:

Artech House	Artech House
685 Canton Street	46 Gillingham Street
Norwood, MA 02062	London SW1V 1AH UK
Phone: 781-769-9750	Phone: +44 (0)20 7596-8750
Fax: 781-769-6334	Fax: +44 (0)20 7630-0166
e-mail: artech@artechhouse.com	e-mail: artech-uk@artechhouse.com

Find us on the World Wide Web at:
www.artechhouse.com